LIAR

Robert S Feldman, PhD, is a fellow of the American Psychological Association and the Association for Psychological Science. He is an Associate Dean of the College of Social and Behavioral Sciences and Professor of Psychology at the University of Massachusetts, Amherst. He has written over one hundred books, book chapters and scientific articles, and his psychology textbooks have sold over one million copies and have been translated into numerous languages.

D1454199

LIAR

The Truth About Lying

Robert Feldman

2 4 6 8 10 9 7 5 3 1

Published under the title *The Liar in Your Life* in 2009 by Virgin Books,
an imprint of Ebury Publishing
A Random House Group Company

First published in the United States by Grand Central Publishing,
New York, in 2009

This edition published 2010

The Random House Group Limited Reg. No. 954009

Addresses for companies within the Random House Group can be found
at www.randomhouse.co.uk

A CIP catalogue record for this book is available from the British Library

The Random House Group Limited supports The Forest Stewardship
Council [FSC], the leading international forest certification organisation.
All our titles that are printed on Greenpeace-approved FSC-certified paper
carry the FSC logo. Our paper procurement policy can be found at
www.rbooks.co.uk/environment

Printed in the UK by CPI Bookmarque, Croydon CR0 4TD

ISBN 9780753515662

To buy books by your favourite authors and register for offers
visit www.rbooks.co.uk

To Kathy

CONTENTS

Introduction   1

CHAPTER 1
Everyday Inventions of Everyday Life   5

CHAPTER 2
The Liar's Advantage   27

CHAPTER 3
Deception 101: How Children Learn to Lie   57

CHAPTER 4
The Evolution of Deceit: Are We Born to Lie?   79

CHAPTER 5
Broken Trust: Loving a Liar   97

CHAPTER 6
Self-Deception: The Lies We Tell Ourselves   121

CHAPTER 7
Cosmetic Deceit: Lies to Make Us Seem Richer,
Smarter, Better   143

CHAPTER 8
Lies with Intent: Deceit to Trick or Cheat   163

CHAPTER 9
Synthetic Reality: Media-Manufactured Lies   181

CHAPTER 10

　　Career Lies: Deception in the Workplace　　　201

CHAPTER 11

　　Web of Deceit: The Brave New World
　　　of Internet Dishonesty　　　223

CONCLUSION

　　Living with Lies　　　245

Acknowledgments　　　261

Sources　　　263

Index　　　283

LIAR

INTRODUCTION

The National Archives, housed in an austere building in downtown Washington, D.C., contains original copies of the founding documents of the United States of America: the Declaration of Independence, the Constitution, the Bill of Rights. These documents, with their talk of unalienable rights and the equality of all, established the country not just in a legal sense but in a moral sense, too. The United States would be, and still aspires to be, a nation where justice and truth prevail.

Yet I did not visit the archives several decades ago to learn more about the brighter moments in our nation's past. Instead, I went in order to listen to scratchy tape recordings made secretly in Richard Nixon's Oval Office, recordings of fraud and deceit that ultimately led to Nixon's resignation from the presidency in the dénouement of the Watergate scandal. I believed, with the great conviction and zeal of a young assistant professor determined to understand the nature of lying, that I might be able to learn more about deceit by listening to the words of one of its most infamous practitioners.

However, when I listened to the Nixon tapes, I was frustrated that I could not determine from tone or intonation the moments when Nixon or his cronies were lying. Instead, to my ears, Nixon's conversations and soliloquies were remarkable most of all for how unremarkable they were. There was talk of political appointments and strategies; there were flashes of insight and of paranoia. Overall, though, from what I could tell, the conversation was not much different from what I might have heard from recordings of any office, oval or not.

After subsequent decades of research and dozens of studies into the topic of deception, I now see that my frustration was misplaced. My failure to distinguish a Nixonian office from any other had less to do with my own inability to recognize lies and more with the fact that there is simply not much distinction to notice. The scale and impact of Nixon's lies set him apart from probably every other president and surely most people generally. But what my research and the research of many others has shown is that lies occur regularly in every office. They occur regularly in every living room, in every bedroom; they occur regularly in conversations between strangers and conversations between friends.

In a sense, the very fact that the National Archives houses both the Nixon tapes and our most esteemed texts is paradigmatic. For in our society, the juxtaposition of venerated truth and notorious deceit is not just a matter of storage; it is a contradiction that plays out in our lives every day. While we talk a great deal about respecting the truth, while most of us regard the truth with genuine respect, the fact is that lies are common in American life, and in Western society in general. I went to the National Archives because I thought lies were hard to find. In fact, lying was then and is now nearly ubiquitous. If I wanted to listen to people lying, I could have listened in on practically any conversation between any two people.

Let me put it another way: there is no question mark at the

end of this book's title. There *is* a liar in your life. In fact, there are a lot of them, We encounter lies not only from the claims of presidents ("I am not a crook" or, more recently, "I did not have sexual relations with that woman") or sleazy sales associates at the local car dealership ("This SUV gets terrific mileage!"); we also hear lies from the people we meet and interact with on a daily basis, including our family, friends, colleagues, and the strangers we encounter in the ordinary course of each day. Dishonesty is deeply ingrained in our everyday interactions and in our broader culture. As we will see, it colors our perceptions of who other people are and our perceptions of their behavior. It even affects how we perceive our own behavior.

The issue we need to confront is not whether people lie to us—they do—but how much and why. Just as importantly, we need to consider why we're so prone to believing and even embracing the deception we hear from others, as well as the lies we tell ourselves. We need to explore why we view certain lies as harmless, while rejecting others as manipulative and shameful. And we need to consider how lies play out in broader societal contexts such as the business world, the media, and the new realm of digital communication. The primary purpose of *Liar* is to describe and explain the prevalence and consequences of lying in contemporary life, as well as to discuss the ways in which these lies affect us.

In this book, I've focused on lying not in terms of its philosophical or moral dimensions but rather as an objective scientist describing what science tells us. Understanding lying is more a matter of discussing how it occurs, not whether it ought to occur. Hence, the emphasis is on clear explanation as opposed to principled judgment.

Yet it does not take an ethicist or a clergy member to recognize that lying exacts a toll—on us as individuals, on our families and communities, and on society at large. Further, from whatever perspective one approaches deception, it is hard not to feel surprised, or even alarmed, at the discovery of just how much lying goes on in our lives. I think it's safe to say that we all share the goal of building a more honest society. The surest way to do this is to come to grips with—and confront—the lies each of us face as individuals.

I hope *Liar* can be the first step in this process.

CHAPTER 1

Everyday Inventions
of Everyday Life

Think about the last time you were lied to.

It may take you a minute. Most of the time when I ask people about when they were last deceived, they need a few moments before coming up with something. Eventually, they will recollect the story of the mechanic who overcharged for an unnecessary repair, or the date who promised to call the next day and was never heard from again.

Lies that took some kind of emotional or financial toll are the ones that generally spring to mind when we think about the deception we encounter. This makes sense. Events that are painful or dramatic tend to be memorable, and tend also to shape our impressions of the circumstances—like being lied to—that surround them. My guess is that the lie you came up with as the one you most recently encountered involved a blow to either your heart or your wallet.

The reality of deception, though, is very different from what such painful memories lead us to believe. Our relationship to lying is far more intimate than the occasional encounter with a duplicitous mechanic or dishonest lover. Think again, more carefully, about the last time you were lied to. Perhaps you picked up your dry cleaning, and when you thanked the person handing it to you, he responded, "My pleasure"—although both of you knew there was almost no chance that doing your laundry had given him any pleasure at all. Or maybe you were in line at the grocery store and you struck up a conversation with the woman in line ahead of you. Maybe she told you she'd never had to wait in line so long before. Really?

Or perhaps the last time you checked your e-mail you were offered a share of a Nigerian inheritance, which you could claim for only a few thousand dollars in taxes. Or maybe you watched television or listened to the radio, and heard about this or that product's miraculous or life-altering virtues. Maybe an infomercial promised you savings, but only provided you "act now."

The truth is, we are lied to frequently, even in the course of a single day. Most of the lies we don't notice, or don't even consider to be deception. Spam e-mail, deceptive advertising, and disingenuous social niceties form almost an omnipresent white noise that we've learned to tune out. Regardless of what we choose to accommodate or ignore, though, the fact remains that lies are a typical feature of our everyday experience. That we do disregard so much deception only underlines how common it really is.

Lying is not limited to one aspect of our society, one type of person, or one kind of institution. As we'll see, lying permeates the way we get to know one another and the way we form relationships. It is a part of how we educate our children and how we elect our leaders. It is essential to our economy, and it is essential to the media.

More strikingly, while lying sometimes occurs as an aberration in these and other arenas, often its manifestations are the rule. We tend to think of lying as something we censure. But just as we smile when the man handing us our dry cleaning lies about the pleasure he took in laundering our clothes, there are lies society accepts, and even encourages. Indeed, deception is so deeply ingrained in the functioning of our society that if we removed it, we might not recognize the society that resulted. We probably wouldn't be very comfortable living in it, either.

The fact is that much of what we think we know about deception is, simply put, not true. Misconceptions too often mask lying's prominence in our society and the ambiguities that surround its operation. So the first step to understanding the role of lying in our lives may be to consider the many ways we *mis*-understand it.

Amanda and the Seven Dwarfs

A former student of mine, whom I'll call Gary, moved to Santa Fe a few years ago to pursue a career in real estate. (You'll forgive me for fudging the names and other minor details in this story, and in other personal anecdotes that appear in the book. My only concern is to protect the innocent, as they say on *Dragnet*. The essentials, of course, are the truth, the whole truth, and so forth.) Gary is a devoted marathoner, and he joined a recreational club of runners in his area. Another member of this club was a young woman named Amanda. She and Gary fell in love.

Amanda told Gary about her troubled upbringing. Her mother had died when she was young, and she was estranged from her father. As a teenager, she had battled cancer. Gary was sympathetic, and impressed at the courage and toughness she showed in overcoming these hardships. After they'd dated for a little under a year, Gary proposed, and Amanda accepted. They bought an apartment together and started to plan their wedding.

In the following weeks, though, Amanda began to complain

of feeling fatigued and lethargic. She showed little enthusiasm for putting together an invitation list or selecting a reception venue. Since this was wholly out of character for the energetic woman he knew, Gary encouraged her to see her doctor—a man Amanda trusted and whom she had been seeing since college. Because she was anxious about her doctor's visit, Gary offered to go with her.

At the doctor's office, Gary and Amanda described Amanda's symptoms. Amanda's doctor said that mononucleosis sounded like a potential explanation, but he would have to examine her. Gary then asked whether a diagnosis of mono was more likely based on Amanda's history of cancer. As Gary described it to me weeks later, the doctor looked at him blankly and asked, "Cancer?"

Amanda had never had cancer. Nor did she have mono. What she did have, or so it seems, is mythomania, more commonly described as compulsive lying. Amanda wasn't estranged from her father, and her mother was very much alive. Amanda had hidden her fairly close relationship with her parents from Gary, along with a whole host of other facts about her basically happy and completely healthy background.

The relationship, and the lies, unraveled quickly but not neatly. Gary had to explain to all his friends and family why he was canceling his wedding. He had to buy out Amanda's share of the apartment, which he eventually sold, at a loss. And he had to start a big part of his life all over again.

I wouldn't be surprised if you've heard stories similar to Gary's. Perhaps you've personally encountered a compulsive liar and experienced the unnerving revelation that everything you know about him or her might be false. Compulsive lying is not a common condition, but the anecdotes that accompany it tend to be remembered.

Now let's consider another incident of deception, one that is also remarkable but that occurred in a far different context from Gary's broken engagement to Amanda. In 1994, seven top executives from leading American tobacco companies, among them the CEOs of Philip Morris, Brown & Williamson, and U.S. Tobacco, testified before the House Subcommittee on Health and the Environment. The "seven dwarfs," as they were later dubbed, had been called as part of the committee's on-going efforts to bring attention to the health dangers of cigarettes. All seven of these men were asked whether they believed nicotine to be addictive. And each man answered in turn, under oath, that he did not. The statement "I believe that nicotine is not addictive" was repeated again and again.

What the seven dwarfs did not volunteer was research Big Tobacco itself had done, demonstrating that nicotine, in fact, is addictive. Nor did they mention that their companies had made efforts to enhance the addictive powers of the nicotine in the cigarettes they sold. Three months after their testimony, the Justice Department opened a criminal investigation into whether they had committed perjury with their "nicotine is not addictive" assertion.

The stories of Gary and Amanda, on the one hand, and the seven dwarfs of Big Tobacco, on the other, would seem to have little in common, other than the fact that they both have lying at their core. But taken together, these stories provide a fairly comprehensive picture of how most of us believe deception functions in our society. Those telling the lies in both stories seem generally representative of the kinds of people we typically think of as liars: lying, as practiced by Amanda, was an abnormal behavior, one indicative of mental imbalance. She may be an extreme case, but liars are generally thought of as standing outside the norm for social behavior. They are more morally lax and more manipulative—or simply more crazy—than an "ordinary" person. The seven dwarfs embody another feature of the lying stereotype. We can see these men in the ruthless liar mold, displaying a willingness to sacrifice the truth in order to make a profit or to escape punishment. They aren't crazy, but they are greedy or guilty enough to be dishonest.

In both of these incidents of deception, too, we can identify innocent victims of the lies. Amanda tricked and emotionally manipulated Gary for her own purposes, whatever they might have been. The Big Tobacco executives perpetrated their fraud against a congressional subcommittee and, more broadly, against the American public in general. In other words, they lied to *us*.

Finally, and perhaps most importantly, in both cases the act of lying was a clear violation of conventional standards for behavior. Amanda's lies violated the bonds of trust she shared with her fiancé, and so Gary broke off their engagement. The tobacco executives broke their oath to tell the truth, and legal action followed. In broad terms, the lies in both cases were *wrong*, and were censured as such.

In sum, then, both of these stories, while different in their particulars, fit our common conception of how lying works. One story played out in a private arena, the other in public, but in both cases the structure was the same: atypical individuals employed deception to victimize innocent people and were justly condemned for it. Indeed, because such stories are so remarkable and draw so much attention, they almost *define* the stereotype of deceit. As with the lies touched on earlier, those of the duplicitous mechanic and the dishonest date, when we think about lying, these are the kinds of dramatic events that shape our impressions. They are also consistent with the "big" deceptions found throughout the history of civilization. Indeed, many of the most notorious historical events—the Greek infiltration of Troy, the Holocaust, the invasion of Iraq—involve deception on a grand scale.

Yet the fact is that most of the lies to which we are exposed on a daily basis, the ones that influence us the most, do not fit the pattern we find in the splashier examples of deception. Indeed, the lies that matter most to our everyday lives come not from compulsive liars or depraved business executives. Extraordinary liars may attract the most attention, but an accurate portrait of deceit reveals that most of the liars in our lives, and the lies they tell, are characterized mainly by how commonplace they really are.

Everyday Inventions

It is probably comforting to believe that we encounter few liars in our daily lives. Perhaps someone with a Machiavellian bent or with psychological problems like Amanda's might lie repeatedly to our face. Ordinary people, though, are less likely to do so. Or, at least, that's what we'd like to think.

This assumption turns out to be wrong. A wealth of psychological research has for decades provided evidence that it's not only the atypically immoral who lie frequently. Indeed, my own research into deception, which has spanned more than four decades now, has repeatedly shown lying to be far more common in daily life than we think. To attempt to find out just how common, I (along with my students James Forrest and Benjamin Happ) conducted a study of more than a hundred people in ordinary social situations. The results of this study have major implications for how we understand the lying in our life—and garnered media attention that ranged far beyond the circles of academia.

The setup of the study was fairly simple. Two at a time, I had participants meet, and I asked these unacquainted individuals to spend ten minutes getting to know each other. I didn't tell the participants, though, that I was conducting a study of lying. Instead, I said I was interested in investigating how people interact when they meet someone new. Something else I didn't mention was that each pair's entire conversation would be secretly videotaped. (Ironically, researchers who study deception end up employing a good deal of it in their research.)

After the conversation finished, I revealed the secret surveillance to the participants. I then asked one of each pair to review the video with me. As the participant watched the video, I asked him or her to identify, moment by moment, any instances in which he or she said something that was "inaccurate." (I purposely didn't ask participants to report "lies," wanting to avoid their becoming defensive or embarrassed and, consequently, not admitting to deception. The term "inaccurate" seemed less charged than "lie.")

There is a difference worth emphasizing between this study and other laboratory studies of deception. Most studies of lying, many of my own included, involve a fairly artificial setup. For example, a participant might be asked to watch a series of short video clips of people describing their upbringing and then identify in which clips participants had been told by the experimenter to lie. That sort of thing doesn't usually happen in real life. However, we meet new people all the time. Maybe the conversations we have with strangers don't usually occur in a small room with a two-way mirror, but meeting and getting to know someone else is a fundamental part of social life. Whatever other conditions my study introduced, at its heart it did seem to reproduce a typical, everyday experience. I hoped, then, that the data I gleaned would be particularly relevant to an exploration of deception in ordinary life.

I did, though, introduce one other twist into the basic structure of the experiment. I wanted to know if the frequency of lying might change with the specifics of the conversation. Perhaps some social interactions were more prone to deception than others.

To try to find out, I told some of the participants to attempt to come off as very likable. In other cases, I told one of the participants to convince the other that he or she was very competent. Everyone else I instructed simply to get to know the other person. I reasoned that while assigning goals to certain people did introduce a slightly greater degree of artificiality into the experiment, social situations in which one person is trying to demonstrate his or her charm or poise to another are very common. And again: none of the people in the study knew I was even interested in lies. As far as the pairs of strangers were concerned, deception had no relevance whatsoever to the study.

The conversations between the participants generally unfolded as you might expect: some initial, tentative "How are you?"s and "Where are you from?"s, followed by a more comfortable exchange of personal details and opinions as the chat got rolling. One conversation between a man and a woman I'll call Tim and Allison was fairly typical. Tim was a college student with a laid-back disposition suggestive of someone at ease with himself. Once he and Allison had gotten a little bit acquainted, he told her about his band.

TIM: We just signed to a record company, actually.
ALLISON: Really?
TIM: Yeah, Epitaph.
ALLISON: Do you sing or...
TIM: Yeah, I'm the lead singer.
ALLISON: Wow!

Another participant, Natasha, also discussed with her partner her musical background, talking about how she entered competitions as a pianist and toured the country with a chamber group. She also managed to weave into the conversation that she'd been a member of her honor society in high school. It was all more or less what you'd expect from two strangers making small talk—one person, directly or just unconsciously, trying to impress another with his or her achievements, or just passing the time by discussing his or her life.

What makes all of the above examples remarkable is that they are all lies. Natasha never toured the country, and never quite managed to be inducted into the honor society. Tim's band didn't sign with Epitaph. In fact, there's no band at all. Tim's musical expertise is limited to, in his words, "a couple chords." And these are only a few examples of what I found to be an extraordinary pattern. Participants in my study didn't just lie occasionally. They lied a lot.

Participants watching themselves on video confessed to lies that were big and small, rooted in the truth and fantastic, predictable and unexpected, relatively defensible and simply baffling. Further, the lying was hardly limited to the participants to whom I had given a directive to appear likable or competent. These people lied with greater frequency, but even those with no specific agenda lied regularly.

All told, I found that most people lied three times in the course of a ten-minute conversation. Some lied as many as twelve times. Bear in mind, too, that after the fact, participants might have been reluctant to confess to their "inaccuracies." This would only lead to an underreporting of the incidences of deception, though. In other words, it's possible that the frequency of lies was even *higher* than three lies per conversation.

My finding that most people told three lies in a ten-minute

"getting to know you" chat attracted national media attention. The *CBS Evening News*, the BBC, the *New York Times*, and the *Washington Post* all covered the story. I was often asked whether my results could be explained by some circumstance unrelated to how people "actually lie" in the real world. Admittedly, it would be easy—and maybe a little comforting—to conclude that the randomly selected participants in my study just happened to be unusually duplicitous. Or one might reason that some factor in my study induced people to lie far more than they normally would. But my later research on conversations between unacquainted strangers has shown, fairly consistently, that they lie to each other about three times every ten minutes, both inside and outside the lab. With apologies to the media outlets that shined a spotlight on my work, the results of this study really weren't extraordinary. They were typical. The extraordinary thing is how much, it turns out, people lie to each other.

High rates of lying are common even outside conversations between strangers, who are unlikely to encounter each other in the future. We might be able to accept that new acquaintances lie to each other with regularity, but we'd think that people with any sort of established social bond would not. Yet this is not the case. Psychologists such as myself have conducted scores of studies examining interpersonal deception: as it plays out in conversations between strangers, as in my study; in interactions between spouses and lovers; within families; and on the job. Lies occur regularly in all such contexts. The exact frequency is difficult to measure. A study like mine works fine to examine interactions between people who are meeting for the first time, but it's not as if this setup lends itself to, say, conversations between a husband and wife in bed.

However, diary research studies, in which participants

are asked to record their daily social interactions and indicate which contained lies, show that lying occurs regularly even in the most intimate relationships. Although deception occurs at lower levels between those with a close bond and often involves lies meant to put another person at ease ("Of course you're not putting on weight"), lying is still a routine part of the rapport between spouses, lovers, close friends, and family members. No relationship has been found to be immune to dishonesty.

The weight of evidence is thus compelling and clear: people are lied to with great frequency in their daily lives. While the extent and content of Amanda's deception of Gary may have been extreme, the fact that she lied regularly is not. Lying in our society is not "abnormal." The normal people who fill our lives do it all the time, in all sorts of ordinary interpersonal situations.

The question becomes, Why? Why do people feel compelled to make up bands they don't belong to or honors they never earned? What are the lies that occur so regularly when we talk with someone new—or sometimes even with a person we know well—all about? To put it simply: Why all the lies?

To answer these questions, we'll need to reconsider some of our fundamental ideas about the motivations behind deception. Stories like those of Amanda duping Gary or the seven dwarfs trying to dupe us tend to make us think about lying in terms of what it does *to* the person who is fooled. The central issue, though, may be what lying does *for* the person telling the lies.

"We Have *So* Much in Common"

In the 2002 film *About a Boy*, starring Hugh Grant and adapted from a Nick Hornby novel, the thirty-something protagonist, Will, pretends to have a son so he can join a single-parents' group to meet women. Predictably, the invention of

"Ned" leads to a series of complications and, because it's a Hugh Grant movie, ends up helping Will find love. The trope is a familiar one in romantic comedies: the hero tells a giant lie—about having a passion for dance or a lucrative career—in order to win the interest of some desirable romantic partner.

We probably don't spend much time wondering why a tobacco executive would lie to a congressional subcommittee about the dangers of cigarettes. Nor does it baffle us when a mechanic tells us a replacement part costs three times more than it actually does. While we might question the character of the people who tell such lies, the reasons for the lies themselves seem straightforward. Tobacco executives want to evade a truth that would harm their business and perhaps leave them legally culpable; greedy mechanics hope to bilk ignorant customers out of a few dollars more. Profit, the avoidance of punishment: these are the sorts of motivations we often associate with deception. If we add Amanda's example into our considerations, we might include mental imbalance as another conventionally understood motive for lies.

Yet greed, evasion of punishment, or some degree of insanity are not adequate explanations for much of the lying that occurs in daily life. Unacquainted strangers usually have nothing material to gain or any consequences to avoid through deception. Nor is there profit involved in many of the other interpersonal interactions that make up a typical day, and which researchers have found to be riddled with lies. Conditions like mythomania are very rare; mental problems can account for only a small portion of lies.

Ironically, the fiction of movies like *About a Boy* may provide more of a clue for the motivations behind the bulk of the deception we encounter than real-life incidents like the tobacco hearing. In the movies, deceptive behavior is exaggerated and played for laughs. Yet using deception to win affection may be so common in the movies because it is so common in reality, too.

To see what does motivate much interpersonal deception, let's examine more closely the lies told during my experiment. As I mentioned, I gave some of the participants particular goals for how to present themselves: some of them were instructed to come off as likable, others as competent. And while participants with no particular goal lied frequently, tellingly, those who had a self-presentation agenda lied more. Tellingly, also, the kinds of lies participants told varied based on their goals.

Let's first consider the participants instructed to impress their partner with their likability. These people tended to tell lies about their feelings. They distorted their true opinions and emotions, often in order to mirror those expressed by their partners. If their partner expressed a preference for Chinese food, for instance, they would claim to like Chinese food, too, even if they hated it. This kind of mirroring behavior is exactly the kind we see enacted for comedic effect in so many movies.

In fact, psychologists have found the mirroring of opinions, even at the cost of the truth, to be a very common strategy for ingratiating oneself with others. The reasoning behind such behavior is rather straightforward. Most people shy away from conflict and disagreement. They build relationships with others based on fundamental things they have *in common*. In order to form a relationship with another person, then, one would want to avoid the areas of dissonance and emphasize the commonalities.

Imagine yourself on a first date. If you find your date charming and attractive, it would be an obvious tactic to try to at least gloss over your disgust for her preferred political party and to maybe feign more interest than you actually have in her discussion of West African folk music. What bears emphasis here is not only that such behavior is common, as psychological research has shown, but also that mirroring of opinion to avoid disagreement and demonstrate similarity is widely considered to be *normal*. If you later tell a friend that you liked your date but spent your dinner with her arguing over politics and expressing disinterest in her hobbies, he might give you credit for honesty, but he would also think you were a complete social moron. Deception is such a common technique for ingratiation that its *lack* strikes us as aberrant.

Now let's look at the participants in my study I told to try to appear competent. The lies of this group reveal another powerful motivation for interpersonal deception, one more directly psychological than social. Participants instructed to come off as competent tended to lie about their biographies. They invented achievements and plans that would enhance the way they were perceived. They spoke of academic honor societies they didn't belong to and of career ambitions they had no intention of fulfilling. In other words, in order to impress their partners as competent, they made up stories about being competent.

I want to emphasize again that I didn't encourage any of the participants to lie. Indeed, when I spoke with participants with self-presentation goals after their conversations, they reported that they hadn't felt encouraged to be deceptive. Deception was a strategy they selected on their own to achieve their goal. But why would so many people lie to appear competent or likable? Why not "just be yourself"?

We can answer these questions if we consider what "just being yourself" means. Often, when someone gives us this advice, the implication is that "just being yourself" is the simplest approach to any social situation. In fact, "just being yourself," if we examine it closely, turns out to be a fairly complicated process, involving a complex balancing of a range of factors.

To begin with, when we interact with another person, there is always a larger social context that shapes the encounter. If we see a friend at a party, for example, we will speak with him differently than we would if we visited him in his cubicle at his office. The different standards for behavior in the different settings have to be taken into account in the "self" we present to our friend. This self is further shaped by the content of the encounter, emotional or otherwise. If a friend has just lost his cat, we wouldn't be much a friend if we didn't express sympathy; if a friend announces her engagement, we wouldn't be much of a friend if we didn't express joy. Such social standards for how we ought to act are weighed against expressions of our "true" feelings.

Finally, working in conjunction with our sensitivity to context is an almost constant interest in projecting a positive image of ourselves. No matter where we are or who we are talking to, we generally want to show our better qualities. Which of these qualities we express is again influenced by the nature of the interaction we are involved in. For example, our excellent sense of humor isn't much use at funerals, but our caring, sensitive nature is. On the other hand, our sense of humor might be precisely what we want to show on a first date, or to a prospective client.

"Just being yourself," it turns out, takes effort. Indeed, psychologists have long discussed it as something that takes *creative* effort. Our expression of who we are involves choices that reflect social and interpersonal context, our mood, our personality, our need to maintain our self-image, and on and on. The fact that we are able to perform this process with little conscious effort every day and in nearly every conversation speaks to our vast intelligence as social beings.

Still, if we consider self-presentation as a creative process, we can see how it can easily slide into deception. Again, every interaction involves decisions about which attributes to emphasize and to minimize, which impulses to follow and which to ignore. At some point, we may not be choosing among our actual traits and our sincere reactions. We may simply fabricate the traits and reactions the social situation calls for, or that we think it calls for. In other words, we might lie.

In addition to this, there is another complexity to "just being yourself." We aren't always confident in ourselves. Insecurities are part of human nature. All of us, at times, question our own good qualities—whether we are really smart enough, attractive enough, capable enough. Lying can allow us to navigate social situations in which we don't feel we quite measure up. Like the participants in my study who attempted to appear competent by making up stories of their competence, if we fear we don't embody the qualities a particular situation calls for, we can substitute a fiction that does.

Think back to Amanda and the lies she told Gary about her deceased parent and her battle with cancer. It's probably not a worthwhile exercise to try to draw thirdhand conclusions about why she did what she did. But if we assume that there was at least some element of wanting to win sympathy and admiration, of attempting to present herself in a way that was more appealing to Gary than she believed the facts allowed for, we can identify elements of conventional social behavior in her mythomania.

The key difference, of course, is that Amanda manipulated Gary practically all the way to the altar. Common interpersonal deception is usually far less menacing. Without a doubt, every lie, by definition, involves deceit and implicit manipulation—but that does not mean that every lie is employed in the service of deception and manipulation. When Tim told Allison about his nonexistent band and his nonexistent record contract, he did so without any larger agenda of fooling her into doing this or thinking that. For all he knew, he would never see Allison again. Tim's lies seemed to involve Allison only secondarily. His primary goal seemed to be fostering his own persona or addressing his own insecurities when meeting a new person. To put it simply, Tim's lies were about *Tim*.

We now see how another aspect of the conventional conception of lying is debunked by reality. Stories like that of Amanda and of the seven dwarfs of Big Tobacco make us think of lying as a tool used to victimize or exploit ordinary people. More commonly, though, ordinary people use lying to quell their own insecurities, to build a friendship, or to avoid a disagreement.

Sometimes, too, lying can be used within a conversation to benefit the conversation itself. There are times in any interaction when a strict adherence to the truth would only interrupt its natural flow, probably needlessly. When a friend wants to tell you about the great time he had in Montauk over the weekend, and asks you, "You know where Montauk is, right?," it borders on the pointless, not to mention the tedious, to stop his story and find out exactly where the town might be. The conversation goes much more smoothly if you nod, and say, "Oh, sure, Montauk." I call such deception "lies of social convenience." These lies grease the wheels of social discourse. They are not about fooling someone or achieving illicit gain. They are a tactic to make communication easier, or sometimes even possible.

As we will discuss more fully in future chapters, psychologists have found an association between socially successful people and skill at deception. In other words, popular people, for whatever reason, tend to be good liars. While it is easy to exaggerate the meaning of this finding (we can't say, for instance, that popular people are popular *because* they are good liars), it can be argued that an ability to lie is a valuable social skill. Consider whether you would really want to form a relationship with someone who pointed out every area of disagreement or could not convince you of his feigned interest in your hobbies. In many ways, deception is not so different from tact; indeed, one could make a case that sometimes they are actually one and the same.

Regardless of the terminology we apply to interpersonal deception, it's important to recognize that it is both a common and an accepted feature of ordinary conversation. Strict honesty is often directly opposed to what we consider to be standard social behavior. Lying, as strange as it sounds, is more normal.

But if lying is more frequently used to keep a conversation moving than to cheat or manipulate, this raises an important question: Does lying matter as much as we think? Perhaps, since there are no obvious victims to much deception, its frequency in our culture should not be so alarming. Maybe lying, outside of the kind practiced by Amanda or the seven dwarfs of Big Tobacco, doesn't really matter so much.

This line of thinking may be comforting, but unfortunately it is also misleading. While many lies don't cost us money or happiness, they do cost us *something*. The idea that some don't is surprisingly common, though. Many of us like to think that there are lies that are so insignificant, they aren't even really lies at all.

The Myth of the Little White Lie

We have seen how deception is pervasive in daily life, but not deception as we commonly think of it. A coworker may claim to like the Yankees in order to steer clear of an argument about the Red Sox. The woman in line ahead of us at Starbucks may feign a familiarity with our company to avoid the inconvenience of saying that she's never heard of it.

When I tell people that ten-minute conversations often include three lies, and sometimes more, they are usually shocked. But when I explain the function of these lies, the shock gives way to a kind of ambivalence. "But those are just little white lies," I've been told more than once about some of the more common forms of interpersonal deception.

This is what I call the Myth of the Little White Lie. According to this myth, "little white lies" are not the same thing as "real" lies. "Little white lies," like a lie of social convenience or the "My pleasure" we hear on receiving our dry cleaning, are so negligible—or so the myth says—that they shouldn't even be grouped with lies like those of the seven dwarfs. "Real" lies are bad: they cost money or cause pain. "Real" lies are morally wrong. "Little white lies," by (somewhat circular) definition, don't hurt anyone.

Unfortunately, the Myth of the Little White Lie is basically a fairy tale. Although "little white lies" may be less egregious than "real" lies, they still—like all deception—involve *some* degree of victimization. If a lie succeeds, someone is always fooled. And, crucially, even if the target of the lie doesn't know this, the liar does.

Bella DePaulo, a researcher at the University of California, Santa Barbara, and her students have found repeated and consistent evidence that lying—even "white" lying—takes a toll on the teller of the lie. Lying can cause a "twinge of distress," in DePaulo's words, making liars feel a little worse than they did before they told a lie. Further, this coloring of mood can last even after the conversation has returned to more honest territory. The sum effect of this is what DePaulo calls an emotional "smudge" on the interaction. Conversations involving lies are less warm, less intimate, less comfortable than those that are more honest.

The common lies in everyday life may not hurt us in an easily measurable way, then. But they have the effect of making everyday life that much less friendly. This is the cost of living in a society so prone to deceit in so many of its aspects: our life is often smudged. The accumulation of these many smudges can erode our trust in one another, it can make us cynical about our media and government, it can make us generally less attentive to the world around us. Whatever our particular response to the lies in our lives, the fact is that we have one. All lies have an impact. It's probably fair to say that some have a greater impact than others, but given their volume, not even the smallest lie can be wholly ignored.

Furthermore, when people find out they are being lied to, the effect is immediate and almost always negative. In a study I conducted in which participants learned that they'd been lied to during a conversation they'd just held with another person, these participants immediately formed a negative impression of the individual who had lied to them. Their conversational partner was seen as untrustworthy, unlikable, and generally more devious. But here's the most insidious consequence: those who were duped typically began to increase the level of *their* lies in a subsequent conversation with the person who lied to them. In short, lies—even the tiny white lies of everyday conversation—beget more lies.

In making the argument that all lies are consequential, we need to consider both the reasons lies occur in nearly every walk of modern life and the effect those lies have on us. As we will see in later chapters, the effects are not exclusively negative—or, at least, they are often no more negative than a strict adherence to honesty might be. As with a lie to keep a conversation moving, some deception can be extremely helpful in accomplishing goals that are essential to an individual's or society's continued functioning.

On the other hand, we will also consider the toll lying takes. Lying can often be more expedient in the short term, but ultimately, in the long term, it may present more social and psychological difficulties than it solves. Furthermore, an analysis of the conditions under which lying promotes or deters effective social interaction must consider the moral and philosophical implications of lying, which we'll also address in future chapters.

First, though, let's examine an aspect of deception we have so far ignored. We've been looking at lying as something we recognize. Very often, though, this is not the case. We've already seen how many of our preconceived notions about deception—who practices it and how often and why—are incorrect. There's another, essential piece to how we think about lying, though: our reaction to it. In the chapter that follows, we'll consider why lies fool us and what we might do to better detect them. As we will see, however, our opportunities to accomplish the latter are very limited—not least because, in some cases, we *want* to live with lies.

CHAPTER 2

The Liar's Advantage

Alexi Santana's application to Princeton University must have stood out right away. Rather than include an essay about a backpacking trip across Europe or the stresses of a private school education, Santana discussed his life as a parentless ranch hand: sleeping outdoors, teaching himself the great works of world literature, and running for miles in the Nevada wilderness. An admission officer's dream, Santana was accepted into the class of 1993. He became a standout on the track team and took six or seven classes a semester, earning mostly A's. He even won admission to one of Princeton's most prestigious eating clubs. As if following the plot of a Hollywood movie, it seemed the self-taught ranch hand had made good at one of America's finest universities.

Then, at a Princeton-Harvard-Yale track meet, a Yale senior recognized Alexi Santana. But she didn't recognize him as Santana. She recognized him as James Hogue, an ex-convict in his thirties who had posed as a high school student in Palo Alto years earlier. As the situation unraveled, the picturesque stories of Alexi Santana's youth were all revealed to be inventions—intended, apparently, to entice an admissions office looking for geographic and economic diversity in its freshman class. Hogue's admission was quickly revoked, and he was eventually jailed for defrauding the Princeton student-aid office of financial assistance.

Although what Hogue did is clearly extraordinary, it's not exactly unprecedented. Although (fortunately for us) extremely rare, stories of con men establishing phony identities for themselves go back hundreds of years. In the nineteenth century, a Scot named Gregor MacGregor claimed to be the prince of a fictional Central American nation called Poyais. He sold titles to land in Poyais, and even convinced European settlers to sail across the Atlantic to establish colonies there. Wilhelm Voigt, an undistinguished German shoemaker, put on a captain's uniform and led a group of soldiers to occupy the small town of Kopenick in 1906. He had the mayor arrested and seized money from the local treasury before being found out. More recently, Laurel Wilson, an American woman born in 1941, claimed to be Lauren Stratford, a survivor of a satanic cult ritual. After that story was exposed, she later posed as a Holocaust survivor named Laura Grabowski.

You could write volumes about the pathology of people like James Hogue—what compels them to deceive, how they live with their fabrications, what their "real" motivations are. The causes underlying impostorism, which we will discuss more fully in Chapter 8, remain a topic both fascinating and elusive. Many psychologists would argue that the perpetrators themselves don't even really know why they've carried out their deceit.

Yet perhaps the most compelling aspect of deceivers like James Hogue is not their underlying motivation but that such impostors can succeed at all. Indeed, an incredible part of James Hogue's unlikely story is that for so long, *he got away with it*. Consider what Hogue accomplished: he moved to a community of some of the brightest minds in the country and integrated himself into a social group composed largely of people nearly half his age. He didn't keep a low profile, either: he joined the track team and an eating club; he had roommates; he even hosted small parties for select female classmates. Yet it took a stroke of extraordinary luck (good or bad, depending on your perspective) for his deception to be uncovered: someone from the other side of the country recognized him from years before. Professors, coaches, classmates, and deans at this Ivy League university were all fooled.

Still more surprising is the fact that Hogue was far from the polished, unflappable charlatan we expect from movie and television portrayals of con men. Just the opposite, in fact: he exhibited some of the most stereotypical "clues" to deceit. He avoided eye contact. He was vague about the specifics of his past. He made extraordinary claims, such as that he'd done stunts for a movie about skiing. In retrospect, it's startling—to us and probably to those who attended Princeton with him—that James Hogue passed as Alexi Santana for so long.

Hogue's success, though, illustrates an essential truth about deception, one we rarely recognize. We usually think that successful lying is difficult. Confident in our ability to sort out what's true and what isn't, we are unnerved when we discover that we've been lied to. We speak of "good" and "bad" liars, ascribing to the former group unusual skills that allow them to pull off the difficult feat of fabrication.

The story of James Hogue suggests something else entirely, something supported by my own and other research: lying is easy. It doesn't take a slick con man to fool dozens of the brightest, most educated people in the country. And it doesn't take unusual calculation and self-control to fool people in the kind of interactions we have on a daily basis. Think back to the experiment that I discussed in the first chapter, in which I studied conversations between strangers and found that they lied to each other about three times every ten minutes. The last time you had a chance encounter with a stranger, did he or she lie to you three times? You would probably say no, but my research and other studies suggest that the answer is yes. Most likely, you simply didn't notice the deception.

The question is, Why not? Why didn't someone at Princeton catch on to James Hogue? Why do we believe it when someone says our pants don't look too tight, even when we struggled to pull them on? Why can't we tell when a colleague's praise about job performance is hollow? In short, why can't we detect deceit?

The answer: the Liar's Advantage. This is my term for the range of factors, some large, some small, that give liars a leg up in getting away with their deception. If we want to understand why so much lying occurs in modern society, it's essential that we understand the many components of the Liar's Advantage. After all, if every time a lie was told—if even most of the times a lie was told—it was uncovered, lying would probably be a lot less frequent. In reality, the Liar's Advantage allows the bulk of lies to pass unnoticed. Consequently, people can, and do, lie with regularity.

As we explore the Liar's Advantage, we will see how more of our basic assumptions about deception are false. We will see why you need not be a silver-tongued salesman—or a calculating sociopath—to dupe people in significant ways. And we will also examine how a large piece of the Liar's Advantage comes not from the liar but from the person being lied to. Startlingly, it turns out that often we don't notice lies because we don't want to notice them.

The Liar's Advantage

Truth Detection

As we begin to discuss the Liar's Advantage, let's examine this notion that lying is easy to get away with. When you first read that assertion, did you believe it? Or did you think, "Other people might not be able to spot a liar, but *I* can?"

The latter sentiment is the typical view. A friend of mine, a middle-aged woman named Maura, told me how she recently warned a new boyfriend, "Don't bother lying to me, because I'll just know." And she is certainly not the only person I've met who sees herself as virtually immune to deception. Study after study has shown that most people have a great deal of faith in their ability to catch a lie, to sense fabrication. Even if we don't share Maura's level of confidence, few of us think of ourselves as pushovers, easily susceptible to cons and dishonesty.

But do we really know when we're being lied to? When it comes right down to it and someone lies, do we "just know," like Maura claims she would? In 2006, Texas Christian University professor Charles Bond and Bella DePaulo of the University of California at Santa Barbara tried to answer this question. These two leading researchers into deception wanted to determine how good, statistically, people are at judging when they're being told a lie. Analyzing tens of thousands of individual performances, Bond and DePaulo found that people can differentiate truth from lies only 47 percent of the time. In other words, we are actually a little *worse* at figuring out when someone is deceiving us than we would be if we just guessed randomly. Bond and DePaulo's research suggests that we might just as well flip a coin to decide if what we're hearing is the truth.

The difficulty of detecting deceit is shown even more starkly when you examine those with a professional interest in catching liars. We tend to assume that certain people—police officers, detectives, FBI agents, and others involved in the criminal justice system—are exceptionally good at determining when they're being lied to. The media has fed this perception for decades. In the hard-boiled crime novels of Dashiell Hammett or Raymond Chandler and the film noir adaptations they inspired, it is a measure of the PI heroes' long experience that no one can "put one over" on them—that is, get away with lying to them. More recently, television shows like *24* and *Law and Order* depict interrogators who can spot a suspect's lies without fail. A recent James Bond film, *Casino Royale*, featured 007 using his exceptional lie-detection skills to compete in a high-stakes game of poker.

While we probably don't expect anyone to have Bond's preternatural expertise in detecting deception, we do assume that truth detection "experts"—those with training and practice in spotting a liar—can identify deception with great consistency. After all, detectives' jobs (not to mention our peace of mind) depend on their knowing whether someone is telling the truth or lying to cover up a recent liquor store heist.

But just how reliable are lie-detection experts? Researcher Paul Ekman of the University of California in San Francisco and colleagues Maureen O'Sullivan and Mark Frank decided to measure their performance. Selecting as their subjects members of groups like polygraph administrators, judges, psychiatrists, and police officers, they sought to test people, in the words of their study, "who have a specialized interest, and presumably more experience, in detecting deceit." The researchers showed these professionals a series of short video clips. Each clip featured the face of a young woman as she described her reaction to a film she was watching. Sometimes the woman was watching a soothing nature film, other times a gruesome horror movie. Regardless, she talked about how enjoyable it was to see scenes of nature. Could the police officers and the rest tell the difference between a clip of a woman honestly describing her reactions and a clip of a woman lying about them?

Ekman's findings were a little unsettling. Most of the trained and experienced lie catchers didn't do much better at selecting the lying women than if they'd used the coin-flipping approach. Of the groups studied, only Secret Service members demonstrated any particular lie-detection aptitude. The rest—polygraph administrators, cops, judges—were no better than ordinary people at detecting deceit. In other words, they were not very good at all. And while we might like to think that the performance of the Secret Service is attributable to the intense training its agents receive to ferret out people who make serious threats against government officials, it may be more likely that a statistical anomaly within the study masked the same incapacity at recognizing lies that every other group showed.

The implications of Ekman's findings to our legal and justice systems, for instance, are serious. Consider the case of Richard Jewell. During the 1996 Olympics in Atlanta, Jewell, working as a part-time security guard, noticed a suspicious-looking backpack on the Olympic grounds. He immediately notified police and began evacuating the area. The backpack exploded moments later, and Jewell's quick thinking probably saved scores of lives. Yet in the days following the bombing, Jewell went from hero to pariah, as he became the FBI's chief suspect in the case. Despite Jewell's repeated denials, despite a total lack of evidence, the FBI spent months investigating Jewell: ransacking his residence, questioning friends and acquaintances, keeping Jewell under twenty-four-hour surveillance. It was months before Jewell was formally cleared, and years before the real Olympic bomber was identified. The FBI's inability, as an institution and on the level of individual agents, to recognize that Jewell was telling them the truth—that he in fact tried to thwart the bombing—cost Jewell his good name and wasted untold resources while the real bomber was still at large.

When we realize that even those with "specialized interest" in identifying deception usually can't do it right more than half the time, we begin to appreciate the true difficulty the average person has in spotting lies. In Ekman's experiment, the subjects knew that they were supposed to be on the lookout for liars. Even then, they weren't very successful in finding them. In our daily lives, no one taps us on the shoulder and says, "By the way, one of the people you are about to meet is going to lie to you." It becomes clearer and clearer how James Hogue, a man in his thirties, was able to pose as a college freshman. We are just not very good at knowing when someone is lying to us.

This forms the first element of the Liar's Advantage. It represents a fundamental reason why liars succeed in deception: spotting a lie is difficult. Very often, federal agents and judges can't do it; you and I can't do it; and probably my friend Maura can't do it as well as she likes to think.

Our poor performance at catching lies probably shouldn't surprise us as much as it does, though. To explain why, let me share a brief anecdote: A few years ago I decided to take up golf. So I went to the local course and rented a club and paid for a bucket of balls. Then I spent the next hour hitting golf ball after golf ball after golf ball off the tee. After every shot I would watch the path of the ball, then adjust my swing accordingly. The fact that I never picked up a golf club again should tell you how much my practice paid off, but my golf game isn't the issue here. What's important is the method: in order to get better at swinging the golf club, I would take a swing and watch the ball to evaluate my performance.

The Liar's Advantage

Now let's go back to lying. Let's assume that lie detection is a skill like any other. The way you acquire and improve upon a skill is through practice. I wanted to learn to play golf, so I practiced. How, though, does one practice lie detection in ordinary life? You might try to pay attention to every statement you hear, and assess whether or not it's true—but the problem is, *how do you know if you're right?* You could ask every person you encounter, after everything they say, whether or not they are lying, but they could easily just lie again—and moreover, doing so wouldn't make you many friends. So you might suspect that someone is lying to you, but there is virtually no way to find out if your suspicion is correct. It's as if when I tried to learn to golf, I played in the dead of night. I could take swing after swing after swing, but without seeing where the ball went, I would have no way of knowing how I was doing. With catching a liar, we can make guess after guess after guess about what is true and what is not, but we rarely, if ever, know when we're right. Thus it's very hard to build our lie-detection skills. Keep in mind, too, that even those who presumably do get some feedback on their deceit detection—FBI agents and detectives and other such experts—still aren't very proficient.

Identifying a lie is difficult to practice and difficult to master—a tougher skill to acquire than even a good golf swing. This forms a significant piece of the Liar's Advantage. In a sense, liars exploit one of our weaknesses, challenging us to use an ability we often don't possess. The difficulty in catching a lie raises an obvious and urgent question: How *can* we spot a liar? What clues to deceit can we look for? Unfortunately, in asking this latter question—or, rather, in assuming there is an answer—we have already made another miscalculation that contributes to the Liar's Advantage.

The Averted Gaze

Let's return to the image of the iconic con man, the one we get from movies like *The Sting* and *Ocean's Eleven* (or *Twelve* or *Thirteen*, for that matter). In such works of fiction, the hustler is portrayed as unflappable, glib, always one step ahead of anyone he is trying to con. The implicit idea is that to pull off deceit, you need the aplomb (and maybe the wardrobe) of George Clooney.

But as we have seen, it's easy to get away with a lie: we're usually worse at identifying dishonesty than we'd be if we guessed at random. So why does the media offer these depictions of ultraslick liars? And, more importantly, why do we respond to them?

The answer has to do with a very common and deeply ingrained myth about liars. We take for granted that liars usually exhibit some signal that they are lying. And we assume it takes extraordinary poise *not* to show these signs. Subsequently, anyone who can tell lies without it being written all over his or her face must be worthy of portrayal on the silver screen. They must have the cool befitting a movie star.

The underlying assumption at work here—that there are frequently clear and noticeable signals that someone is lying—forms an essential piece of the Liar's Advantage. We think that when someone tells a lie, there are red flags: A person lying will avert his gaze. He'll shuffle his feet or drum his fingers. Perhaps his face reddens. If it's a particularly big lie, he might even start to sweat. When we don't see these red flags, we often conclude that the person is telling the truth.

To see how all this functions as part of the Liar's Advantage, let's consider one red flag in particular: the averted gaze. Charles Bond, a researcher I mentioned earlier, conducted a study in which investigators asked over two thousand people in scores of different countries what they look for to tell someone is lying. The most frequent answer was the averted gaze. Clearly, the idea that liars shift their eyes in the course of deceit is widespread and crosses most borders.

But is it true? Startlingly, it seems that "gaze aversion," as psychologists call it, is not, in fact, related to deception. Numerous researchers have conducted experiments, and all conclude that a shifted gaze is not a telltale sign of a liar. Gaze aversion may signal other things—such as submissiveness, an association dating back from our animal ancestors, who signified their deference by looking away—but it is unrelated to lying.

Yet the stereotype that gaze aversion signals deception remains a powerful one. I had a colleague whose husband avoided almost all of the social events in academia—receptions, parties, graduations—that most spouses attend (if grudgingly). The first few times I did meet him at such an event and tried to engage him in conversation, he made little eye contact. He simply would not look me in the face, instead looking off to one side or the other. Despite my best intentions, I couldn't help but feel that the husband was a dishonest and shifty guy, someone who could not be trusted.

I later found out that my colleague's husband had a deeply rooted social anxiety disorder that led him to dread social situations. His evasion of eye contact signaled only that he felt extreme unease and apprehension when having to carry out conversations with people he didn't know.

The power of the gaze aversion stereotype is so great that even after I learned the true reason behind his behavior, I was still unable to shake the initial suspicion that he was lying to me. And as a psychologist I knew full well that the link between gaze aversion and deceptiveness is a myth!

Just as we cannot conclude that an averted gaze necessarily signals deceit, we also cannot conclude that the *lack* of an averted gaze signals honesty; this also holds for the lack of a sweaty brow or a hunched-over, tense posture. Experts on deception have concluded that there are no physical tics that universally signal that a person is lying. Individual differences in how people lie are strong. One person might blink rapidly when she lies; another might stare at you, taking elongated pauses between blinks. Further, practiced liars learn their own giveaways (or the conventionally assumed giveaways, like gaze aversion), and teach themselves to avoid them.

To understand how difficult it really is to tell, from someone's behavior, if he's lying, consider polygraph machines. Movies like *Meet the Parents* suggest that if you want to know if someone is telling the truth, all you need to do is hook him up to a polygraph. The suspect's lies will be recognized by the machine's instruments, and his deceit will be uncovered.

This is a compelling idea, of course: a mechanical Pinocchio's nose, revealing beyond any doubt when someone tells a lie. Despite the media myths, though, polygraphs are not actually "lie detectors" in the strictest sense. They don't buzz when someone tells a lie or ring pleasantly when someone tells the truth. Instead, the polygraph is predicated on the idea that when people lie, they experience anxiety. Anxiety is connected fairly strongly with a range of physical responses—a pounding heart, an elevated pulse, sweating, heavy breathing. It is these responses that a polygraph machine measures.

The earliest polygraphs, developed around the turn of the century, were little more than elaborate blood pressure monitors—an elevation in blood pressure was interpreted as a signal of anxiety and, hence, deception. Modern polygraphs are far more sophisticated. They record a range of physiological responses simultaneously: monitors on the fingers track the activity of the sweat glands; tubes around the chest measure changes in breathing; a blood pressure cuff is used to note changes in pulse and blood pressure. The polygraph thus functions under much the same principle we use when we look into a person's face to determine if he or she is telling us the truth: lying triggers detectable physical signals. A polygraph machine is really only a scientific tool for picking up these signals.

Because humans are such poor detectors of lies, a machine that can do it for us holds obvious appeal—provided it actually works. And this, it turns out, is the problem. Though the polygraph is still in wide use, its effectiveness is far from certain.

Although many studies have concluded that polygraphs work more than 80 percent of the time, a recent report issued by the National Academy of Sciences National Research Council questioned the value of much of this research. As the report said, "The general quality of the evidence for judging polygraph validity is relatively low: the substantial majority of the studies most relevant for this purpose were below the quality level typically needed for [federal] funding." And even if you accept the figure claiming above 80 percent accuracy (and many researchers do not), that still means that one out of five times, the polygraph yields a false result.

This is troubling when you consider that polygraphs are used by the police to determine guilt or innocence, and by federal agencies to ferret out moles. Yet cases of polygraph failures abound. For example, Aldrich Ames, the American spy who sold Cold War secrets to the Soviets, passed multiple polygraph tests while acting as a double agent. Eleven CIA operatives were killed as a result of Ames's continuing duplicity. In another case, Gary Leon Ridgway, known as the Green River Killer, passed a polygraph when he was a suspect in the murder of his fourth victim. Set free, he went on to kill another forty-four people. And Charles Cullen, a nurse, was convicted of killing dozens of his patients via lethal injection. After the death of his first victim, police suspected Cullen of foul play, but he cleared himself by passing a polygraph test.

The flaw with polygraph machines is that what is true of the averted gaze is also true of the physiological responses a polygraph measures: they are not always connected to lying. If you ran up five flights of stairs and then sat down for a polygraph, everything you said would look like a lie, because you'd be panting, sweaty, and your heart would be pounding. The physical signs of exertion are often the same as the signs for anxiety. More to the point, if you were extremely nervous while you took a polygraph—but only because you'd been wrongfully arrested for a triple homicide—your physical responses would still look like deception on the machine's instruments. The polygraph can record only that a subject is anxious; it can't determine *why*. Think back to the example of my colleague's anxious husband. Just because you are showing signs typically associated with lying doesn't mean you're lying. This remains the inherent flaw of polygraph machines. The National Research Council report on polygraphs states it clearly: "Although psychological states often associated with deception (e.g., fear of being judged deceptive) do tend to affect the physiological responses that the polygraph measures, these same states can arise in the absence of deception. Moreover, many other psychological and physiological factors (e.g., anxiety about being tested) also affect those responses. Such phenomena make polygraph testing intrinsically susceptible to producing erroneous results."

The report thus acknowledges that people sometimes show signs of nervousness even when they're telling the truth. By the same token, people lying sometimes don't show signs of nervousness. We are wrong to assume that everyone who lies feels guilty or anxious about it. Liars can rehearse their fabrications to the point where repeating them becomes second nature, an automatic response that elicits no particular physical arousal. Further, we have all known people who lie to themselves as well as to us. These individuals can embrace a lie so fully that it seems to supplant the truth even in their own minds. (We'll look more closely at this type of lie, and this type of liar, in Chapter 8.) The essential point is that while you and I might feel nervous when we lie, that feeling is no more universal than the averted gaze. And as Aldrich Ames showed, even if 80 percent of liars exhibit signs of nervousness, the detection gaps remain extremely significant.

The shortcomings of the polygraph have led scientists, researchers, and entrepreneurs to explore new lie-detection technology. After all, there is money to be made: the polygraph business brings in hundreds of millions of dollars every year. Over the last decade, several tools have been celebrated as the key to unlocking the secrets of honesty and deception: electroencephalogram (EEG) monitoring of the electric activity in the brain; thermal imaging, directed at the observation that sometimes people's eyes heat up when they lie; and, more recently, functional MRI scanning, which shows the flow of blood in the brain. All of these technologies have demonstrated flaws, though. The electric signal the brain gives off when someone lies can't be distinguished from other signals, undermining the effectiveness of the EEG. The eye-heating effect thermal imaging traces is actually just another indicator of nervousness, not necessarily of deception. And while the brain scans of the functional MRI have shown promise, there remains much debate over whether the brain processes deception in a way that is significantly different from how it processes other types of thoughts. Ultimately, as the National Research Council report declares, no alternative technology "has yet been shown to out-perform the polygraph."

For the foreseeable future, then, the tool used by the government to identify spies and by the police to identify killers remains the polygraph—one that is "intrinsically susceptible to producing erroneous results." Considering that the best science can offer in the way of physiologically based lie detection is decidedly flawed, it shouldn't surprise us that our own efforts to discern a liar from how he or she acts are often futile as well. And remember that in a setting in which a polygraph is used, the entire focus is on whether a certain person is telling the truth. In our daily lives, our attention is far more divided.

The lack of reliable physical clues to deception contributes to the Liar's Advantage in two ways. First, and simply, since there are no universal behaviors that signal deception, liars can't be given away by them. Most liars don't do anything in particular when they lie. This makes it easier for them to pass off their deception as truth. Second, and more subtly, we think there *are* physical clues to deception. We rely on stereotypical behaviors like the averted gaze to help us spot dishonesty. In effect, we're waiting to hear an alarm bell that doesn't exist. And because we don't hear it—because the liar we're talking to doesn't shift her eyes or mumble or blush—we fall back to our erroneous default position: she must be telling the truth. This faulty assumption—that a *lack* of certain behaviors signals a *lack* of deception—forms a key component of the Liar's Advantage.

Clearly, the absence of telltale signs of deceit also contributes to the first aspect of the Liar's Advantage discussed earlier: that we are pretty inept at determining when someone is lying. Yet there is more to the Liar's Advantage than our ability (or inability) to spot deception. To understand the next part of the

Liar's Advantage, we'll return to James Hogue, alias Alexi Santana, Princeton class of '93.

The Truth Bias

So far, we've been examining the physical dimensions to lie
detection. "Look me in the eye and tell me that!" is the old adage for detecting deceit. It is also an adage that neatly encom-
passes many of the common notions about lies: that there are
physical signals to deception, that these signals often occur in
the eyes (in the form of an averted gaze), and that with a long,
hard look, we can know if someone is lying. We know by now
that all of these notions are mistaken. Yet the difficulty of notic-
ing a lie goes beyond what we do, or do not, see in a person's
eyes or face. The Liar's Advantage, it turns out, extends even
into the very way we think.

To begin to understand how, write down a list of all the conversations you had today. Include conversations in any form—
through e-mail, on the phone, face-to-face—and of any length.
The pleasantries you exchanged with the tollbooth worker on
your morning commute count as much as a long talk with your
spouse. If you spoke with the same person twice—say, with
a coworker in the morning and then again later in the afternoon—that counts as two separate conversations.

Now look over the list and put a check mark beside every
conversation you had during which you wondered if the person
you were conversing with was lying. Note that this isn't a question of whether, in retrospect, you now believe someone could
have been lying to you. Make a check only if you *considered at the
time* whether your partner in the conversation was lying.

Unless your job involves collecting homework or evaluating felons for parole, you probably haven't made a lot of check
marks. Most of us, in fact, don't spend a lot time in our daily

lives wondering, "Am I being lied to?" What's interesting about this is that, as we know by now, we are lied to fairly regularly. Yet look again at your list—if you're like most people, you never even considered whether the person on the other end of the phone or across the kitchen table or e-mailing you from Cincinnati was being honest. You just assumed it.

This psychological phenomenon, in which we assume that we aren't being deceived, is known as the *truth bias*. The truth bias means that rather than objectively judging the honesty of those with whom we interact based on their behavior and what they say, our default belief is that they're telling the truth. Someone needs to give us a compelling reason to think they're lying; otherwise the idea never occurs to us. Recent thinking in the psychological community suggests that the truth bias operates as a judgment heuristic. *Judgment heuristic* is the term research psychologists use for a cognitive rule of thumb. Judgment heuristics simplify the world for us—rather than assess every situation based on all the available information, we use subconscious mental rules to make quick determinations about things. The truth bias is one such mental rule. It lets us get through the day without scrutinizing the face of the gas station attendant giving us directions or assessing the potential ulterior motives of the man on the train platform who tells us the Patriots won last night. We lead our daily lives with the belief that most people are being honest with us.

When you think about it, it isn't difficult to see why we need a truth bias. Who wants to spend their day wondering if even the most straightforward information they've been given is a lie? Many people don't even count the change they get at the convenience store. Who, then, would take the time to wonder whether the clerk *really* heard that it's going to rain tomorrow? The truth bias makes daily interactions a lot simpler.

The Liar's Advantage

Remember, though, that the truth bias functions as a judgment heuristic—a cognitive rule of thumb we aren't really conscious of utilizing. Indeed, the usefulness of judgment heuristics is that we *don't* have to think about them. The effect of this, though, is that judgment heuristics like the truth bias can operate in unexpected ways.

A pair of Japanese researchers, Toshiji Kawagoe and Hirokazu Takizawa, conducted an experiment that measured the effects of the truth bias. The experiment involved having two people compete in simple word games. The details of the games are less important than two essential points: First, within the games, the two people were adversaries—one would win, the other would lose. Second, Kawagoe and Takizawa explained to both players that the person playing the role dubbed "sender" could, if he chose, deceive the other player. This deception would give the sender an advantage, if he could get away with the deceit.

What Kawagoe and Takizawa wanted to know was whether the other player would trust the sender. We'd probably expect that he wouldn't, given that he knew the sender had motivation to lie. The surprising result that Kawagoe and Takizawa found, though, was that the other player *did* in fact trust the sender, accepting what he said within the game as credulous. The truth bias trumped the suspicion that the opposing player had every reason to feel toward the sender. Kawagoe and Takizawa found that even when two people are pitted against each other—even when both know that one has both motive and opportunity to trick the other—there is still a strong bias toward trust and belief.

This gives us an idea of the truth bias's unexpected strength. It is not something we can switch on and off, even when logic would suggest we should. The truth bias is like any unconscious bias—it affects our behavior in ways we don't expect and can't easily control. For instance, several years ago I was stopped at a red light in New York City when a man in a suit tapped on my window. He told me that he was a lawyer who had been mugged, his wallet, car keys, and cell phone stolen. He needed twenty dollars, he explained, to contact his family and pay for a train ticket home. If I gave him my address, he assured me, he would repay me. I gave him the twenty dollars. Needless to say, I am still awaiting repayment.

Everyone to whom I tell this story says, "You should have known better." In retrospect, it does seem foolish to have given money—along with my home address—to a total stranger. But the fact is, like the rest of us, I was operating under a deeply ingrained truth bias—a bias that Kawagoe and Takizawa found could indeed trump logical suspicion.

Another of our cognitive processes also contributes to the Liar's Advantage—and it frequently works in concert with the truth bias. To explore this idea, let's return to a scenario I touched on earlier: someone wondering whether a convenience store clerk *really* heard the weather report. Let's imagine there's a man out there who is actually suspicious enough to consider that question. And let's imagine that this man—let's call him Sherlock—is equally suspicious of everyone he interacts with; in whatever conversation Sherlock engages, with whomever, he is always wondering if he is being told lies. Sherlock wonders whether his daughter really needs a ride home from soccer practice later that day. Sherlock wonders if the man at the newsstand really did just sell his last copy of the *Times*. Sherlock isn't convinced by his coworker's remark that he'll be ready for lunch as soon as he gets off the phone.

Besides leading a fairly unpleasant life—trusting no one, questioning everything—Sherlock would also probably find himself mentally exhausted by lunch—unless, of course, he were a fictional detective. For us in the real world, it takes cognitive energy to consider ulterior motives and hidden agendas, to scrutinize every single phrase for fabrication. This fact contributes to the Liar's Advantage.

While we're often curious and engaged by the world, we're also careful with how we spend our mental energy. For instance, when we walk down the street, we don't examine every crack in the sidewalk, every car on the road, the face of every person we pass, the shape of each cloud in the sky, the path of every bird. First of all, we'd never make it to the corner. But also, we simply don't have the cognitive capacity to consciously consider every aspect of what we encounter. We pay attention to a few things and don't spend much time thinking about the rest.

This model of thought considers us *cognitive misers*. The cognitive miser model holds that we typically spend as little mental energy as we can on various situations and social interactions. To put it simply, we can be mentally lazy. We try to figure things out as quickly and efficiently as possible.

Our imaginary scenario of a man who questions everyone suggests how the cognitive miser model adds to the Liar's Advantage. To scrutinize a statement for the truth takes mental energy—and we like to save our mental energy when we can. This allows liars to float beneath our cognitive radar. They may lie to us, and we may simply be too cognitively miserly to try to consider whether they did. Assuming we're being told the truth saves our mental resources for other things—thoughts about work, about family, about the crossword puzzle.

Of course, we're not always cognitive misers. If we're in a situation of high concern, one that focuses our attention—perhaps we're questioning our teenage son about just how a bottle of vodka came to find its way under his bed—our cognitive miserliness will be put aside, and we'll focus on ferreting out the truth. But most of the time we're a lot more mentally lazy, and the cognitive miser within us significantly lowers our level of curiosity about whether we're hearing the truth.

As we can tell by now, the Liar's Advantage is fairly significant. First, we're not very good at recognizing lies, and we don't get much chance to practice. Second, it's often impossible to determine whether someone is lying from their gestures or facial expressions. Third, we all operate under a powerful truth bias that gives liars an immediate edge in duping us. Further, we're often disinclined to spend our cognitive resources to even consider if we're being lied to. Yet there is still another element to the Liar's Advantage, perhaps the most important of all. This element turns on its head many of our basic beliefs about why people tell lies and why they get away with them.

The Willing Accomplice

I take piano lessons, and despite my better judgment, periodically I participate in recitals with my fellow students. Following every one of my performances, my piano teacher praises my playing. No matter how many mistakes I make, no matter how much my execution varies from recital to recital, I'm always told I did an excellent job. And despite my "Aw, shucks" protests, I'm always pleased to hear it—more than willing to accept that once again, yes, I did an excellent job.

This is the kind of deception we're likely to encounter in our everyday lives. The fact of the matter is, we'll probably never meet someone using a false identity. James Hogue could pose as Alexi Santana for so long in part because—in addition to all the reasons we've discussed—people so rarely fabricate their entire life story, down to their name. No one at Princeton was on the lookout for a thirty-one-year-old posing as a freshman, in great part because such an occurrence is far beyond the norm of typical behavior.

Deception in general, though, is not exceptional. The deception we're regularly exposed to is not the fraudulent variety of James Hogue but, rather, interpersonal lies told by those we meet and those we know well. Many lies serve only to keep a conversation moving—to grease the wheels of social discourse. Other lies mostly relate to the liar—to make him or her appear more appealing or successful in the short term.

We make a mistake if we think that all lies are of the James Hogue variety. Most lies aren't part of a grand web of deception, and many lies are far less calculated than we might assume. Further, not all deception even serves the needs of the person doing the lying. Consider, for example, how my piano teacher tells me I did an excellent job after every piano recital, regardless of my actual performance. That's a kind of lie we're all told from time to time: the false compliment. We say that our child looks great with his new hair color; we say that our friend got a great deal on her SUV; we say that our coworker really deserves a promotion.

False compliments are lies, but the liar is not telling them for malicious reasons. Usually, the motivations in giving a false compliment are both immediate and benign: the falsehood is designed to make the recipient of the lie feel good or to avoid hurting his feelings.

We hold a common conception of deceiver and deceived: that the latter is a victim of the former. But when we consider false compliments, we see how this conception is too simple. Often, we lie because we *don't* want to victimize, through the use of a harsh truth, those we're lying to. In order to spare their feelings, we lie to them. Even when we spare their feelings for selfish reasons, to avoid the fallout of telling the truth, the effect is still to support and encourage the person being deceived.

The fact that some lies benefit their recipient underscores another piece of the Liar's Advantage. Think about being on the other side of a false compliment, as the recipient instead of the teller. How motivated are you to find out that yes, you have been putting on weight? Or that no, you really don't deserve a promotion and a higher salary? Or that this time, your playing in the recital was clearly mediocre? If you're like most people, you're not terribly vigilant in uncovering your flaws, mistakes, and shortcomings. And because certain lies protect us from these harsh realities, we don't scrutinize them.

Perhaps the most important piece of the Liar's Advantage, the factor that prevents a lie from being uncovered, is what I call the *Willing Accomplice Principle*. The Willing Accomplice Principle states that sometimes we simply don't want to uncover a lie. It's not only less strenuous cognitively, it's also more flattering and comforting to accept certain statements at face value. With regard to false compliments, we all want to believe the best about ourselves. Hence, we tend to be unsuspicious of those who seem to believe it, too.

This seems like an obvious point: when a lie flatters us, we don't spend much time trying to determine whether it's true. But like the truth bias, our tendency to believe lies that make us feel good may operate more powerfully than we might expect.

How strong is the bias toward believing statements that flatter us? Roos Vonk, a social psychologist at the University of Nijmegen, in the Netherlands, designed a series of clever experiments to try to answer this question.

Vonk realized that it can be difficult to isolate from other factors the role flattery plays in gaining trust. For instance, imagine you've just been introduced to your brother's fiancée. The first thing she tells you is that your brother never told her how good-looking you are. Naturally, you believe her! The reasons you believe her, though, are a little fuzzy (psychologists might say that there are too many "relevant variables," but they really mean fuzzy). Maybe you believe her because it's important to get along with your brother's future wife, and so you're inclined toward liking—and therefore trusting—her. Maybe you believe her because you already know you're good-looking, and we tend not to scrutinize information that conforms with our preconceived notions. Maybe you haven't seen your brother in a while, and there is a lot you want to ask him and his fiancée. Like any cognitive miser, you're not going to focus your thinking on a passing compliment.

Vonk wanted to construct a situation in which none of these other explanations would be relevant. He wanted to know to what extent we are more inclined to believe flattery just because it's flattery—not because of our vanity, or who is doing the flattering, or the other things on our mind when we hear it. He wanted to test the power of compliments to win trust with as much specificity as possible.

Vonk's experiment worked like this: He told the participants in his study that he was doing research into how people collaborate and form impressions of one another. To that end, he had each participant sit alone in a cubicle and take a personality test. Afterward, he told them that another group was going to read the results of the personality tests, and write up descriptions, evaluating each participant as a potential partner in a supposed later stage of the study. The trick Vonk pulled was that there was no second group and no later stage—Vonk's real interest was in how participants judged the descriptions.

These descriptions, ostensibly based on the results of the personality tests the participants took but actually written by Vonk and his assistants beforehand, read like this:

I understand that I will work with [participant's name or other name]. I have seen her test results. I noticed that we have the same ideas about many things. Especially in how we deal with other people we are very much alike. It seems to me that anyone can get along with [name], but I will certainly get along great with her myself. I'm very glad that I will work with [name] because we seem to be so similar. And I'm sure that she will take her responsibility very seriously and that she'll do an excellent job at whatever it is we're doing, because she seems to have many talents. Also, she seems like a great person to go out with or to talk with, but anyway, that's not the issue now. I think she'll find the right way to do the task. She's given many responses that appeal to me. All in all, my impression is that she's a really nice person, easy to get along with, and someone who has many qualities. I'm looking forward to meeting her.

Sometimes the name in the description was the participant's name; other times it was a name of someone the participant didn't know. The participants were asked to evaluate the person who had written the description on a number of criteria, such as "sincerity" and "sliminess."

Vonk added a number of twists to this basic setup. He told some of the participants that the author of the description believed that her financial compensation for the experiment was being determined by the participant. Hence, the participant believed that the author of the description had a financial motive to offer false praise. In some cases, Vonk told the participants that they would later meet the description's author. Vonk also asked questions about the participant's mood to see if that made any difference to how they assessed the author of the description.

Adding all these different wrinkles to his study allowed Vonk to discover that participants who read their own name in the description evaluated the author as more honest and more credible than those who read someone else's name in the same description. In other words, participants who were flattered believed the author was sincere; those who weren't flattered were skeptical. And unexpectedly, Vonk found that this was true regardless of whether the participants thought they would ever meet the author, regardless of the participant's mood, his or her self-esteem, or the amount of compensation the participant believed the description's author stood to earn through false praise.

Our impulse to trust flattery turns out to be extremely strong. Vonk's study suggests that you would have believed the compliment from your brother's fiancée even if she wasn't your brother's fiancée, if you'd never met her before and would never see her again, if you were in a terrible mood, if you hated your looks, or even if you knew that she could make some money by flattering you. Vonk's surprising results indicate that even weighed against all that, you'd still believe the woman who said she thought you were good-looking.

Our need to receive praise and tame our insecurities seems almost automatically to trump a healthy skepticism. Our bias toward believing compliments seems to operate a lot like the truth bias: it isn't something we can turn on or off depending on the situation. To a certain degree, it's as if I can't help believing my piano teacher's praise of my playing.

Our complicity with liars isn't limited to explicit personal praise of the variety Vonk studied. For the same reasons we're almost uncontrollably trusting of compliments to ourselves, we're also given to believing compliments about our work, our children, and our possessions. Indeed, the partnership we sometimes form with liars in our acceptance of their deceit can be very broad and have great implications.

Let's examine the Willing Accomplice Principle, about our readiness—even eagerness—to be deceived, in another context. Imagine that a real estate agent is showing you a house. Not surprisingly, the real estate agent is falling all over herself praising it: the condition of the roof and the flooring, the neighborhood, the size, the value—all first-rate. You know enough to be skeptical of someone with an obvious financial motive in your purchasing the house, but there's a problem: you love the house, too. What's more, you've been looking for the right house for months, this one is in your price range, and it's just a quick commute away from work. If you are like most people, your initially skeptical assessment of what the real estate agent says probably begins to change: instead of being on guard against deceit, you will start to *want* to believe her.

In this way, we enter into a kind of unstated conspiracy with liars. In the case of the real estate agent, there is tangible benefit on both sides to believing her description of the house: she gets a commission, and you get a house you want. The situation is really fairly similar to that of a false compliment. When my piano teacher tells me I did a great job playing, she saves herself the awkwardness and guilt of disparaging my performance, and I get to walk around thinking about what a great piano player I am.

This point is so straightforward that it is often overlooked, but it forms an essential component of our complicity with liars. In many cases, a liar and the target of the lie both benefit from the lie's success. Given this, it is not hard to see how powerful our own contribution to the Liar's Advantage can be. If a liar can hit upon deception that we'd like to believe, too, we're both—liar and target of the lie—hoping on some level that the lie won't be revealed for what it is. Now *that* is a significant edge in pulling off deception.

This characterization of deceit—in which liar and target of the lie both have an interest in the lie succeeding—is far different from the typical conception of how fabrication operates. We usually imagine deception along the lines of the story of James Hogue. In such circumstances, one person is the liar, and the other—or others—are victims. Again, though, incidents of large-scale deception like that committed by James Hogue are the exception. Far more common is deception that follows the Willing Accomplice Principle. Consider how many false compliments you give—and likely receive—every day.

This raises an obvious question: If so many of the lies we hear are ones we embrace, perhaps we should be less concerned with deceit? The fact that we're accomplices in so much deception signals that we're already more enmeshed in it than we usually acknowledge. However, simply because lies sometimes stoke our egos does not mean we should uncritically accept them. Consider again the scenario of the real estate agent praising the house you want to buy. In the short term, you are willing to accept her lies about the house because you are already inclined to buy it. In the long term, though, accepting what the real estate agent says at face value could prove very dangerous. However much you'd like to believe that the house has been cleared for termites by multiple inspectors, this is an assurance that demands scrutiny.

On a larger scale, consider the collapse of the subprime real estate market in 2008. Lenders extended loans to those with terrible track records of repayment. There was mutually convenient deception on both sides: borrowers with miserable credit assured lenders that this time they would repay their loans; lend-ers assured borrowers that astronomical interest rates wouldn't lead them to financial ruin and eventual default. Both sides had a financial stake in allowing the deception to continue. Eco-nomic forces, though, rarely tolerate such arrangements. The (now seemingly inevitable) collapse of the subprime market triggered global repercussions that are still being felt.

Although it seems clear in retrospect that vigilance in seek-ing the truth would have been appropriate, the problem is that the cognitive rules we play by—the truth bias, the trust in flat-terers that Vonk explored, our need for cognitive efficiency—are not ones we can easily alter. Just as there is no way to explain to someone else all the kinds of lies we'll accept, and all the kinds we don't want to hear, we can't really make this explanation to ourselves, either. The Liar's Advantage, then, can seem in some ways permanent. It exploits mental processes over which we largely have no control.

Nonetheless, the Liar's Advantage is only that—an advan-tage. While it gives liars a leg up on deceiving us, it does not mean we are bound to be always fooled—assuming, of course, that we don't want to be fooled. Acknowledgment of the true complexity of deception—that it is more often practiced by piano teachers with their students' complicity, rather than con artists pulling the wool over the eyes of an entire university—is a good first step toward gaining a better handle on the deceit that surrounds us. It is also helpful to consider where our no-tions about deception come from. Why do we assume that liars always deceive us maliciously? Where do our misconceptions about the averted gaze come from? Why aren't we more aware of our own role in successful deception? The next chapter takes up these and similar questions, as we explore the lessons chil-dren learn about lying.

CHAPTER 3

Deception 101:
How Children Learn to Lie

Testing day at Forest Brook High School in Houston probably was not what George W. Bush had in mind when he signed into law the No Child Left Behind Act, which mandated periodic competency testing. Some students taking the high-stakes Texas Assessment of Knowledge and Skills (TAKS) test in March 2008 were sitting close enough to share answers. In another classroom, a proctor read a newspaper while students took the test, and students left the room for bathroom breaks, unaccompanied by proctors. In a third classroom, students talked to one another before handing in their answer sheets. Overall, the testing took place in a chaotic atmosphere.

Perhaps the incidents at Forest Brook simply indicated administrative disorganization. But the history of testing at Forest Brook suggests otherwise. Until 2005, Forest Brook was another urban school with a dismal record of failure. Suddenly, though, its TAKS scores soared, and 95 percent of eleventh graders passed the state science test. The students at Forest Brook became poster children for the benefits of school reform, brought about by a partnership of its teachers and students.

If it seemed too good to be true, it was. After an exposé by the *Dallas Morning News,* it became apparent that the rise in scores had more likely been brought about by systematic subterfuge than true academic improvement. Investigators came to believe that some teachers doled out answers to their students during the test or later changed their students' answers. When the state assigned independent monitors to oversee test administration the following year, the science scores plummeted, with only 39 percent of students passing. Indeed, testing irregularities were identified at hundreds of schools in Texas, and in the fallout of these revelations teachers and administrators were fired, suspended, and demoted.

Testing was the centerpiece of the No Child Left Behind Act: The results of the competency tests would then be used as a yardstick to determine school success. Schools that performed poorly would face penalties such as teacher or administrator firings or, in extreme cases, takeover by the state.

No Child Left Behind, which also promised schools billions of dollars in new federal funding, received bipartisan support. Even lawmakers who traditionally opposed increases in federal money for education lined up behind the act, attracted by the new accountability schools would face in keeping up their test scores. Our culture is one that customarily judges performance in numerically quantifiable terms: movies are hits if they earn a lot of money in ticket sales; politicians are doing well if they are ahead in polls; CEOs are successful if they drive up their company's stock price. Perhaps it was inevitable (or unavoidable) that schools would start to be assessed in the same way.

Further, tying a school's future to its students' test scores apparently has a track record of success—at least inasmuch as raising the scores on those tests is concerned. (Whether standardized test performance really ought to be the measure of an education is an argument for a different book.) Many schools have reported dramatic increases in test results when these results had consequences for teacher employment and school funding.

There is a problem underlying this emphasis on test performance, though, one that relates not to the fairness of tying an entire school's destiny to a standardized test but, rather, to the integrity of the test performance itself. Students and teachers might respond to higher-stakes testing with increased study time and effort. Or they might respond by cheating.

Raising the specter of cheating is not just a matter of cynicism. Research shows that students cheat, and cheat frequently. A 2006 study by the Josephson Institute of Ethics examining 36,000 high school students found that 60 percent of them cheated on a test during the previous year, and 35 percent of them did so more than once. A third of them admitted to plagiarizing material from the Internet. A separate study of 4,500 students conducted by Donald McCabe of Rutgers University found even higher rates of cheating. Nearly three-quarters of those surveyed by McCabe admitted to cheating on an exam or a test.

Cheating, then, is not an aberration. These studies suggest that it is typical, a practice the vast majority of high school students engage in. And McCabe also found another surprising result, one particularly relevant to a discussion of how cheating might undermine the results of mandatory tests such as those required by No Child Left Behind. McCabe determined that while 90 percent of teachers reported knowing that cheating was occurring in their classrooms, a third of them took no action to prevent it.

Given these attitudes, it is easy to see how cheating could skew the results of standardized tests. And in many cases when jobs and funding were on the line, cheating is exactly what occurred. State officials in Mississippi had to throw out test results in nine different schools after evidence of widespread cheating emerged. In Arizona, test results were discarded across nine school districts where teachers had read portions of tests to students in advance or had given them additional time to finish. In 2005, an Indiana third-grade teacher was suspended when administrators discovered her practice of tapping her students on the shoulder when they marked an incorrect answer.

Recent years have seen cheating scandals in schools from New York to Florida to California. Importantly, in nearly all these instances the cheating was collaborative—teachers worked with students in achieving dishonest results. In some cases, teachers would give students the actual tests to study from ahead of time. In other instances, teachers would simply write correct answers on the blackboard while students took the test.

Indeed, the origins of deception in children almost always involve a relationship between the child and someone else. As in the cheating scandals discussed above, the relationship sometimes seems clear: adults use their influence to guide children into dishonesty. We often assume children are indoctrinated in dishonesty, in overt or subtle ways, by more morally compromised grown-ups. Many children, at least, seem to take this view. In his study of high school students, McCabe found that the most common reason students gave for their cheating was the example set by adults. Yet this conception is probably too simplistic. Even parents who stress the value of honesty the most frequently find that their children lie to them, and to others, with regularity.

Just as the uses and purposes of lying by adults are complex, deception as practiced by children is no different. The dishonesty on tests like those mandated by No Child Left Behind turns out to be one of the simpler forms it takes. Like adults, children lie for a range of reasons and in a variety of circumstances—

and, surprisingly, their lying may actually be a by-product of their increasing cognitive and social sophistication, which in other manifestations are welcomed by their parents.

Don't Peek!

A five-year-old boy we'll call Jonah is facing a dilemma. He had just been playing a game with a friendly-looking woman. As she explained it, the game sounded easy. She would play the sounds of toys behind Jonah's back, and all he had to do was guess what each toy was. The initial two sounds were easy for him to identify. The first was the sound of a fire engine— simple enough to match with a toy truck. The second sound was a recorded voice saying, "To infinity and beyond!" As Jonah knew, this is the motto of Disney's Buzz Lightyear.

The sound of the third toy, though, left Jonah stumped. It was a simple melody that Jonah couldn't associate with any particular toy. Just as he was about to give up, the woman playing the sounds was told by an assistant that she had a phone call. She prepared to leave Jonah alone in the room, instructing him not to peek at the mysterious toy behind his back while she was gone. As she left, she warned him again, "Remember, no peeking!" For a minute or so, Jonah held out, but finally the temptation was too great. He turned around and saw that the toy was a Barney doll. Then he heard the doorknob rattling, and he turned back around quickly. The friendly woman returned to the room and asked him if he had figured out what the toy was. He happily declared that it was a Barney doll. Then she asked him, pointedly, whether or not he'd peeked—and Jonah had his dilemma: to lie or tell the truth.

At the beginning of the chapter we discussed some of the statistics that reveal the high rates of cheating that occur among high school students. While the ubiquity of cheating is probably surprising, the fact that it goes on may not be. Our preconceived notions about teenagers probably allow for the fact that they cheat in high school. As any teenager who has been followed around an electronics store by a salesclerk can tell you, adult attitudes toward "children" once they reach thirteen are less than wholly trusting. But let's turn the child development clock back a few stages and look at our attitudes toward younger children.

The idea of young children as innocents, unsullied by the experiences of later life, is a common one. It also has an impressive philosophical pedigree. Enlightenment philosopher Jean-Jacques Rousseau believed that young children are, by nature, virtuous and good. "There is no original perversity in the human heart," he asserted; the "perversity" that people acquire comes from the corrupting influences of society.

American culture in particular seems to embrace Rousseau's ideas about the innate goodness of children. Our educational system, with its emphasis on creativity and individual attention, is largely based on the idea that a child's natural disposition is toward the good. Further, unlike in, for instance, Scotland, where children are punished as adults starting at the age of eight, our justice system grants younger members of society special leeway, as if crime is not indicative of the true nature of their characters.

This attitude is reflected in the views of many parents I speak with, who believe that their children possess an innate, and powerful, moral compass. "My children don't lie," I've been assured by many a kindergarten mother. When we look into the face of a child, it's hard to believe he or she could be capable of the cunning, much the less the malice, we generally associate with deceit.

However, developmental psychologists who have been studying questions of deceptive behavior in children for decades would argue differently. Indeed, what they have found stands in contrast to the simple goodness we typically attribute to young children. One of the primary tools psychologists utilize in studying childhood deception involves what's called the "temptation resistance paradigm," or, in simpler terms, "peeking experiments." It is in such an experiment that Jonah finds himself in the scenario described at the beginning of this section. Peeking experiments can have many variations: they can involve flash cards, or cloths covering the toys, or different types of cautions about peeking. At their core, though, the scenario is always the same: a child is tempted into looking at something he or she has been instructed not to, and then the experimenter confronts the child to see if he or she will lie about the behavior.

The specifics of the experiment described above are derived from a study conducted by Victoria Talwar of McGill University, in Montreal. And the results of her study, broadly speaking, are typical for peeking experiments. Of the more than one hundred three- to seven-year-olds Talwar studied, 82 percent peeked at the third toy. (Talwar intentionally used a sound that had no connection to the actual toy, in order to induce children to peek.) And of those who peeked, the vast majority lied about it. Depending on the variation of the peeking experiment, sometimes as many as 95 percent of the guilty peekers lied.

The peeking experiment demonstrates that young children are not as honest as we might like to think. As with teenagers cheating on tests, the typical behavior in scenarios like the peeking experiment is for children to lie. The fact of childhood deception is not limited to the lab, either. Observed in preschool or elementary school, interacting with peers or with their parents, most children lie. Lying is not limited to any particular demographic, either. Children from upper-class, middle-class, and lower-class backgrounds lie. Girls lie as well as boys. Children at all IQ levels lie. And children of all cultures lie; there is nothing about modern Western society that induces more dishonesty than that found in children in the developing world or in Eastern cultures.

Deception in children is common enough, in fact, that psychologists have been able to identify clear patterns in how children lie as they age. Verbal lies start in most children around the age of three, though in some children they can occur as early as two. Lying typically accompanies children's understanding of the fact that their parents have rules and that there are punishments associated with breaking them. The earliest are almost reflexive attempts to avoid these punishments. In other words, the first lies children tell are often of the "I didn't do it" variety. Importantly, these lies are as unsophisticated as the phrasing suggests. A three-year-old will claim "I didn't do it" even in the face of clear evidence that he or she broke the vase, hit the sibling, or ate the last cookie. Three-year-olds have the ability to feign denial, but not the understanding or insight to make this denial believable.

Children's lies become more nuanced around the age of four or five. The indiscriminate "I didn't do it" is replaced by the more calculated "The dog did it." (We will discuss why children are able to take this step in deception later in the chapter.) Also, it is around the age of four that children begin to tell social lies, such as those discussed in the first chapter. As children begin preschool and have greater peer interaction, the need for lies that ingratiate or boost a fragile ego increases. Again, in these early forms such lying is crude, but it often serves the same psychological needs as adult lying. Whereas an adult may brag about exaggerated success at work, a child may brag about a trip he took to hunt down the Loch Ness monster.

By kindergarten, most children also start to engage in the

socially useful (and, as we saw in the previous chapter, psychologically powerful) practice of false flattery. Kang Lee, director of the Ontario Institute for Studies in Education at the University of Toronto, and Genyue Fu of Zhejiang Normal University, in China, asked a group of children aged three to six for their opinions of drawings, both when the artist was present and when the artist was absent. The three-year-olds didn't alter their judgments of the drawings when the artist was there to overhear their evaluations; they were simply honest in their criticism or admiration. The five- and six-year-olds, though, praised drawings more in the presence of the artist. By this age children have the social wherewithal to use deceit to shade their own opinions.

Clearly we can see that as children grow up, the lies they tell become increasingly complex. In less than three years, they move from basically transparent attempts to escape blame to subtle maskings of their true opinions that reference the sensitivities and egos of others. And there is also another important way in which childhood deception alters with age.

I conducted a study of childhood deception involving three age groups: first graders, seventh graders, and college students. I gave participants in each group two different drinks to try; one tasted pleasant, the other like cough medicine cut with gasoline (at least, that's how Kool-Aid without the sugar tastes to most people). I told the participants that their goal was to convince an interviewer that they liked the repulsive drink as much as the good one, as they might if they were acting in a commercial. I videotaped their reactions and descriptions of the two drinks, and then showed these videos to a group of adult observers.

The observers could usually tell when the first graders had tried the unpleasant drink. Despite some attempts at masking their displeasure, their puckered lips and frowns gave them

away. The seventh graders, though, consistently fooled the observers. Their lies about how the drink tasted were successful.
And the group of college students dissembled so successfully
that they convinced many observers that they were tasting the
good drink when, in fact, they were tasting the bad one.

This study shows a clear progression, one that is echoed
in many other studies and that parallels the development in
complexity of the lies children tell as they age: the older children get, the *better* they are at lying, to the point where eventually their lies become indiscernible from the truth. A lot of
parents claim that lying is something that children grow out of.
In fact, the opposite is true: children grow *into* lying, learning
to become more thoughtful and more nimble liars as they make
their way into young adulthood.

For decades, surveys of parents have shown that honesty
is the trait they most hope their children will display. How,
then, to account for the fact that children become only more
adept at dishonesty as they grow up? There are a number of
answers to this question, which we will explore in the following section. Perhaps the most important, though, is one we
have already seen throughout our discussion of deception in
our lives: while adults may pay lip service to the value of honesty, their behavior often sends a more ambiguous—and even
contradictory—message.

Model Liars

Once upon a time, a young boy named George Washington
was given a new hatchet. Eager to try out his new toy (child
safety standards were different then), young George chopped
down a cherry tree. When George's father saw the dead tree,
he was horrified. He confronted the future Founding Father
and demanded to know whether he was the one who had cut

down the tree. George declared, "I cannot tell a lie!" and confessed. George's father wasn't angry, though. He explained that George's honesty was more valuable than any tree, and forgave him.

Or so the legend goes.

The story of George Washington and the cherry tree remains a popular one in elementary schools across the country. And why not? It adds a patriotic flourish to a lesson every child is taught from preschool on: don't lie. Yet even this seemingly straightforward tale contains ambiguity with regard to the truth. Scholars agree that the legend of Washington and the cherry tree is just that: a legend, one invented by an ex-parson-turned-bookseller in his nineteenth-century biography of the first president.

Teaching our children a made-up story to instill in them the value of honesty is in some ways emblematic of society's larger lessons to children with regard to truth and lies. Even when we feel we are being clear, the message is often mixed. Perhaps this shouldn't surprise us. As we have seen, our own relationship with dishonesty is more complex than we generally acknowledge.

It's important to keep this complexity in mind when examining how children learn to lie. Many children have heard the story of George Washington and the cherry tree. Many others have also heard stories with parallel morals, such as those of the boy who cried wolf or Pinocchio. Yet as common as these stories may be, children's exposure to lies is probably much more frequent—daily at minimum. As we've seen, lies are a common feature of everyday life. A parent tells her boss that she's as sick as a dog and can't come to work, yet makes an amazing recovery as soon as she puts down the phone. A father tells his son he's too tired to play with him, yet later goes out to a bar with his friends. A mother assures her neighbor that she loves her new lawn gargoyle, then tells a friend that it looks hideous.

Children are witness to these lies. We might like to think that preschool children can't recognize fabricated evening plans or a false compliment, but within a few years these are just the kinds of lies children themselves are telling. Mirroring others' behavior—what psychologists refer to as *modeling*—is a powerful aspect of child development. We may *tell* children that honesty is more valuable than any cherry tree—but their observations and experience show that dishonesty is an important part of social life, too. It probably shouldn't surprise us so much to hear children lying in the service of their social and psychological needs. They are only doing what their parents, teachers, aunts, and uncles do.

I call the people who, through their actions and behavior, implicitly teach children to lie, *Model Liars*. Model liars don't set out to teach dishonesty, but because children see them lying and observe the benefits that lying brings, the message is clear: lying works as a social tactic.

Of course, children's lies don't always reflect a deliberate effort to manipulate others. As we have seen, despite our conventional conception of deceit, the bulk of lies we encounter don't have a malicious character—they serve to mask an insecurity, keep a conversation moving, avoid offense. This is true of the lies children tell, as well. Because their thinking is immature, children's lies are often more blatant—again, they'll lie about a hunt for the Loch Ness monster instead of inflating their title at work. Nonetheless, their primary concern is not usually to manipulate or defraud their fellow kindergartener, any more than this is the intent of the woman in line ahead of us at the movies who fibs about her résumé.

It may be possible, then, to reconcile the fact that children do lie frequently with our image of them as innately good (or, at least, largely better than most adults). Lying is not necessarily evidence of wickedness. It's merely evidence that children are human beings too, and, in social situations, employ some of the same tactics as their elders.

There is also another important way in which children are led to deceit by the example, and even the explicit instruction, of adults. To understand how this occurs, imagine that you are the parent of a child involved in the flattery experiment I described earlier. Your kindergartener is being asked to evaluate a series of drawings, sometimes with the artist present, sometimes not. When sitting across from the creator of a drawing you know your child hates, would you really want your child to be honest? Or would you hope your child would do the polite thing and couch his true opinions with some false praise?

These are difficult questions because parents want their children to be honest *and* polite. Often, though, these two values come into conflict. For young children, it's not easy to grasp the nuances of situations in which they are "supposed" to lie. A preschooler might be defensibly confused when she is punished for lying about eating Grandmother's freshly baked cookies, then is punished again for being honest about how unhappy she is to receive Grandmother's hand-knitted sweater. While eventually children do, usually with the help of their parents, master the art of "little white lies," this simply means they've mastered a form of deceit. Despite the stories we tell children, then, the fact is that there is honesty we punish and deception we encourage.

The message of honesty we preach to children is further undercut by the fact that adults themselves don't always practice it—not only in conversations with other adults but also in their dealings with children. I think any parent would confess to having lied to his or her child at some point. Often, these lies are intended to protect the child from a harsh or complex truth. When Jamie Lynn Spears, the then-sixteen-year-old star of Nickelodeon's popular series *Zoey 101*, revealed she was pregnant, parents across the country were faced with some very difficult choices about what to explain to Zoey's young fans. We probably couldn't blame a parent who lied to his or her young child rather than elucidate some of the finer points of conception and teen pregnancy. While some of the lies parents tell are more self-serving—used to steal a few minutes' peace after a long day or simply to evade a discussion of why the sky is blue—many falsehoods are told in the name of good parenting. Children often do lack the mental and emotional sophistication to comprehend issues of death, sex, and violence that lying shields them from. Unfortunately, when children realize they have been lied to, the motives behind the deception are often less important, and less comprehensible, than the fact of the deception itself. Even parents with the best of intentions can end up signaling to their children that lying is an acceptable practice.

When one examines the broad range of exposure children have to the practice of dishonesty, we can see why they lie with the frequency they do. They overhear the adults in their lives, their models for more sophisticated social and mental behavior, lying to one another regularly. Their parents and teachers often explicitly instruct them to lie when civility demands it. And they themselves are lied to, often by the people they trust most in the world.

However, as we've discussed, the bulk of the lies children tell are told without malice. Moreover, it is overly simplistic to view the manifestation of deceit in children in a wholly negative light. Sometimes, a lie means a child has learned to be polite. Or he or she can be demonstrating a sensitivity to someone else's feelings. Importantly, too, we can tell something significant about the child who lies: not necessarily that he or she is "dishonest" but, rather, that he or she has made an important advancement in mental aptitude.

Specifically, a crucial step in children's mental growth is their development of what's called *theory of mind*. Theory of mind doesn't refer to a theory held by psychologists to explain a particular phenomenon. Rather, it is a set of ideas that every one of us holds about how the human mind functions. But theory of mind is not something that we're born with. Instead, it gradually develops as our cognitive abilities become more sophisticated. Before children develop a theory of mind, they have little awareness of the consciousness of other people. Their theory of mind represents their comprehension of how both they themselves and other people think: that people have beliefs, intentions, desires. Prior to theory of mind, children see the world only from their own perspective. What they see, think, and believe they assume everyone sees, thinks, and believes.

Rudiments of a theory of mind begin to emerge after infancy. For example, by preschool age, children can distinguish between something in their minds and physical actuality. A three-year-old knows that he can imagine something that is not physically present, such as a zebra, and that others can do the same. A three-year-old can also pretend that something has happened and react as if it really had occurred. This skill becomes part of their imaginative play, as well as a crucial building block for their earliest attempts at deception.

There are limits, though, to young children's theory of mind. Although three-year-olds understand the concept of "pretend," their understanding of "belief" is still not complete. The difficulty experienced by three-year-olds in comprehending "belief" is illustrated by their performance on what's called a false-belief task. In a typical false-belief task, preschoolers are shown a doll named Maxi who places chocolate in a cabinet and then leaves. After Maxi is gone, though, his mother moves the chocolate somewhere else. After viewing these events, a preschooler is asked where Maxi will look for the chocolate when he returns. Three-year-olds answer (erroneously) that Maxi will look for it in the new location. In contrast, most four-year-olds correctly realize that Maxi has the erroneous false belief that the chocolate is still in the cabinet, and therefore that's where he will look for it.

Lying, of course, beyond the crudest forms, demands an understanding of the concept of belief: that what a person thinks is true is not the same as what is true. Hence, a child who successfully lies demonstrates that he or she has mastered a crucial element of theory of mind. Indeed, telling a plausible lie shows a great deal of sophisticated thinking: an awareness of the beliefs of another person, an ability to manipulate those beliefs through language, and an understanding of what another person might regard as credible. In a sense, then, lying represents an important cognitive milestone.

Further, what's crucial to keep in mind as we assess children's deception is that they arrive at the milestone divorced from its moral implications. Concepts of morality, of right and wrong, involve a whole other order of thinking beyond theory of mind, one that many children have yet to master. Children have the cognitive skills to lie before they have the cognitive skills to comprehend that it is "wrong." For many of them, lying closely resembles playing make-believe, an activity that also allows them to explore their understanding of theory of mind. They do learn quickly that lying is disapproved of in a way that playing make-believe is not—but, as we have seen, they also learn that this disapproval is far from unqualified.

Indeed, for children with certain kinds of developmental disabilities, the inability to lie can be viewed as a symptom of the disorder. The best example is children with autism, a profound disability in which children exhibit language difficulties and such social deficits as the inability to recognize and respond to others' emotions.

Parents of children with autism often report that their children are simply incapable of lying. While at first glance unrelenting honesty might be seen as a virtue, in fact it is at the heart of the social difficulties children with autism experience. For instance, playing children's games becomes an impossibility if the games require children to engage in pretend play. Children with autism are thought to lack a theory of mind allowing them to understand that others have their own perspectives and emotions. In order for a child with autism to lie, they have to understand that two different perspectives are possible simultaneously: the true one ("I broke the lamp") and a false perspective ("Someone else broke it"). Not only are children with autism unable to imagine that false perspective, but they may be unable to understand that the perspective that others hold is different from their own. The inability to understand that multiple perspectives exist makes them feel that what's in their own mind ("I broke the lamp") is apparent to everyone else.

Consider the irony of the situation. Honesty in children with autism is viewed as a manifestation of their disorder. Subsequently, autistic children who were originally unfailingly honest but have begun to show signs of lying effectively are considered to be showing improvement in their condition.

Once again, the view that honesty is good and lying is bad proves flawed.

The Lovable Liar

The daughter of an acquaintance of mine began dating a boy who—at least in her father's view—was a total loser, unworthy of his daughter's affections. The suitor, sixteen years old, didn't do well in school, and he had a large group of friends who were constantly in trouble in school. Yet the daughter—an honor student and all-around high achiever—was entranced with him, despite the fact that she'd caught him in a lie on more than one occasion. And even her father had to admit that there was a certain charm to the boy, who, when he visited the daughter, was unfailingly polite to the father.

We don't usually think of charm and deception as being tied together, and yet that's certainly the case with adults. As I mentioned in Chapter 1, there's a clear connection between skill in lying and more general social aptitude, at least for adults. For adults, good liars also tend to be good at forming friendships, to be more empathetic, to have greater social insight. But does the same hold true for children and adolescents? Is convincing lying associated with a broader array of social skills?

In order to answer the question, I conducted a variation on the experiment with the sweet and bitter drinks I described earlier. In this case, I examined older children, using adolescents aged eleven to sixteen as the participants. As before, I had the adolescents drink and describe both drinks, falsely claiming to like both equally. I videotaped these responses, then showed them to a panel of observers, asking them to judge whether the adolescents actually liked the drink or if they were lying. But in this study, I looked more closely at the participants to get a sense of their social skills. I asked the adolescents' parents and their teachers to rate the participants' social skills, to estimate how many friends they had, and to indicate how many different activities they participated in; from that information I constructed an index of the adolescents' popularity.

As in the previous iteration of the experiment, I found that the older the children were, the better they were at convincing the observers that they liked the awful drink as much as the tasty one. Apparently, skill in lying continues to grow well into adolescence. But the more intriguing result was that the greater the social competence of the adolescents, the more successful they were at deceit. Just like adults, the more popular adolescents were better able to fool the observers with their lies than the less popular ones.

After the study was published, it garnered some attention in the national press, but the results were twisted into a more sensationalistic form. Generally, reporters used a hook claiming I had discovered that lying makes adolescents more popular. That claim is misleading. My study didn't show that adolescents are popular *because* they lie. My study showed that adolescents who are good liars are also successful in other aspects of social life. The results are correlational, not causal, as psychologists like to say. Think of the distinction this way: socially successful adolescents tend to be good liars, and fire engines tend to be red. We can't conclude from these statements that adolescents are socially successful because they're good liars any more than we can conclude that a truck is a fire engine because it's red.

The connection between lying and social aptitude in adolescents is real, though, and has several possible explanations. It may be that socially competent adolescents are better liars because they have more opportunities to practice their deception. Since they are socially competent, they have a lot of friends, and in interacting with all these people, they have ample opportunity

to hone their lying skills. Adolescents who are less socially competent, on the other hand, have fewer friends, and so fewer chances
to practice deception. It is also possible that socially competent
adolescents are more comfortable with social situations in general, and this comfort allows them to be relaxed enough to pull
off a lie. As we've seen from the previous chapter, anxiety is the
foremost clue people look for in detecting deception.

Yet neither of these explanations seems fully satisfactory.
First, just because an adolescent is socially competent does not
necessarily mean that he or she has more social interactions
(and so more opportunities to practice lying) than an adolescent with less social competence. Social incompetence doesn't
mean an adolescent can't have an after-school job, play a school
sport, or come from a large family. Such a teenager, on balance, would probably have more social interactions than a socially skilled teenager who is an only child and spends time after
school studying. Second, comfort in social situations is not, as
we have seen, a prerequisite for pulling off a lie. Indeed, many
people lie because they *aren't* comfortable in social situations.

Perhaps the best explanation for the connection between
social skills and deceit becomes clear if we don't draw such a
sharp contrast between the two. In other words, we might think
of deceit as a social skill itself—or, rather, as a component of
many social skills. Almost by definition, socially skilled people
tend to be tactful, polite, and ingratiating. All these qualities
can involve a distortion of one's true opinions and reactions.
Sometimes, they are little more than distortion. Taken in the
context of children, we can also say that qualities like tact, as
well as the knowledge of when to employ them, signal a certain
maturity in social interactions.

By this reasoning, then, lying not only demonstrates important steps in cognitive development; it also has implications

for social development. Children who integrate deception into their social lives show that they have mastered some of the more subtle forms of interpersonal interaction. And given how frequent lying is in daily life, they also show that they have mastered one of the more common forms.

The manifestation of deception in children is not simply a matter of falling short of the standard set by George Washington. Lying in children is typical, it shows a sensitivity to adult behavior, and it demonstrates mental and social acuity. In fact, a parent might have more cause for alarm if his or her child does not lie than if the child does.

Of course, most parents don't see it this way. And, as we have seen throughout our discussion of lying in our lives, while lying is in some ways more benign than we usually think, in other ways it is more harmful. Certainly, the widespread deception surveys show that in children it has negative consequences. Consider again its implications for the multibillion-dollar No Child Left Behind Act.

Further, if we are interested in building a more honest culture, this should start with raising more honest children. And while lying is a common feature of child development, rampant dishonesty is not inevitable. One of the easiest ways adults can help children be more honest is not to box them into deception. This happens, ironically, in real-world scenarios that closely resemble the peeking experiment. Adults will often confront a child about something the adult knows the child has done. ("Were you the one who cut the tablecloth into a dress?" is an example from my days of raising children.) In such situations, children are essentially encouraged to lie—they will often see deception as their last chance to avoid punishment. Such tactics by adults undercut what might be a sincere wish in children to try to be honest.

Rather than taking the approach of snuffing out any and all instances of lying, adults might do better to teach children that honesty is a difficult but still achievable goal. They might point out that while the moral of the story of George Washington and the cherry tree is a valuable one, even the most honest people lie on occasion. The point is to make a sincere effort to be truthful, while balancing a sensitivity to other people's feelings. While some parents may feel such a message is too complex for their children, it bears noting that being honest is perhaps no less complex for adults, either. And regardless of how they are introduced to this complexity, they will discover it one way or another.

The fact that children lie drives home the point that deception is a fact of modern culture. Indeed, it may be a fact of human *life*. Vasudevi Reddy of the University of Portsmouth, in England, recently conducted a study of deception in the youngest children: infants. Through her research, Reddy identified what she considers deceptive behavior starting in children as young as six months old. Infants, Reddy asserts, use tactics such as fake crying and laughing to win attention.

This research is new, and the intention, deceptive or not, behind any infant behavior may ultimately be impossible to fix. Still, Reddy's research raises an intriguing question: If children are lying in the crib, is it really a behavior they learn from adults? It's possible that lying may have a deeper source: the DNA of every human. As we will consider next, the reason children become such proficient liars may be, in fact, that they are born to lie.

CHAPTER 4

The Evolution of Deceit: Are We Born to Lie?

Even at seventy-seven, Elva Giddings was a sharp, competent woman; she lived alone and managed her own household. Like many people, though, she had dreams of instant wealth and loved to fill out cards to enter sweepstakes. And one day, her dreams came true: she received a telephone call informing her that she had won second place in a lottery and had $240,000 coming her way. All she had to do was pay the taxes on her winnings, which came to only $10,000.

After Elva sent a check for the $10,000, she got more good news. The first-place winner of the lottery had been disqualified, and now Elva would be receiving $2 million. All she needed to do was pay the additional taxes on the grand prize—to the tune of over $70,000. For Elva, this money constituted almost all of her savings, money she'd intended to give her grandchildren to help them pay for college. Still, the prospect of a multimillion-dollar payday proved all too enticing. Elva sent the check.

As you have probably already guessed, she never received her $2 million windfall. Elva Giddings had fallen victim to a lottery scam, variations of which have cheated Americans out of billions of dollars. Luckily for Elva, by the time she sent the

$70,000 check, her phone calls with the con man perpetrating the lottery scam had begun to be monitored by law enforcement officials. They were able to break up the fraud before the check was ever cashed.

Many victims of lottery scams and other such schemes aren't so lucky. By some estimates, each year one out of every three adult Americans receives a call from a con man. Often the cons are cloaked with the prospects of easy wealth: your wishes for prosperity have been granted; all you have to do is pay. Frequently, too, these scams make use of the digital technologies that are ubiquitous in modern society. The con men hide their tracks using a web of pagers, stolen cell phone numbers, and calling cards.

Up to now, we've looked mostly at forms of deception that are normal—in the sense that they are common, in the sense that nearly everyone practices them, and in the sense that our daily lives would appear to us as *abnormal* without them. Lies outside the realm of civility or advertising or cocktail-party chatter, though—lies, say, of the variety used to defraud Elva Giddings—are hardly normal in any sense. Lottery scams and other such schemes are perpetrated relatively rarely, and by unusually unscrupulous people. Also, nearly everyone else in society would agree that we'd be better off without these sorts of lies. There is, however, one perspective from which a lottery scheme could be considered normal. One could argue that such deception is *natural*.

Consider the portia spider. The portia is a hairy creature about the size of a button on a dress shirt, and species of it are found in Africa, Australia, and many parts of Asia. Most spiders we're familiar with eat insects, but the portia has a taste for other spiders—not to mention sophisticated methods for catching them. Portias regularly attack larger spiders, sometimes as big as twice their own size. Like humans, the portia compensates for its physical limitations with exceptional cunning.

The portia has excellent vision, but most other spiders see poorly. They rely on the vibrations they feel in their web to identify what has landed there. Spiders can tell the difference between the shaking in their web made by a trapped, helpless insect and that made by an approaching predator or a potential mate. The portia spider uses this reliance on vibration against its prey. When landing on or moving across the web of its potential meal, it waits for natural cover provided by a falling leaf or a breeze. In this way, the vibrations made by its approach are masked. Its prey is not even aware that it is under attack. And this is only the beginning of portias' extraordinary predatory skills. Portia spiders are actually able to manipulate the webs of their prey to mimic the vibrations of trapped food or a hopeful suitor. The unsuspecting spider heads toward what it thinks is a tasty meal or a likely mate, only to be ambushed and eaten by the portia. Still more extraordinary is the fact that different types of spiders "feel" for different types of vibrations, and the portia will change how it manipulates a web depending on what it is hunting. The vibrations that attract one type of spider will have no effect on another, and the portia adjusts accordingly. Sometimes, the portia will employ trial and error to hit upon a deceptive vibration that attracts its prey, even spending days patiently testing false cues until something works.

A predator uses the promise of a false reward to manipulate its prey into a compromised position. It's hard not to think of Elva Giddings and the lottery scheme that ensnared her. However, there are important distinctions between the behavior of the portia spider and the behavior of human con men—or of any human. While the portia spider might appear to be using reason and knowledge of its prey to draw conclusions about how to attack it, this is only an appearance. Portia spiders aren't capable of such sophisticated thinking; really, they aren't capable of thinking at all. Their behavior is a function of instinct, formed by way of evolution over thousands and thousands of generations. Only humans can "think up" ways to trick and attack a meal or a mark. Our capacity to devise and enact noninstinctive plans is one thing that sets us apart from other animals.

Still, even if the cognitive process behind the deception of a portia spider and that of a human con man is different, the behavior itself remains remarkably similar. Both species send false signals—the spider through web vibrations, the human through language—to create the illusion of a benefit. They then exploit this illusion for their own profit—caloric or monetary, as the case may be.

As skilled at deception as humans are, we do not hold a monopoly on the behavior. The portia spider plucking out false signals on its prey's web is just one example of the falsehoods and manipulations that occur across the natural world. As we will see, nonhuman deception can be almost as varied and complex as the kind practiced by humans.

The ubiquity of deception in nature presents an intriguing possibility as we investigate the lying in our lives. We often think of the practice of deception as a kind of falling away from the natural order of things. But given that the youngest of children often lie (as discussed in the previous chapter), given that animals so often deceive one another, perhaps the deception in modern life is not a falling away from the natural order, but, rather, a sign of consistency with it. In other words, perhaps deception is something humans are born to do.

The Evolution of Deceit

Lie or Die

Before Charles Darwin published *On the Origin of Species,* in 1859, it was widely believed that the earth had been created only a few thousand years ago, by God, in seven days, as described in Genesis. All the animal and plant life on earth had been created in that week, and it existed in the same form then as in modern times. Creation was more or less static, and was ordered in a hierarchy with human beings at the top.

So it's hard to overstate the importance of Darwin's theories to the way we view ourselves, the world around us, and how it all came to be. The static model was replaced by a model of constant adaptation and change. Instead of humanity being above nature, we were thrust into the thick of it, an animal as much as any other. And the creating hand of God was replaced by Darwin's engine of natural selection, an engine fueled by competition and death.

Darwin's theories suggest that anything that gives an individual creature an advantage in surviving its environment or in finding a mate can be selected for and passed on. In hummingbirds, larger beak size provides an advantage in survival, as it increases the kinds of flowers from which the birds can draw nectar. In an example of what's called sexual selection—the selection of traits that provide an advantage in attracting or winning a mate—male peacocks have developed their elaborate plumage. In nineteenth-century England, the peppered moth changed color, going from speckled gray to black, as darkness in color provided better camouflage against trees now covered in industrial soot. And, in an example of the selection of a trait that provides protection against a specific predator, there are spiders that have evolved a sort of alarm at the approach of a portia spider; they will abandon their web in a panic if they sense the subtle signs of the approach of this deadly foe.

All this brings us back to lying. We usually think of Darwinian adaptations as things like wing color and beak size. But in a range of contexts, deception has proven an advantageous trait for survival and procreation. To put it simply, nature has selected deceit, and we see it in a vast array of plants, insects, and animals. The forms of this deception are also highly varied, being played out as adaptations to the range of environments in which living things struggle to pass on their genes.

In its crudest forms, natural deception can be entirely passive. This is the case with one of the most pervasive forms of deceit, as well as perhaps the simplest: camouflage. It's not hard to see the advantages it gives a creature to be able to blend in with its surroundings. If a predator can't find you, it can't eat you. Frequently, though, camouflage goes beyond a simple matching of background colors, as in the case of a peppered moth perched on a soot-covered London tree. Zebras have stripes to make it difficult for a predator to differentiate between the individuals in a herd. Some creatures are camouflaged to look like something they are not: insects of the order Phasmatodea have the color and long, slender appearance of a stick; the wings of certain praying mantises are wide, flat, and green, so that viewed from above they look almost identical to a leaf. The portia spider has developed a similar characteristic: its coloration makes it look like a piece of forest detritus, such as a scrap of bark, a trait that further exploits the poor eyesight of its prey.

In other cases, creatures are camouflaged to look like different creatures. Certain harmless butterflies have the same wing patterns as the poisonous heliconid variety—a bluff to fend off hungry birds. Many other butterflies and moths have "eyespots" on their wings, dark, circular markings that may give the impression to a predator that it is being watched—

and affording its prey crucial time in which to escape. Animal impersonation can even occur across species. Young bushveld lizards are black, in order to mimic the toxic oogpister beetle. The mirror orchid has a flower that looks like a female wasp. It augments this deceptive lure with the release of a scent similar to a female wasp's pheromones. In this way, the mirror orchid attracts male wasps looking to mate, allowing the flower to spread its pollen despite the fact that it contains no nectar.

Deception carried out by way of appearance is only the simplest form of natural trickery, though. Many animals are capable of *acting* deceptively, too. A huge variety of creatures employ the tactic of "playing dead" when threatened. Opossums are so notorious for their imitations of a dead or sickly animal that their name has become synonymous with the strategy. But the prize for the most dramatic imitation of death should probably go to the hognose snake. In playing dead, a hognose will roll over onto its back, excrete fecal matter and a disgusting odor, and let its tongue hang limp as drops of blood fall from its mouth.

The behaviors animals can fake go beyond imitations of death. The methods animals use for communication can also be the methods they use to deceive one another. It's a stretch to say that animals tell one another lies. This implies a capacity for intention and behavioral insight that all but a few species lack. But the signals they send to one another do not always communicate what the recipient understands them to, and this misunderstanding frequently benefits the sender.

For example, fireflies use their luminescence in order to seek out a mate. Male fireflies signal their presence to prospective partners by illuminating near an area where a female might be found. Females, who are flightless, illuminate back to signal to a male that they are willing sexual partners. At least, that is how it usually works. In some firefly species, a female signals a willingness to mate, but only as a hunting tactic. When the duped suitor arrives, she eats him.

Frogs, too, communicate false signals to one another. Male green frogs use their croaks to announce their size. Larger males have a lower-pitched croak. Sometimes, though, small frogs will lower their croaks, imitating the signals of a bigger male. This can serve to ward off the challenges of competitors. Or, taking a page from the behavior of certain female fireflies, males will give voice to their distinctive mating call, only to attack the female who is duped into approaching.

The urge to procreate, which underpins the mechanism of evolution as a whole, can also be used by one species against another. Bolas spiders do not spin webs. Instead, they are fishermen who use a synthetic form of moth pheromone as bait. This bait is contained on a sticky glob at the end of a single line of silk. The bolas spider lowers this line and swings it to ensnare the male moths attracted to the scent of a sexually aroused female.

But no discussion of cross-species animal deception would be complete without mention of social parasites. These natural spongers are able to trick their hosts—often socially organized insects such as bees, wasps, and ants—into caring for them and their offspring. Often, they achieve this by synthesizing the chemicals that the exploited species uses to identify members of its own group. The staphylinid beetle, for example, can make ants believe that it is a larva of their own colony, and the ants will feed it and care for it even as it repays their hospitality by eating the colony's real ant larvae.

The variety and frequency of deception in nature demonstrates that it offers its practitioners an advantage in the great game of survival and procreation. Note, also, that in many of the examples mentioned above, we've been discussing some of the least intelligent forms of animal life: frogs, fireflies, beetles. Clearly, it does not take a large brain to execute some fairly cunning acts of deception.

Yet as we consider the question of whether the deception that humans practice has evolutionary roots, it is important to keep in mind that animals of the intelligence of a bug don't employ deception the way we do. As in the difference in the behavior of a portia spider and the con man who scammed Elva Giddings, creatures like beetles and fireflies enact their deceit purely as a function of instinct. Their behavior can be thought of as reflexive: it neither requires learning nor exhibits understanding.

In this, humans differ even from animals that can, in a limited way, alter their deceptive behavior based on the response of their targets. Piping plovers have evolved a very cunning way of protecting their nests. When predators threaten their chicks, plovers will fake a broken wing and scurry in the opposite direction, hoping to draw the attention of the hostile animal away with the promise of an easy meal. If they see that they have lost the predator's attention, they will squawk more loudly and flap their "broken" wing more elaborately. Yet while this demonstrates some ability to tailor an automatic response to a specific situation, one could argue that even this is merely a function of instinct—a hardwired behavior honed by natural selection over thousands of generations of fleeing plovers.

Human deception operates in clear contrast to this. Unlike animals, we don't lie only when presented with particular stimuli—say, when an intruder enters our home and threatens our children, or when we hope to lure a mate into what will be a less-than-permanent relationship. Our deception is flexible, it is creative, and we can employ it in almost any context or environment. In this way, our lying makes use of our truly characteristic adaptation, the one that more than anything else sets us apart from our fellow animals: our minds.

Tic-Tac-Toe or Calvinball

In Bill Watterson's comic strip *Calvin and Hobbes*, Calvin and his imaginary tiger friend Hobbes play a one-of-a-kind game they dub Calvinball. The rules of Calvinball are simple: you make the rules up as you go along. The action is fast as players reveal themselves as double agents, scores climb as high as Q to 12, and equipment from eye masks to volleyballs to croquet wickets enter the fray and are then declared irrelevant. Calvinball is spontaneous, borderless, and requires wit more than athleticism.

Contrast that to a game of tic-tac-toe. A player has only one of nine squares in which to mark an X or O. The possibilities for strategy are limited, at best. Most games end in a tie.

As we've discussed, the deception most creatures on earth enact is instinctive. Given a particular stimulus, they respond in a particular deceptive way. When a plover with chicks senses the approach of a predator, it is wired to run away while feigning a broken wing. In rough terms, it's playing tic-tac-toe. A predator makes an X, and the plover responds with reflexive O to block it. The variety in nature means that these contests are played out much more elaborately than four crossed lines on a piece of paper allows for. But the mechanism of the behavior is basically the same: stimulus X elicits deceptive behavior O.

When humans lie, we're playing Calvinball. We are not bounded by particular stimuli or particular behavior. We can invent and fashion our lies to suit the situation or in response to whomever we are "playing" against. The forms of deceit humans are capable of are as limitless as the human imagination.

It's important to keep in mind, when evaluating the cunning of a portia spider, the intelligence of the creatures it is fooling. While its hunting tactics may be impressive for an animal with the brain the size of a pin, its prey species have pin-sized brains, too. The spiders the portia hunts aren't capable of insight into their attackers or of devising new solutions to the problem of predation.

When humans attempt to lie to other humans, on the other hand, they are trying to fool the smartest animals on earth. Human deception demands the flexibility and creativity of a game of Calvinball because humans are, relatively speaking, so difficult to fool. Just because a con man makes an X, that does not mean his target will make an O.

The key distinction biologists make between the deception practiced by humans and that seen in much of the animal kingdom is that the former involves what's called "mind reading." This is not the application of psychic powers, though that would surely be a useful tactic in deceit. Rather, reading minds means applying our understanding of what other people think, believe, or expect. Recall our discussion of theory of mind in the previous chapter. The awareness of the minds of others and how they operate is a crucial asset in our ability to manipulate one another. We can assess what we know other people think, as well as how they think, in order to fool them.

Mind reading is the fundamental element in the huge diversity of human deceptive behavior. We address our knowledge of what others think when we give a sensitive friend a false compliment, when we deceive our boss about our workload, and when we invent an excuse to avoid an unappealing social invitation. The mechanics of how we deceive—our decision as to when a lie might be necessary, the attention we give to persuasion and plausibility, the cues we look for to see whether our lie is successful—all hinge on our reading others' minds.

Consider, for instance, the mind-reading dynamics of even

a very straightforward lie. Let's say Eve asks her husband, Adam, whether he cleaned the gutters yet. Adam didn't—and he knows his wife will be upset to find that out. So he tells her a lie: "Yes, I cleaned them this morning before you got up." He knows that Eve is going out later in the afternoon, and this will give him a chance to actually clean the gutters, thereby covering up his lie. Again, it is a simple, seemingly uncomplicated lie, the kind of lie even a child could tell.

Yet even such a basic example of human deceit involves complexity on the mental level. Adam has to assess, first, what Eve knows. He can't trick her if she's been outside and seen the clogged gutters. Second, he has to make an assessment as to what Eve will believe. His addition of the "I cleaned them this morning" has to be plausible, and must contribute to the overall plausibility of the deceit. Finally, he has to make a judgment about what Eve will do. For the lie to succeed, he needs to know that she won't immediately check the gutters, and that later in the day she will go out and give him a chance to really do the work. Hence, even a lie like "Yes, I cleaned them this morning" demands accurate assessments of the target's knowledge, judgment, and intentions. The portia spider's behavior is impressive, but let's give our species some credit, too.

Without question, our great capacity for mind reading makes us distinct from all of nature's other liars. But the question of whether mind reading, to any degree of sophistication, is something humans alone can engage in is less clear. While we may be the best mind readers on the planet, we might not be the only ones.

Cheating Monkeys

I have never been sure why, but we humans seem to find endless amusement in primates. We dress chimpanzees up in

The Evolution of Deceit

tuxedos and laugh when they stick out their tongues. Images of monkeys adorn greeting cards and baby clothes. For years, my daughter asked for a pet monkey for her birthday. (No, I didn't oblige.) We seem to have cultivated an image of primates as lovable scamps—just like us but, well, *cuter*. I don't dispute that some monkeys are cute, of course. But when we choose our greeting cards, we may not give enough consideration to the first half of this characterization: how much like us they truly are.

Richard Byrne and Andrew Whiten, evolutionary psychologists at the University of St. Andrews, in Scotland, have spent decades studying primate behavior. They have compiled a database of hundreds of incidents of monkeys and apes cheating, tricking, and manipulating one another. In some of these cases, their behavior seems to resemble very closely the less admirable habits of their more evolved relatives.

For instance, male monkeys who live in social groups are generally ordered in strict hierarchies. The dominant males control the access to females in the group. Primatologists have observed subordinate males sneaking off with females to have sex out of sight of the dominant male leaders. The clandestine lovers will even muffle the sounds of their copulation, in order to further hide their tryst. In a similar incident, a baboon was crafty enough to keep her head and shoulders visible to the dominant male in her group, while behind a rock, her hands were busy grooming a subordinate male.

Primates also frequently use deception to cheat each other out of another of life's essentials besides sex: food. Whiten and Byrne recorded the story of one young baboon in the Drakensberg Mountains of southern Africa, whom primatologists called Paul. Paul noticed another baboon digging up a tasty plant bulb. Once the bulb was loose, young Paul let out a scream, and his frightened mother quickly came charging over, fright-

ening away the baboon who'd been digging up the bulb. Paul
was now free to take the bulb for himself. In another example,
a Dutch primatologist, Frans Plooij, saw a chimpanzee come
upon some food, only to hide it when another chimp appeared.
The first chimp waited until the other had departed, sitting
placidly as if nothing was out of the ordinary, before retrieving
the food for himself.

The complexity of the deception in these examples sepa-
rates it from the reflexive, programmed deception of spiders
and fireflies. Clearly, the higher-order intelligence of primates
is at work in their deceit. Yet the question of whether any of
these acts demonstrates mind reading, the hallmark of human
deception, is the source of a heated debate among ethologists.
In some cases, it certainly appears that apes and monkeys manipulate the thinking of others. When Paul cried out for his
mother, he seemed to comprehend in some way what her response would be, and to exploit this comprehension to his own
benefit. The female baboon who showed just enough of herself
to convince the dominant male in her group that she wasn't up
to any illicit grooming did seem to have an awareness of what
the dominant male might suspect and what he might be reassured by. On the other hand, these behaviors could simply be
the result of trial and error—a basic form of learning possible
for animals of far more limited intelligence than primates, and
one that doesn't require understanding of the minds of other
creatures. Perhaps, for instance, Paul had noticed that calling for his mother often resulted in his getting food, and so his
behavior was not so much manipulation of her reactions as a
learned response drawn from other, similar situations.

The question of whether baboons, chimps, or other of our
closest animal relatives can read minds ultimately comes down
to whether they understand what a mind is at all. Recent stud-

ies along the lines of the Maxi doll experiment described in the previous chapter have suggested that some nonhuman primates do, in fact, have some understanding of theory of mind. Yet ascribing theory of mind to monkeys and apes may always be a matter of conjecture, since on some level it seems fundamentally impossible to know what any nonhuman creature is *actually thinking*. Their behavior may be indicative of theory of mind, but so then is the behavior of a portia spider.

Yet even if we grant that monkey or ape methods of manipulation are less sophisticated than human methods, the fact that their deceptive behavior is so similar to ours offers some intriguing clues about the origin of lying. Indeed, these clues may take us beyond an understanding of the source of our deception and even offer insight into the source of humanity's advanced intelligence in general. Some scientists believe that human deception is not only a function of evolution but also the driving force behind it. Lies, in other words, may have made us who we are today.

The Arms Race of the Mind

We've been looking at some peculiar animal behavior. Now let's look at an oddity among us humans. Every December, members of *Homo sapiens* adorn their homes in multicolored electrical lights, festoon their lawns with plastic likenesses of elves and reindeer, and sometimes go so far as to inflate enormous plastic depictions of a man in a red suit with a white beard. I'm talking, of course, about the annual habit of putting out Christmas decorations—a human behavior that if not you, someone living very close to you engages in.

Now let's look at another aspect of this behavior. Perhaps one of your neighbors—let's call him Kris—takes enormous pride in having the splashiest, showiest Christmas display in town. And another neighbor we'll call Nick has the same ambition. So when Kris gets a ten-foot Christmas tree for his yard, Nick gets a twelve-footer. Nick spells out "Merry Christmas" in lights on his roof, so Kris spells out "Merry Christmas and Happy New Year!" Kris hires carolers to serenade passersby; Nick pays for a twelve-piece orchestra. And so forth.

The point of this (only slightly) exaggerated story of one-upsmanship is that without the other's presence in the neighborhood, neither Kris nor Nick would ever achieve such heights of jollity or electrical usage. The principle at work is escalation. Each man raises the stakes for the other, and each responds by raising them again, in a cycle that spirals upward.

Now let's turn back to the question of deceit, and whether it can be considered a behavior humans developed as a product of evolution. As we've discussed, deception provides an advantage in survival and procreation to a myriad of creatures. But if we think of the animal kingdom as static, we're making the same mistake pre-Darwinian thinkers made. Evolution is an ongoing process. If deception manifests itself as a trait that provides an advantage, the ability to detect that deception might be an advantageous trait, too. If a firefly has a better chance of survival by tricking other fireflies into thinking it wants to mate when it really wants to eat, a firefly who can tell the difference has a better chance of survival by avoiding that risk. Following this line of thinking, an even more cunning firefly might then come along who can trick even the more discerning fireflies— seizing an advantage until natural selection turns out another, still more discerning version of the firefly. And so forth.

This "arms race" conception of evolution, the same one mirrored in the decoration war between Kris and Nick, has recently been applied to humans and the development of their intelligence. Richard Byrne and Andrew Whiten, who created a catalog of hundreds of instances of monkey and ape deceit, hypothesize that for early humans, deception and manipulation provided key advantages in survival. The first humans, many anthropologists agree, lived in social groups of shifting composition and frequently changing alliances. In these circumstances, Byrne and Whiten believe, the ability to lie, cheat, and swindle effectively would have been invaluable in winning food, status, and opportunities to mate. Perhaps equally advantageous, though, would have been the ability to *detect* the liars, cheaters, and swindlers who beset early man. And just as these opposing pressures push Kris and Nick to further Christmas extravagances, the evolutionary battle between liars and the need to detect lies pushed early man's mind to greater and greater capacity. In what they call their "Machiavellian intelligence hypothesis," Byrne and Whiten posit that the struggles among our ancestors to outsmart and outwit one another were the key to the evolution of intelligence in *Homo sapiens*.

Obviously, such a hypothesis is all but impossible to confirm, but there is mounting evidence in support of it. A correlation has been found in primates between a species' average neocortex size and the group size in which the species' members live—pointing to a connection between mental capacity and the complexity of social interactions. Also, mathematical simulations modeling the growth of intelligence show that competition can spark an explosion in cognitive capacity.

But if our intelligence has its roots in deception, what are the implications for our culture? If our brains are in some way selected to be deceptive, can we be anything but?

It's important to keep in mind that the Machiavellian intelligence hypothesis remains merely that—a hypothesis. Many anthropologists would agree that living in social groups does spur intelligence but would disagree with Byrne and Whiten that it is specifically *Machiavellian* encounters that are at the heart of this phenomenon. Almost any social interaction, especially within the context of a large group, can have a complexity that might drive intelligence. Collaboration and cooperation have their nuances, too, after all.

Yet even if our ancestors made deception part of our genetic inheritance, it does not mean we are destined to lie. Human society functions because we are able to resist many of our "animal instincts." Probably more than theory of mind, it is this ability to deny our impulses that truly makes us different from the rest of the earth's inhabitants. We may see the opportunity to lie; we may even feel, we might imagine, some primordial tug to do so. That does not mean we must follow through with it.

These issues of denying our instincts probably have their most frequent applications in the realm of relationships. In this arena, the urge to deceive and the risks of being deceived are particularly urgent. In the next chapter, we will examine how our values, our commitments, and our inescapable sex drive shape and erode the honesty between spouses, lovers, and boyfriends and girlfriends.

CHAPTER 5

Broken Trust:
Loving a Liar

Perhaps the most dramatic and notorious example of broken trust in recent years played out, as these matters often do, against the backdrop of politics. Eliot Spitzer arrived in Albany with great ambition. Having won the governorship of New York by a landslide, Spitzer promised to reform stagnant Albany politics once and for all. During his eight years as New York's attorney general, he had earned a reputation as a tireless fighter of corporate corruption, clashing with business titans who tried to stand in the way of his reforms. The self-styled "sheriff of Wall Street" was now going to bring his ethical crusade to a whole new arena. But the man who had built his career on fighting dishonesty in the financial world was undone by his own deceptions, ones enacted in a wholly different realm. In March 2008, it was revealed that Spitzer had been recorded on a federal wiretap arranging to meet a prostitute at a Washington, D.C., hotel. Within days of this disclosure, Spitzer, who was married and the father of three children, resigned.

The incident triggered a frenzy in the national media. The ironies seemed simply too choice for the press to resist: the paragon of justice caught red-handed in a crime, the symbol of virtue enmeshed in something so patently tawdry. There was another element to the story, though, of which many commentators made special mention. At the press conferences Spitzer held as the scandal unfolded, his wife, Silda Wall Spitzer, stone-faced and stricken, appeared by his side. For many, she was a sad and unsettling figure. And the attention she received was probably not simply a matter of sympathy or embarrassment on her behalf. Surely, there was some element of identification.

An old soul song sums up the situation nicely: "Everybody plays the fool." Sooner or later, all of us will fall victim to emotional betrayal in some form. Loved ones may break their promises; we may catch them in a pattern of calculated deceit; spouses or lovers may cheat. The feelings accompanying the revelation of such betrayals are often devastating. It can seem as if all the positive feelings associated with love and trust have been pulled inside out, transformed into their own inverses: hurt, humiliation, fear, and loneliness, to name just a few. It was emotions like these that many people saw on the face of Silda Wall Spitzer, perhaps catching echoes of painful episodes in their own emotional histories.

Most of the lies we encounter in our daily lives have fairly low emotional stakes. We might be surprised to learn that the stranger we've struck up a conversation with on the train platform hasn't, as he says, seen *The Third Man*, but it's unlikely we'd be truly hurt by this revelation. Some lies, though, have the potential do real, and deep, emotional harm. And while these lies are relatively rare when compared to the deceptive social niceties we encounter in nearly every interaction, their potential consequences make them extremely important to understand.

The problem, of course, is that they are by nature *difficult* to understand. The first question that follows the admission of deception is almost inevitably "Why?" But the "Because" is elusive, sometimes even for the liar. First, the varieties of emotional betrayal are as diverse as the individuals who enact them and the particular relationships they violate. What is for one couple a minor bending of the truth may be for another a wholesale violation of the bonds that hold that couple together. Further, the reasons a person might trick her spouse or manipulate his closest friend are often particular to that individual. Further still, as suggested above, the individual who enacts the betrayal may not fully understand the *why* behind the behavior any more than the person betrayed does. Our motivations for many of our actions are opaque—this can be especially true with regard to an act as complex, and with as complex consequences, as the betrayal of trust.

Nevertheless, psychologists and other researchers have made progress in seeking to understand why the bonds of trust can be broken. For many of the same reasons that the press gave so much attention to Eliot Spitzer's downfall, their focus has often been on infidelity. It is an act that is both common and dramatic, making it something we can all understand and at once all be (ostensibly) horrified by. Plus, it has the added benefit of being associated with sex—an appeal that should not be overlooked, even for academics. Most of all, though, among all the emotional wounds we commonly inflict on one another, infidelity is probably the one that cuts the deepest. And while the dynamics of infidelity are often relevant to other forms of betrayal, cheating, as we all have witnessed or even felt, inflicts a unique brand of pain.

Cheating: How Much and How Often

Eliot Spitzer was hardly the first politician to have been caught up in a scandal involving infidelity and prostitution. But the events that followed his resignation probably gave even the most proudly cynical residents of New York pause. Spitzer was replaced in office by his lieutenant governor, David Paterson. Paterson, legally blind and the first African-American to become governor of New York, had been married for fifteen years when he took office. But the day after being installed as governor, he, too, admitted to infidelity. Indeed, he confessed that he had had multiple extramarital affairs—as had his wife.

Most likely, few of us retain many illusions about the sanctity of the marriages we observe in public life. Still, when consecutive governors in one of the largest states are revealed to be unfaithful (and let's not forget an earlier New York governor, Nelson Rockefeller, who reputedly died in flagrante with a young female aide in 1979), it can't help but make us wonder how ubiquitous infidelity really is. If people with so much to lose aren't faithful, what about those who risk only the trust of their spouse or lover?

Even if all the Bill Clintons and John Edwardses and Eliot Spitzers guilty of infidelity suddenly, as a group, stopped cheating (not likely, but theoretically possible), we probably still wouldn't lack for opportunities to wonder and worry about the frequency of infidelity. Most of us personally know people who cheat. Not a few of us have likely been cheated on in the past. Sometimes, it may seem that monogamy is the exception in our society.

Psychologists, as well as other social scientists, have struggled to answer the question of how common infidelity really is. The first problem is one we discussed earlier in the context of lying in general: definition. Simply put, what counts as infidelity? Is it exclusively extramarital sexual intercourse? Should sex acts short of intercourse count as infidelity or (as Bill Clinton might argue) not? And what about nonphysical relationships?

Is it possible to commit emotional adultery? Cyberadultery? And in what sort of relationships is the question of infidelity even relevant? Most people would agree that marriage is not a prerequisite for cheating, but at what point does a casual relationship become a monogamous one?

In addition to this problem of defining infidelity, there is the nature of infidelity itself. As with any violation of another person's trust, cheating is something those who practice want to keep secret. No guarantee of anonymity may be sufficient for an adulterous spouse to admit his or her behavior to a researcher. One study showed that those currently in a marriage were far more likely to deny infidelity than those whose marriages had already ended. This reluctance to confess is not always simply a matter of discretion, either. Admitting infidelity to a psychologist also means admitting it *to yourself*. Because definitions of infidelity are so flexible, it can be easy to construct reassuring notions about what is and is not cheating.

With these caveats in mind, though, we can address some of the insight researchers have gained into the frequency of infidelity in our society. Psychologists Adrian Blow of Michigan State University and Kelley Hartnett of St. Louis University conducted an in-depth review of recent studies of infidelity. In looking at the range of work done on the question of the frequency of infidelity, they determined that most researchers have found cheating occurs in less than 25 percent of marriages. While much data supports this statistic, again, it is important to keep it in context. Blow and Hartnett's figure holds for heterosexual married couples engaging in extramarital sex. Rates of infidelity are not necessarily the same for, say, unmarried cohabiting couples or homosexual couples or with regard to sexual behavior that is not intercourse. More specific statistics on how frequent infidelity is will require broader research. (It's worth noting that sexuality is generally among the trickier subjects for psychologists to sort out empirically, even when they are not focused specifically on a taboo behavior like infidelity.)

One conclusion about infidelity that psychologists can make with confidence, though, is that most people have a clear opinion about it. They don't like it. Surveys show that an overwhelming majority of Americans consider infidelity to be wrong. In a 2001 Gallup poll, 89 percent of respondents said that "married men and women having an affair" is wrong. Interestingly, this same study found that attitudes about infidelity have become *more* conservative in the last few decades—in contrast to attitudes toward other aspects of sexuality, such as premarital sex. It seems the consensus that infidelity is immoral is growing, in spite of (or perhaps because of) the prominent adultery scandals of recent years.

In this way, infidelity and other serious breaches of trust differ from many of the other types of lying we've discussed to this point. Most people would likely argue that false flattery or the protective lies we tell children and friends are a beneficial aspect of social discourse. But surveys such as the Gallup poll cited above indicate that few of us would defend sexual or emotional dishonesty. As a society, we seem to recognize that behavior like infidelity has corrosive and painful results. Infidelity, for example, is among the leading causes of divorce, of battery, and even of murder. Yet as we all know, through the stories of friends or the headlines in the *New York Post* or firsthand experience, infidelity is a fact of modern life. Many decry it, but statistics indicate that some of those who call it wrong must also engage in it. As we will see, this is only one of many paradoxes that cloud attempts to understand the act of cheating.

The Affairs of Madison County

Several years ago, a woman I know (let's call her Hera) suffered the dissolution of her marriage when her husband of ten years declared that he wanted a divorce so he could marry his mistress, a woman fifteen years his junior. I remember very clearly a phone conversation I had with Hera about her breakup in the weeks that followed. At some point during the conversation, she asked me something along the lines of "Why did this happen?" And I took the opportunity to expound on some of the latest research, and probably hoariest clichés, about why men leave their marriages, what the psychology is behind their behavior, whether women are wired in the same way, and so forth. But about five minutes into my (hopefully at least a little comforting) monologue, Hera interrupted me. "No, no," she clarified. "What I'm asking is, what did *I* do?"

When we are stabbed in the back, through infidelity or some other violation, the initial response is almost always that of a victim. This is appropriate, of course. After all, it's our back that just got stabbed. Upon reflection, though, there often comes a point where we start to wonder what our role in our victimization was. We ask ourselves, metaphorically speaking, "What was my back doing there in the first place? Was my back asking for it?"

In these terms, such notions may seem silly, but the idea that victims share the blame for what befalls them in cases of infidelity and such resonates with conventional thinking. In the aftermath of the Spitzer scandal, Dr. Laura Schlessinger, the author and nationally syndicated radio host, argued that women bear responsibility when their husbands cheat. "I hold women accountable," she was quoted as saying, "for tossing out perfectly good men by not treating them with the love and kindness and respect and attention they need." And while this is an extreme position (Dr. Laura is a syndicated radio host, after all), virtually all the men and women I've known who have been stung by betrayal have looked inward at some point, questioning whether they might have done something that caused the offense.

The tendency toward self-blame can manifest itself in the victims of all manner of crimes, outside the realm of trust and honesty. Victims of robberies and of rape often go through a period of wondering what they might have done differently to prevent their maltreatment. Further, for those of us on the outside of a betrayal of trust looking in, it can be comforting to assign cause to the victim. If we feel an act of infidelity, for example, might have been caused by something the faithful partner did, we can believe we have some control over similar behavior in our own partner. In other words, it can be empowering to blame the victim. We tell ourselves that our own actions toward our loved one can shield us from deceit and betrayal. A small industry has grown up around this way of thinking, featuring books with titles like *Avoiding the Greener Grass Syndrome* and *Emotional Infidelity: How to Affair-Proof Your Marriage and 10 Other Secrets to a Great Relationship*.

Beyond the visceral comfort the possibility of "affair-proofing" your relationships might provide, there is a straightforward logic to looking to the wounded party, or at least the violated relationship, in trying to determine the cause of betrayal. Betrayal is, almost by definition, a violation of the bonds and obligations a relationship entails. It can be seen, by extension, as a failure of that relationship. To put it more simply, if one person isn't respecting the obligations of the relationship, the whole relationship must not be working. In regards to infidelity in particular, the critique can be even more pointed: if one partner needs to look elsewhere for emotional or sexual satisfaction, then the other partner must not be doing his or her part to provide those things.

I call this the Madison County model of infidelity. In Robert James Waller's novel *The Bridges of Madison County*, and the film adaptation starring Meryl Streep and Clint Eastwood, lonely Iowa housewife Francesca finds the fulfillment her marriage fails to provide in a torrid affair with dashing *National Geographic* photographer Robert Kincaid. Hollywood and the media often recycle this trope: the bored or unsatisfied spouse finding illicit happiness in the arms of another. Psychologists have tried to determine whether the Madison County model really does explain infidelity, seeking the factors within a relationship that might lead to (or discourage) cheating.

There is certainly evidence that relationship dissatisfaction can trigger infidelity. Studies have shown that women who report unhappiness in their marriages are more likely to engage in extramarital affairs. The same is also often true for men, though the emphasis for them seems to be on attaining sexual satisfaction. This parallels a larger trend researchers have found in studying infidelity: in their illicit relationships women more often seek emotional fulfillment, while men seek sexual thrills. Perhaps the most cogent system psychologists have devised for understanding why relationships might yield to cheating involves what's called the "investment model." In this approach, *commitment* is regarded as the core of any relationship. Commitment in this context, as explained by psychologists Stephen Drigotas and William Barta in their article "The Cheating Heart," means "a psychological attachment to, and a motivation to continue, a relationship." If a person's commitment to a relationship is weak, he or she does not feel "invested" in it; he or she has little at stake, emotionally or otherwise, in its success or failure. If, on the other hand, a person's commitment to the relationship is strong, he or she has a definite interest in its continued success and will work toward this goal. Breaking down the idea of commitment further, the investment model holds that commitment is influenced primarily by three factors: *satisfaction*, which refers to a person's happiness in a relationship; *alternative quality*, a person's judgment about how happy they would be with someone else; and *investments*, the things a person stands to lose (financial security, for example) if the relationship fails.

To understand what these terms mean more concretely, let's return to the fictional example provided by *The Bridges of Madison County*. In evaluating why Francesca had an affair, a psychologist using the investment model would point to her loneliness as the wife of a somewhat dull farmer (satisfaction); the romantic and sexual qualities she ascribed to the alternative to her husband, Robert Kincaid (alternative quality); and how relatively little she had to lose with the dissolution of her marriage (investments). These three factors combined meant her larger commitment to her marriage was low, and hence the likelihood that she might engage in an extramarital affair was relatively high.

Things are always neater in fiction, of course (in addition to being more steamy or weepy, depending on the author). As applied to real people, the three factors that drive commitment often overlap, and sometimes one far supersedes the others in importance. The essential point, though, is that the investment model has had success not only in *explaining*, retrospectively, why infidelity may have occurred, but also in *predicting*, to some degree, which relationships might be prone to it. Drigotas and colleagues C. Annette Safstrom and Tiffany Gentilia conducted a study of dating college students and evaluated their relationships based on their commitment and the factors that contribute to it. They found that those who were more committed, those who were satisfied and invested and had fewer alternatives, were less likely to engage in infidelity than those who registered more weakly in these criteria.

This is a powerful finding. Drigotas and his colleagues managed to identify aspects of relationships that could signal their vulnerability to adultery and cheating in the future. It's important, though, to keep these findings in perspective. It overstates the case to argue that if a person is "highly committed" to a relationship, in the investment model sense of the phrase, he or she won't engage in adultery. Drigotas found that relationships with high commitment levels were *less* prone to infidelity—not immune, just perhaps more resistant. There is no reason to believe that one can "affair-proof" a relationship.

It's also important to consider Drigotas's sample: heterosexual college students who were not married, but dating. The dynamics of such relationships and those within, say, a twenty-year marriage are usually very different. In some ways, dating college students are probably more prone to infidelity but in others, it could be argued, less. A nineteen-year-old, for example, does not have to deal with the waning sex drive of an aging partner, to name just one challenge to longer-term relationships. Furthermore, the logistical constraints of carrying out an affair are very different for dating college students living in separate residence halls and for married couples who share the same bed every night.

Regardless, though, the predictive capacity of the investment model, even if limited, remains instructive. It demonstrates that the popular Madison County model for understanding infidelity has some empirical validity. There do seem to be dimensions to relationships that encourage or discourage their members from cheating.

What is frustrating, though, is the fact that it remains difficult for psychologists to pinpoint what exactly is at work in successfully monogamous relationships. Terms such as "satisfaction" and "commitment" are vague and, ultimately, subjective. Further, one could fairly criticize a theory that posits commitment as the key to avoiding infidelity, since avoiding infidelity is itself an indication of commitment. We may be only a step away from saying that the best way to ensure monogamy is to remain monogamous.

Moreover, looking at betrayal more broadly, the fact that your partner is "committed" to you doesn't exactly guarantee that you won't be lied to by him or her. Sometimes, betrayal occurs *because* of commitment. A friend related a telling anecdote to me: For over two years, a woman dated a man she'd first met in a bar. The relationship was on the point of engagement when the woman made a troubling discovery: her boyfriend was in fact ten years older than he'd claimed. The lie had started when the couple met at the bar. Wanting to appear attractive to her, the man had shaved a decade off his age. As the relationship progressed, he'd felt he had to maintain the lie in order to maintain the relationship, and so employed further fabrication, digging himself deeper and deeper. When the truth was finally revealed, the relationship quickly ended. This is an example of serious and continued deception precisely *because* a member of the relationship was happy with it, invested in its continuation. On the other hand, I know several men and women who are desperately unhappy in their relationships yet who would never lie in a significant way to their partner. Their commitment to honesty trumps their relationship dissatisfaction.

The nature of a relationship, then, is ultimately an insufficient—or at least unsatisfactory—explanation for infidelity or for any sort of betrayal. In a strange way, though, this can be reassuring. When we are stabbed in the back, we can at least spare ourselves the certainty that it is necessarily somehow *our fault*. There is no evidence that a victim always plays a role in his or her victimization. Sometimes, we are just unlucky in the people we form relationships with or in the people we are bound to by blood.

Some psychologists would add a corollary to this notion. They would suggest that we may sometimes be unlucky not in our own relationships but, more precisely in the relationships of everyone else. In pinpointing the source of betrayal, they suggest we start by examining not our spouses, lovers, and family but, rather, our neighbors.

Sex Because of the City

America has often been criticized (and occasionally praised, too) for being a sexually conservative society, at least as compared to other Western countries. Perhaps as the legacy of our Puritan heritage, American values regarding marriage, sex, and divorce often seem more stringent and restrictive than those of France or Italy. Within months of being elected president of France in 2007, Nicolas Sarkozy finalized a divorce from his wife; only months later, he married former supermodel Carla Bruni. It's hard to imagine an American president getting divorced and remarried in the space of his first year in office. Attitudes toward cheating are also different across the Atlantic. While infidelity is far from a given, many Europeans seem more broadly tolerant of, or at least resigned to, cheating than do their American counterparts.

Social psychologists understand such differing cultural values in the context of *social norms*. Social norms are socially agreed upon rules—not so much written laws as broadly encouraged behaviors. Think of norms in terms of a game of Monopoly: there are the rules of Monopoly printed on the box, which everyone follows, and then there are the twists particular groups of players add to the game, such as collecting $400 when landing on Go. Social norms are like this latter category. Social groups form and enact them outside of codified systems of behavior. To use another example: there is no law against men wearing bras, but there are very powerful social norms that discourage it.

When it comes to infidelity, social norms operate strongly. In the United States, these norms seem unambiguous: marriage and committed relationships demand monogamy. As demonstrated by the public (and sometimes borderline enthusiastic) shaming of Eliot Spitzer, violating these norms of monogamy can carry strict social penalties. Outside the arena of politics, the penalties for violating the social norms against infidelity can include a loss of friends, estrangement from loved ones, castigation from the wronged party, and so forth.

Yet while it may seem clear that social norms serve to discourage infidelity, things may not be quite so simple. Often in large and complex social groups multiple norms can exist, and these norms are not necessarily harmonious. And while many elements of social life might push individuals away from cheating, some psychologists argue that we have other social norms that actually encourage infidelity—and encourage it powerfully.

Psychologists make a distinction between *injunctive* norms and *descriptive* norms. Injunctive norms are the more formal social laws of society, ones that are commonly known and largely obeyed. Not smoking cigarettes when you're pregnant, not littering in a national wildlife preserve, not picking your nose in a fancy restaurant—these are examples of injunctive norms. Descriptive norms operate more subtly. They are the norms we learn from the behavior we observe in those around us. If you want to see an example of descriptive norms at work, go to a baseball game and watch people during the playing of the national anthem. Everyone will stand (that's an injunctive norm), but whether people take their hats off or cover their hearts will often be governed, I have observed, by the actions of those sitting in the seats and rows nearby. One fan taking off his hat can trigger a cascade of hat removals. You might see one section in which every hand is on a heart, and other sections in which all hands are clasped behind. Descriptive norms can operate subtly, but the power of the behavior of our closest neighbors—physically and metaphorically—should not be overlooked.

Further, it's possible for injunctive and descriptive norms to run counter to one another. This might happen if a pregnant woman finds herself in a Lamaze class full of smokers. The injunctive norms encourage one behavior; the descriptive norms operate differently.

What is surprising to anyone seeking to understand betrayal is that researchers have found evidence that descriptive norms with regard to infidelity are more powerful than injunctive norms. Studies have shown that individuals who know someone who has been unfaithful are more likely to be unfaithful themselves. It's as if the same factors that make people take off their hats at baseball games also make them cheat on their partners.

This is what I call the Sex and the City model of infidelity. On the wildly popular HBO series *Sex and the City*, four single women navigate the relationship landscape of New York City—and in so doing, have a lot of sex. Indeed, the New York of the show is depicted as one of nearly continuous hookups, liaisons, affairs, and trysts. Monogamy is depicted as a struggle, for both men and women. Leaving aside the social norms of the real New York City, the social norms of the place portrayed on the show *Sex and the City* are ones that might make even a Frenchman blush (well, maybe). The Sex and the City model posits that many cheaters carry out their infidelity because in their social lives, as on the HBO television show, cheating is widespread. The most immediate social precedent is one of infidelity, and this is the one people follow.

The Sex and the City model has obvious implications for betrayal more broadly. If descriptive norms can trump injunctive norms in the sexual arena, they can surely do so in other arenas, too. Many parents have experienced this firsthand when their children find a group of friends disinclined to obey the admonitions of adults. What had been close and trusting parent-child relationships can devolve quickly if the child's peers commonly engage in behavior his or her parents frown upon. The excuse the child gives may seem frustratingly trite—"Sheena does it!"—but remember the fans at the baseball game: descriptive norms have a powerful role in our behavior.

On the other hand, this model provides an important tool to those who want to make betrayal less likely in those around them, be it in their family or their social circle. Quite simply, if you don't want to be betrayed, don't betray anyone else. While you can't guarantee that you will never be wronged, setting a precedent where such behavior is at all normal (or normative, as psychologists like to say) probably introduces you to greater risk. Again, the example of parents is relevant. If you don't want your children to be untrustworthy, don't model untrustworthy behavior for them. The descriptive norms children absorb from their parents can be incredibly powerful.

Yet as with the Madison County model, the Sex and the City model can also seem insufficient. Turning back to infidelity specifically, there are certainly instances in which cheating occurs to the surprise and shock of the immediate social circle. This was the case, for example, when a couple my mother had known for forty years split up in the wake of adultery. Perhaps in the urban jungle social norms condone cheating, but it certainly seemed to be a scandal in my mother's Florida retirement community. And in general, if illicit behavior is somehow triggered by the illicit behavior of others, who started this unfortunate chain of misconduct? At some point, the Sex and the City model can start to resemble a chicken-or-the-egg paradox.

The truth is that while the behavior of others can facilitate certain bad acts, we don't need the example of friends and neighbors to act treacherously. For instance, when it comes to infidelity, the Sex and the City model leaves something essential out: sex. After all, even the weakest of relationships in the most sexually liberal environments might not yield to infidelity if the human sex drive weren't so powerful. Perhaps cheating is not so much a matter of breaking the rules that we see everyone breaking, but rather human beings simply following their natural biological impulses.

The Primal Urge

Swans enjoy a special place in the human heart—particularly when those hearts appear on Valentine's Day cards. But more than their elegant necks or lovely white plumage, swans win human esteem in romantic matters because of a peculiar aspect of their behavior. Unlike most creatures, swans mate for life. They form pairs at two or three years old and usually maintain them until they die. When the female lays eggs, the male defends the nest. Both swan parents help rear their young once they've hatched. Remind you of anyone?

The image of swan fidelity is an appealing one for a species like ours, which places so much emphasis on lifelong monogamy. It's reassuring to see an echo of our romantic ideal in the animal world: it affirms our belief that it's both possible and natural. But the truth of swan behavior is more complicated than the illustration on a Hallmark card suggests. Swans, it turns out, fall short of total monogamy. Scientists studying the DNA of young swans have found that one in six of them has been fathered by a male outside the swan social pair. In other words, swan females are unfaithful, as are the males siring children outside their primary "family."

Indeed, if humans look to nature to reinforce our values regarding fidelity, we'll be disappointed. The simple truth is that virtually every animal on the planet seeks multiple sexual partners, even those who form pairs in order to raise their offspring. DNA research has shown that anywhere from 10 to 70 percent of the progeny of animal social pairs are the product of an illicit encounter. David P. Barash, a psychologist at the University of Washington, was quoted in the *New York Times* describing a variety of flatworm, *Diplozoon paradoxum,* as the only truly "faithful" creature in nature. "Males and females meet each other as adolescents," Barash told the *Times,* "and their bodies literally fuse together, whereupon they remain faithful until death. That's the only species I know of in which there seems to be 100 percent monogamy."

The ubiquity of infidelity in nature suggests that there is something *unnatural* about strict monogamy—that it is a human construct, no more innate than our other peculiar behaviors, like wearing clothes or voting for an *American Idol* contestant. Viewed from the other side, this idea suggests that our nature predisposes us toward sexual promiscuity. We are wired to have multiple sexual partners; when it comes to relationships, we are somehow programmed to betray. I call this conception the Primal Scream model of infidelity. Here, cheating represents the expression of *Homo sapiens'* true primal urges—the scream in the face of societally driven monogamy.

Evolutionary biologists who explore this idea discuss the human sex drive as part of the larger biological drive toward *reproductive success*. This is the fundamental act of successfully passing your genes down to another generation—a Darwinian imperative. Evolutionary biologists argue that much of human behavior, particularly that related to infidelity, is essentially an often unconscious attempt to achieve reproductive success.

Men and women, given their different biologies, go about pursuing reproductive success in different ways. Men are able to sire a theoretically unlimited number of children. Hence, their surest way to pass their DNA to another generation is to mate with as many women as possible. From a reproductive success point of view, it's much better to mate with ten potential mothers than to take a chance with just one. To torture a phrase, it's not evolutionarily effective for a male to put all his sperm in one basket.

Women, on the other hand, are limited in the number of children they can produce; at most, they can bear about one every nine months for the limited number of years they are fertile. Their opportunities to achieve reproductive success are thus relatively few. So they have to make the opportunities they do have count: by mating with a male whose genes are most likely to produce offspring that will thrive.

According to the Primal Scream model of infidelity, the drive for reproductive success explains not only the fact that men and women cheat but also the specifics of *how* they cheat. For example, studies indicate, again, that male infidelity is usually motivated by the desire for sexual satisfaction. Other studies show that men are more likely than women to engage in one-night stands, and less likely to form emotional bonds with their illicit partners. This data is consistent with the conception of male infidelity as a best attempt toward reproductive success: men seek out short-term encounters focused on sex—a good tactic if the goal (conscious or not) is siring as many DNA carriers as possible. Women, on the other hand, cheat based on their own set of reproductive success criteria. Research suggests that a woman's sexual drive is most urgent during the most fertile phase of her menstrual cycle, and that women are most likely to cheat on their partners during this time. Again, this fits a model that places the impetus for infidelity in a woman's drive for impregnation. Furthermore, researchers have found that women are actually more thoroughgoing in the use of contraception with their husbands than with their partners in extramarital affairs. (Recent DNA analysis indicates that fully 10 percent of people have fathers other than the men they believe conceived them.) This meshes with the idea that through infidelity, women are seeking to "trade up"—conceiving a child with a more genetically appealing individual than their life partner.

There are obvious flaws with the Primal Scream model, of course. Primarily, perhaps, it fails to explain homosexual infidelity. How does a man cheating on his male lover with another man further his reproductive success? Or a woman cheating on her husband with a woman? Yet placing biological urges at the core of infidelity does account for one puzzle that surrounds cheating that other models leave unsolved. I've known my share of individuals who have sabotaged seemingly terrific relationships with attractive, intelligent people through infidelity. When we observe such behavior, it *doesn't make sense*. The Primal Scream model affirms precisely this response. Infidelity doesn't make sense because it is at its core not about reason but about animal instinct. Cheating may at times appear absurd through the lens of logic, but through the lens of reproductive success, it can be seen as something close to reasonable.

As we search for the sources of betrayal generally, or try to pick up the pieces when we ourselves are betrayed, we often come to wonder whether there is some fundamental element of human nature involved. It's easy to suspect, also, that this element may not be limited to a manifestation of reproductive urges. Maybe part of us is just, well, *bad*? Freud pointed to something like this in his identification of the death drive in the human psyche. And history, particularly recent history, furnishes more than enough examples to indicate that at least some element of human nature is inclined toward evil. Perhaps we betray one another just for the sake of betrayal.

We need to keep in mind, though, that history—both our personal histories and the history of human civilization—furnishes plenty of examples of the possibility of human goodness. However painful our relationships, however badly behaved our neighbors, however loudly biology squawks in our ear, we retain control over our behavior. It is not inevitable that we will betray, or that any individual must betray us.

On the other hand, whatever accounts for the many forms of betrayal, at some point, we will likely encounter one of them. It's worth exploring, then, what the aftermath of broken trust can be—and, specifically, if it is bound to forever stay broken.

The Mornings After

I can still remember the first feelings of despair while my heart stopped beating. Within moments, I felt devastated, destroyed. My world crumbled in a moment and it seemed as though everything I thought to be true about my marriage and my life was nothing more than an illusion. In that in-

stant, I lost my identity as well as the identity of my
wife....A split second later I fell into the deepest
despair I've ever felt before and never felt since.
The emotional pain in my heart became physical.
A mental anguish that was as painful as the worst
torture one could imagine.

The above quotation is Richard Alan's account of his reaction to learning that his wife has had an affair, excerpted from his book *First Aid for the Betrayed*. This description might seem overblown, but given the context, it has the ring of cold truth. Perhaps one can't exaggerate the level of pain that accompanies the revelation of a partner's deceit, of a lifetime of trust violated, of a relied-upon promise shattered.

As Alan suggests, the damage betrayal causes occurs on many levels. Psychologists and family therapists can actually have a hard time compiling a complete list of all the kinds of harm and potential harm broken trust can wreak. In the most extreme cases, the aftermath can trigger feelings of rage, betrayal, isolation, anxiety, and despair; it can lead to depression, substance abuse, even suicide; it can crush self-esteem and erode every other social bond. And these are just the consequences for the victim. The perpetrator may suffer, too: from overwhelming guilt, from crippling regret, and from the fraying of relationships connected to the broken one, such as those with children or mutual friends. Also, we should not overlook the cost of "getting away with" serious deceit. Think of the shame and embarrassment that must have been felt by the man who had to trick the woman he loved into believing he was ten years younger than his actual age. It's also telling that 95 percent of those who admit affairs to their partners do so out of guilt or a desire to repair the primary relationship. It seems the weight of keeping a dalliance secret often outweighs the happiness it might yield.

Yet despite the plethora of painful consequences, broken trust does not have to be fatal to relationships. While every individual is different, as is every lie, in some cases trust can be repaired, even in the wake of deception as serious as infidelity. It's important to note that such repair may not always be wise. Unfortunately, we may encounter people who are not worth trusting, who will betray our faith as many times as it is restored. Yet there are also cases in which deception can stand as an exception, or in which the factors that led to the deception can be removed or altered. Addictions can be conquered; acquaintances can be discarded; relationships can become more fulfilling.

It is the case, then, that someone who lies or betrays and promises "never to do it again" may, in fact, *not* do it again. But what's essential to keep in mind is that such an assurance is only a precursor to restored trust. Restored trust means believing the assurance, having faith in the honesty of someone who has, at least once, proven to be untrustworthy. No one should think that the promise to never repeat a transgression is tantamount to repairing the damage of that transgression.

Equally important is the other precursor for restored trust: *wanting* to restore that trust. Overcoming betrayal is a two-way street. It means repentance and change on the one side and, at minimum, forgiveness on the other. It is often surprising how attached we can become to our own feelings of injured pride and righteous indignation. Finally, though, if we are serious about moving on with a life that includes our betrayer, we must let go of these feelings.

One final point I'd like to emphasize about restoring trust is that the goal should not be to restore the old relationship. First, why would anyone want to? The old relationship was the one that gave way to infidelity or manipulation or dishonesty. In repair, we should strive for something better. Second, overcoming betrayal is not the same as, and will not feel like, stepping into a time machine and living life as it was before the betrayal occurred. The betrayal *did* occur, and that experience needs to be learned from and assimilated into the new relationship.

There are benefits to such a process. Family therapists point to cases in which infidelity has actually strengthened relationships in the long term (though few would recommend it). Overcoming betrayal can have the affect of bringing people closer together, as dealing with a breach of trust can lead to a rededication to the value of a relationship and to a partner's needs. More importantly, repairing trust can, and should, create a new atmosphere of honesty and openness. We all pay lip service to the truth. But no one likely values it as much as those who have suffered from its violation.

CHAPTER 6

Self-Deception:
The Lies We Tell Ourselves

The break in the case unfolded as if it had been pulled from a cheesy mystery novel. Ten years had passed since the body of six-year-old JonBenét Ramsey had been found in the basement of her parents' Colorado home. Even though the case garnered national media attention, with JonBenét's haunting face appearing on magazine covers and the nightly news for weeks, police had been unable to find her killer. For a time, suspicion fell on JonBenét's family, but no arrests were ever made. The case seemed destined to go unsolved.

Then a professor of journalism at the University of Colorado brought to police attention anonymous e-mails he had received that referenced the JonBenét Ramsey murder. The professor, Michael Tracey, had followed the case closely and produced multiple documentaries about it. He believed the author of the messages might be involved in the murder. Colorado police traced the man writing to Tracey to Thailand, and he was arrested there by Thai officials. John Mark Karr, a former substitute teacher with an arrest record for child pornography, quickly confessed to the murder. Saying that her death was "an accident," he claimed to have been with JonBenét Ramsey when she died. When asked by reporters whether he was innocent, he answered, "No."

For a few days, at least, many believed the case had finally been solved. But what seemed a dramatic conclusion proved to be merely another dead end. DNA found at the crime scene did not match Karr's. His family insisted that he had no connection to the Ramseys and that he had not been with them at the time of the murder. The charges against Karr in connection with the JonBenét Ramsey case were soon dropped, the confession dismissed as a product of Karr's troubled mind.

False confessions, in which an individual confesses to a crime he or she did not actually commit, may strike us initially as an utterly inexplicable behavior. Why accept blame for something you didn't do? Yet false confessions are not wholly unusual within the criminal justice system. Over fifty people confessed to murdering Black Dahlia actress Elizabeth Short in 1947. The Innocence Project, a nonprofit organization of lawyers dedicated to using DNA evidence to overturn wrongful convictions, estimates that over a quarter of the clients they have exonerated made at least partial false confessions. Over two hundred people falsely confessed to kidnapping the Lindbergh baby. In the infamous case of the "Central Park jogger," five teenagers confessed to violently assaulting and raping a twenty-eight-year-old investment banker in New York's Central Park. Years later the confessions were all thrown out, when another man, whose DNA was found at the scene, claimed sole responsibility for the attack.

Often, false confessions are the result of coercive interrogation techniques. Physical abuse can eventually induce almost anyone to confess to a crime, the truth becoming secondary to the alleviation of the immediate torment. Coercion does not have to take a physical form, either. Relentless psychological pressure or outright deception can also persuade innocent people to take responsibility for crimes they did not commit. Especially with regard to young or mentally challenged suspects, the wrongfully accused can become convinced that simply confessing is their best option—one that will allow them to "just go home."

In other instances, though, the psychological dynamics of the false confession are not so straightforward. There are numerous documented cases of innocent suspects, under lengthy and intense interrogation, actually starting to believe—at least temporarily—that they are, in fact, guilty. In Karr's case, there were no angry detectives badgering him. It is possible he confessed to murdering JonBenét Ramsey as a macabre publicity stunt. It is also possible, however, that he had come to believe that he really had killed her.

Indeed, researchers have found that it is easy to induce people to confess to transgressions of which they are actually innocent. For example, social psychologist Saul Kassin of the John Jay College of Criminal Justice asked individual participants to type a list of letters read aloud quickly in what was supposedly a study of reaction time. Right before starting, each participant was warned that if they pressed the Alt key, the computer would malfunction. Just sixty seconds into the task, the computer seemed to crash, and the irate experimenter accused the participant of hitting the forbidden Alt key. In reality, each participant was innocent, having avoided the Alt key entirely. Yet when accused by the experimenter and a supposed eyewitness of hitting that key, a significant number of participants not only signed a written confession but appeared to be convinced of their guilt to the point of manufacturing details of their supposed misdeed.

We generally think of our perceptions as reliable, of our

memories as stable. Yet there is a great deal of evidence that both these assumptions are false. Our mental processes often stray significantly from the dispassionate and the objective; our memories of what we witnessed and experienced almost always erode, and sometimes even transform. We can't always depend on ourselves to form a strictly "truthful" impression of reality. Humans are capable of deceiving themselves into thinking they murdered people they never even met. Very likely, we are all engaged in multiple mundane acts of self-deception that influence our behavior and impressions on a daily basis.

Lying is a behavior that makes sense to us when it comes from other people. At the very least, we can understand that others might have motive—defensible or nefarious—to deceive us. But the question of why we would deceive ourselves is much more difficult to reconcile. Why would we be anything but completely honest within the boundaries of our own mind? More fundamentally, how *could* a person even lie to him or herself?

Consider the idea of self-deception from a logical perspective. To employ a shorthand definition, let's say lying means knowing the truth but distorting it to fool another person. For instance, you might (if you're feeling greedy) tell your friend you haven't seen the hundred-dollar bill he dropped, masking the truth that it ended up under your loafer. Using the same definition, though, lying to yourself would seem to require that you both know the truth and fool yourself into not knowing it. It's almost as if you're hiding the hundred-dollar bill without knowing where it is. You are both the teller of the lie and the one it deceives.

Yet self-deception is a fact of human thought. It is possible largely because our experience of reality is far more complicated than the knowledge of where a dropped hundred-dollar bill might have ended up. Indeed, it is these complications that seem to make self-deception necessary. Just as the lies we tell one another help us navigate the psychological complexities of social life, the lies we tell ourselves help us carry on in the sometimes tricky endeavor of simply *being ourselves*.

"I Disagree with Myself"; or, How to Think Two Things at Once

Imagine you've just spent an hour as a participant in a psychological experiment—an excruciatingly boring one. For what seemed like an unendurable sixty minutes, you were charged with the task of placing spools on a tray and twisting a series of square pegs around and around. You'd mastered the task after ten minutes, and you spent the remainder of the time berating yourself for ever agreeing to spend your time this way. Finally, you're finished. But then the psychologist running the experiment, with a sheepish look on his face, makes an unusual request.

The researcher says that, due to a scheduling problem, he needs your services in working with the next participant. The experiment, he explains, concerns the effects of motivational preparation on task performance. The next participant is due to arrive at any minute. All you have to do, the experimenter explains, is tell her that the experimental task is fun, fascinating, and exciting. For this, you'll be paid a dollar.

If you agree to the researcher's request and tell the next participant how thrilling the task will be, receiving a dollar for your trouble, something you probably never thought possible will likely happen: your attitude toward the initial task will change, and you'll come to feel more positively toward it. Even more surprisingly, your attitude toward the task will be more favorable than if the experimenter had offered you twenty dollars to be his confederate.

The scenario and findings described above are taken from a groundbreaking experiment conducted in the 1950s by Leon Festinger and James M. Carlsmith. Festinger and Carlsmith were not, as they told their participants, interested in the connection between preparation and performance. Rather, their interest was in how their participants' attitudes toward a painfully boring task changed when those participants agreed to describe it as exciting. Their central finding—that describing the task as engaging somehow made it seem more engaging in the participants' minds—yielded great insight into the way we deal with conflicting ideas. Specifically, it helped validate a psychological theory that has remained essential for over fifty years: *cognitive dissonance*. Cognitive dissonance is one of the key elements to understanding the mechanics of self-deception.

"Cognitive dissonance" is the term psychologists use for the tension that arises from holding two contradictory ideas in mind simultaneously. For example, a man with high cholesterol might know "I need to avoid red meat" but at the same time be faced with the contradictory fact "I am eating a T-bone steak." The conflict between these two ideas, or *cognitions*, as psychologists refer to them, creates the mental discomfort labeled dissonance.

According to cognitive dissonance theory, in order to resolve the dissonance, the mind, consciously or unconsciously, alters one of the two competing ideas. The man with high cholesterol eating the steak might decide that he eats so little red meat that the steak shouldn't count; or he might conclude that the evidence linking red meat to high cholesterol really isn't so convincing; or he might add a new idea that helps ease the tension, such as "After this meal, I will never eat red meat again." These are the kinds of rationalizations and conditions we all employ when we're doing something we know we probably shouldn't be. What is important to realize, though, is that such altering of ideas and reevaluations of judgments represent an apparently natural and fundamental mechanism of the human mind.

Go back to Festinger and Carlsmith's experiment, in which participants changed their attitudes toward the boring experiment once they agreed to describe it to someone else as exciting. Cognitive dissonance theory provides a neat explanation for this finding. The participants were suddenly faced with two contradictory thoughts: first, that the experiment was boring; second, that they had agreed to say it was stimulating. In order to reconcile these ideas, the participants mentally altered the first one. They came to believe that, in fact, the experiment really *wasn't* boring; thus there was no conflict created by saying it was exciting.

The other wrinkle to Festinger and Carlsmith's experiment was offering participants either one dollar or twenty dollars for talking up the fun of the experimental task. They found, as I mentioned, that participants who received one dollar ended up viewing the task as more enjoyable than those who received twenty. Cognitive dissonance theory explains this, too. Participants who were being paid twenty dollars did not face the same level of dissonance as those who received only a token sum. The former group could think, "The task was boring" and "I am taking twenty dollars to say it wasn't boring." The conflict there is ethical, not psychological. (And, as far as an ethical evaluation goes, it's worth noting that in the 1950s, twenty dollars went a lot further.) The latter participants, those given only a dollar to claim the task was exciting, could not use money as a mental excuse for their behavior. They had to change *how they thought* to resolve their cognitive dissonance.

Now we can start to see the connection between cognitive

dissonance and self-deception. When our opinions, our behavior, or our beliefs contradict each other, we are compelled to alter our thinking. The ideas that result are more internally consistent with one another, but they are not necessarily *consistent with reality*. Is any steak ever really the last one? Do we really think the scientific links between red meat and cholesterol are so flimsy that they can be ignored? The answer to such questions is almost inevitably no, but that doesn't mean that under the pressure of cognitive dissonance we can't convince ourselves that the answer is yes.

As we consider the influence of cognitive dissonance, another key element of self-deception also comes into focus. As mentioned earlier, it's strange to think we could lie to ourselves about the location of a hundred-dollar bill. Physical reality resists easy mental distortion. It has tangible aspects we can't simply change in our minds. Our thoughts, our beliefs, and our attitudes, though, are different. They have no physical dimension—no dimension at all, really, beyond the confines of our thoughts. And within these confines we can alter them almost limitlessly. We can be proud on the days we eat a healthy diet; we can question the science of nutrition on the days when we don't.

But while some of our ideas are easily changed, others can be surprisingly stubborn. When the outside world conflicts with our thinking, sometimes we can find ways to preserve the latter at the expense of how we perceive the former. This mental inflexibility is probably nowhere more apparent than with regard to how we think about ourselves.

Believing in Yourself – *No Matter What*

A few years ago my son decided to join some friends in a weekly poker game. Like a lot of people, he had gotten caught up in the Texas Hold 'Em poker fad, a game that involves some combination (the exact proportions are debatable) of luck and skill. He reasoned that he had seen enough poker on television to do moderately well. Further, he'd heard enough around the dinner table about the research on lying to think he might have a leg up in the game—if only because the other players might think that he'd somehow gleaned some secret knowledge about how to spot a liar.

Suffice it to say, he did not participate in the game for very long. But besides some endurable financial losses, there was another reason he didn't stick with poker. There was a player in the game he really couldn't stand. For purposes of this example, let's call him André. André, who outside of poker was a perfectly amiable person, had an extremely irritating personality when it came to cards. Whenever he won a big hand, he would cluck about how skilled he was—how he had bluffed his opponent perfectly, played his hand with textbook precision, and on and on. More annoyingly, when he lost a large hand, he would spend the next ten to twenty minutes lamenting his bad luck—he had made all the right moves but the cards had come up wrong, it wasn't fair, he was a superior player but his opponent had caught a break. After a few nights of this, my son had had enough: André was preternaturally skilled when he won and amazingly unlucky when he lost.

It turns out, though, that my son got something for the money lost in his brief poker dalliance, because André provided an excellent example of a very common—and very insidious—form of self-deception. Looking at matters objectively, it is fair to say that André's victories weren't *always* attributable to his skill. Sometimes, he got lucky—the cards came his way. On the other hand, when he lost, it was not a question of bad luck every time. Sometimes, he was simply outplayed. But André did not, or could not, see it this way.

We've already examined how the mind responds to cognitive dissonance. When we hold two competing, contradictory ideas, we change one of them, consciously or unconsciously. Red meat goes from forbidden to occasionally allowable; a boring task becomes tolerable, and perhaps even a bit enjoyable. Cognitive dissonance can be most urgent, though, when one of the contradictory ideas relates to our view of ourselves.

Consider André's situation when he loses at poker. He holds a very strong view of himself as a great poker player. Yet this opinion is contradicted by the fact that he has just lost at poker. In order to resolve this dissonance, André engages in self-justification that allows him to retain his positive self-image. It's not that he is a bad poker player, or even a less good poker player than he thinks. In his mind, he is an *unlucky* poker player. In this way, André can preserve his opinion of himself in the face of contradictory facts. What's important to understand, too, is that André does not perceive the facts as contradictory. He believes that he is always unlucky when he loses. In other words, he lies to himself.

Psychologists and researchers have found this need to protect one's self-image to be an extremely powerful force in shaping our perceptions of the world. On one level, it can even create a kind of filter that blocks out information that could be challenging to our self-image. Roy Baumeister of Florida State University conducted an experiment in which he gave a group of participants a phony personality test. The "results" of this personality test were distributed at random. Some participants received highly favorable feedback; others received extremely harsh, negative feedback. Baumeister and his colleagues found that the participants who received the negative response spent far less time looking it over than those who received the positive response. In other words, participants gave less attention to criticism than to praise.

Self-Deception

Psychologists call this phenomenon *selective exposure*. We seek to minimize our exposure to, and even avoid altogether, information that contradicts what we think, particularly what we think about ourselves. Imagine you are at the home page of your local newspaper and you see the headlines of two editorials, one praising your favorite political party, the other decrying it. Not wanting to read attacks on your party's positions and candidates, you click on only the link to the favorable editorial. The theory of selective exposure operates in just this way, except that instead of our political party, the subject matter is our self-concept. We avoid information that challenges us and embrace that which reinforces us.

An important difference, though, between the psychological reality of selective exposure and the example of the newspaper home page is that with selective exposure, in extreme cases we somehow *deny the existence* of the link to the negative editorial. We can perceive only the praise. This is why André can carry on in his belief that when he loses at poker, he is always unlucky. His mistakes, the flaws in his play, don't register with him in his self-evaluations.

Just as importantly, André may also interpret the mistakes he does recognize in a way that protects his self-image. For instance, if he makes a bad bluff, he might tell himself that it was not because he is fundamentally a bad bluffer but simply because he had one beer too many, and this detracted from his performance. Our ability to analyze events in a way that protects our preconceived notions about ourselves is another powerful element of self-deception. And the examples of such thinking are myriad. We like to think of ourselves as having special insight into financial markets, so when our stock trades turn out badly, we tell ourselves it was just a fluke. We think of ourselves as competent, so when we back the car into the closed garage door, we blame atypical exhaustion. We think of ourselves as intelligent, so if we fail a test, we chalk it up to unfair question sets or a neighbor with a distracting cough. In other words, we embrace the possibilities of interpretation to keep bad outcomes at arm's length. Poor results don't have to do with us, we tell ourselves. They have to do with—well, whatever we can imagine.

Psychologists have also noted the inverse of this type of thinking: the tendency to ascribe positive outcomes almost totally to personal performance. So when our stock trades make us money, *that* isn't a fluke. It's a direct result of intelligence and insight. Obviously, almost any success can be ascribed to a combination of luck, circumstance, and individual traits. Yet our interpretations tend to highlight the importance of the last one at the expense of the former two. We can see an exaggerated form of such thinking when lottery winners say, "Well, I must have done something good for somebody." Even when an event is *purely* a product of chance, the mind searches for ways to assign it to personal performance.

Again, a critical point here is that when we view negative outcomes as bad luck and positive outcomes as a consequence of our own abilities, we don't realize we are applying a bias. We believe we are looking at events objectively. And it is just this perceived objectivity that allows us to use these events as evidence to support our notions of ourselves. To put it simply, in order to build or defend our self-esteem, we tell ourselves lies about how we perceive our experiences. Without fully realizing it, we interpret what happens to us in ways that are comforting, flattering, or both.

On a personal level, this tendency can lead to persistent self-delusion. The book *He's Just Not That into You* (adapted as a film in 2009) took as its best-selling theme the necessity of accepting difficult truths in the face of stubborn romantic self-deception. It is all too tempting to imagine that a lost phone number or an unexpected business trip are the explanations for a potential mate's lack of contact. Unrequited romantic interest carries a particular sting, touching, as it does, on so many inevitable insecurities about appearance and desirability. We probably all have friends who have tied themselves in speculative knots rather than accept that an unreturned phone call signals simple disinterest in a second date. If we're honest, we can probably admit that we've tied ourselves in such knots, too. At its worst, self-deception in our private lives can make us cling to relationships that don't work, partners who aren't interested, friendships that have soured.

In the public and professional realms, though, the consequences of self-deception can perhaps be even greater. Indeed, the attempt to preserve one's self-image through self-deceit can have consequences that extend far beyond the individual who does the lying to him- or herself. Scott McClellan worked as the press secretary in the George W. Bush White House for close to three years. During that time he was fiercely loyal to the president, and dogged in selling his policies to the media. Then, in 2008, McClellan published a memoir recounting his work for Bush. Titled *What Happened: Inside the Bush White House and Washington's Culture of Deception*, the book was less than flattering. In it, McClellan asserts that President Bush was a victim (or practitioner, depending on one's perspective) of "self-deception." McClellan writes, "As I worked closely with President Bush, I would come to believe that sometimes he convinces himself to believe what suits his needs at the moment." McClellan describes how the president's tendency to bend the truth in his own mind had costs for his policy toward Iraq and for the administration generally.

It is always dangerous to make assumptions about the workings of someone else's mind, particularly if those assumptions are based on third-party accounts. The difficulty is only compounded when those accounts carry political implications and are filtered through the media. Still, if we consider the challenges presented to President Bush—or to any president, for that matter—it isn't difficult to see how he could fall victim to self-deception. For powerful leaders, be they in the business world or in government, the necessity of maintaining an aura of strength and competence can make it difficult to accept policy failures and mistakes. It goes back to the issue of cognitive dissonance. Powerful people can have difficulty reconciling their faith in their abilities with the fact of their errors. In order to resolve this dissonance, the fact of their errors can become subject to interpretation. As with André's refusal to believe that he can make a mistake at poker, a president may find it impossible to believe that his decisions as commander in chief are wrong. Evidence of failure is viewed as an anomaly in a larger picture of success; disagreement is regarded not as reasonable but as mulish partisan resistance.

We have seen such thinking played out again and again in the careers of prominent leaders. The valuable ability to remain objective, even when it means conceding error, is elusive enough in ordinary life. When factors such as outsized ego, the high stakes of failure, and the glaring spotlight of public attention are added to the mix, objectivity can be even harder to attain.

The costs of self-deception are not hard to identify, as we have seen. Decisions based on what we'd like to think as opposed to what is factually accurate, whether the context is romantic or geopolitical or something in between, rarely serve us well. Wishful thinking can take us only so far.

Self-Deception

On the other hand, to construe self-deception as a wholly negative phenomenon would be to oversimplify matters. Clearly, there is value to accurately apprehending the truth. There may also be benefit, though, to indulging in a measure of fiction. Some research suggests that lying to ourselves can at times be advantageous.

The Lake Wobegon Effect

Garrison Keillor, the host of the public radio show *A Prairie Home Companion*, describes his fictional hometown of Lake Wobegon as a place where "all the women are strong, all the men are good-looking, and all the children are above average." It's a good joke. It is also one that captures a powerful psychological truth. Although we may recognize that we can't *all* be above average—indeed, that it's a logical impossibility—we still tend to think of ourselves this way.

In one survey of over 800,000 high school students conducted by the College Board, 70 percent of respondents said they had "above average" leadership skills; 60 percent rated themselves as in the top 10 percent in the category of getting along with others; and none of the respondents considered themselves below average in relating to their peers. It is not just teenagers who engage in Lake Wobegon thinking, either: 64 percent of professors rate their teaching as above average, and 25 percent consider it "superior." Most businesspeople think they are more ethical than the average, most drivers think they are better drivers than the average—even those who have been hospitalized after car accidents. Generally speaking, the majority of adults think of themselves as smarter and more attractive than the average.

The logic of math tells us there is some self-deception going on here. Apparently we like to think of ourselves as a little smarter, better looking, and more competent behind the wheel than those around us. Clearly, some of us must be fooling ourselves. Yet it's not necessarily the case that we would be better off with a clearer understanding of where we fit on the attribute hierarchy.

Researchers studying depression have found that clinically depressed people often have surprisingly accurate views of themselves—a phenomenon known as *depressive realism*. People suffering from depression make better assessments than nondepressed people about their control over events, their role in effecting positive outcomes, their good qualities, and their shortcomings. Their perceptions are not irrationally pessimistic. On the contrary, they are unusually clear-eyed.

We don't know for sure whether being depressed somehow leads one to greater accuracy or whether having greater clarity into oneself leads to feelings of depression. What is clear is that at least some depressives are unable to find the comfort that self-deception brings to most of us.

Freud understood self-deception as a kind of protection mechanism. Guilt or fears that might threaten the ego were buried in the unconscious. Modern psychology does not take such a clean-cut view of things; the idea that the mind can be neatly divided into components such as the ego and the unconscious has been replaced by more complex models. Yet Freud's core idea may be valid. The world can be a harsh, capricious place. There are limits to what humans are capable of controlling. It is entirely possible that even as you read this, a broken-off chunk of a satellite is hurtling toward you with lethal force. Living in fear, though, is crippling. If we really took seriously the number of car-related fatalities, would we ever get behind the wheel again? Distorting the reality of what goes on around us may be necessary for us to function.

More specifically, Lake Wobegon thinking—that we are all a little better than average—can empower us not merely to merge onto the highway but to strive toward and achieve larger goals and ambitions. If we truly believed ourselves to be ordinary—of typical intelligence, of mundane attractiveness, of average likability—could we really retain the motivation to seek a better job, a higher grade, a loving partner? Self-deception can help preserve our optimism. If we believe we are in some ways superior to others, whether we are or not, we can use this attitude to aspire to goals we believe superior people normally achieve.

The connection between confidence (whether earned or imagined) and performance has a great deal of scientific support. Numerous studies over the years have found that thinking you will succeed helps you succeed, in a variety of contexts. For this reason, deceiving yourself about your intelligence when taking a test or about your competence during a job interview can have tangible benefits. Whether you are above average or not, *thinking* you are can assist you in achieving above-average results.

Researchers Richard Gramzow, Greg Willard, and Wendy Mendes at Northeastern University reported a fascinating finding in line with this idea. They discovered that students they interviewed who exaggerated their grade point average—bumping it up to a few notches above reality—generally later went on to improve their grades. Further, the change in the grades often reflected the exact number they'd reported earlier. In other words, they improved their performance to make their lie *true*. Such lies can be thought of as a sort of expression of inner yearning. Students reported what they perhaps unconsciously wanted their grades to be, then followed through to make this wish reality.

Self-deception can also help one attain more grandiose goals than improved grades. If we honestly assess the odds against opening a successful business or making a radical career change later in life, we might, perfectly rationally, decide not to attempt such an endeavor. But if we offer ourselves an unreasonably optimistic appraisal of the challenges ahead, it can be easier to find the motivation to strive toward realizing such unlikely ambitions. It's important to keep in mind that the odds against achieving most of humanity's greatest accomplishments seem, in retrospect, hopelessly long. Who would have thought we could put a man on the moon before the invention of the pocket calculator?

Furthermore, self-deception has also been shown to offer benefits to those who are struggling with a past misfortune, as opposed to striving toward a future goal. Victims of trauma who can convince themselves that they do, in fact, retain control of their lives cope better than those who take a harder, more realist view of things. Cancer survivors who develop the notion that they can prevent the return of the disease, be it through diet or blind faith, tend to adjust better to life after their sickness. The false sense of security self-deception creates does contribute to psychological health.

Lying to ourselves, then, about our attributes, our ambitions, or our vulnerability can benefit us in ways both mental and concrete. But self-deception can also be helpful in our dealings with other people. Sandra Murray of the University of Buffalo and John Holmes of the University of Waterloo in Ontario have done extensive research into the ways lovers and spouses view each other. Their studies have found that people hold an idealized view of their close romantic partners. Positive attributes become exaggerated; flaws are minimized. This sort of partner glorification has actually been found to be a factor in relationship success. Relationships in which the partners see each other with this positive prejudice tend to last longer and be more mutually satisfying. In a similar vein, psychologists studying relationships have found that people in more success-ful relationships tend to lie to themselves about their options for other partners. The same way people mentally burnish the qualities of spouses or lovers, the qualities of potential mates outside the relationship are often viewed with irrational harsh-ness. Here, the positives are overlooked or minimized, the neg-atives inflated or embellished. Perhaps the realities of sexual competition make long-term relationships all but impossible. We need to see our partners as close to perfect and everyone else as hopelessly flawed.

More broadly, self-deception can be an essential component of social living in general. Consider the fact that however much we idealize them, the people in our lives remain, in the end, people. Our closest friends, husbands or wives, coworkers and family members inevitably indulge in acts of selfishness or mal-ice. Sometimes, unfortunately, these acts are directed toward us. Would it really serve our interests to think of our network of associates as selfish and malevolent? Or, to consider the ques-tion another way, would we maintain this network if we did?

In order to get at such questions, a group of American and Canadian anthropologists created a computer simulation of a two-player game. In the game, each player decides whether to contribute to a common investment pool. They both also have the option of excluding their partner from accessing the pool if the partner is not contributing enough to the common pot. After running the simulation for several generations of interac-tions, the researchers found that players who had established a history of cooperation were willing to ignore isolated acts of selfishness and continue the partnership. Furthermore, the researchers concluded that in the long term, this pattern of behavior was the most beneficial for the larger community. In other words, the ability to overlook the occasional malignant act proved helpful to the society at large. Serial offenders had to be excluded. But the simulation suggested that more harm was done ending imperfect but workable relationships than by continuing them, warts and all.

What this suggests for us is a model of relationships in which we deny, as best we can, the anomalous cheating and stealing of others so that society in general can function. According to one view, this is actually an evolved behavior. Early humans benefited from the ability to overlook minor acts of cheating, the theory holds, because this practice kept the small groups in which they lived more stable and tightly knit. By this reasoning, then, we didn't learn to overlook the flaws of those around us early in life; our genetic heritage makes them somehow invisible.

Other theories also trace self-deception to evolution. Some psychologists conjecture that we learned self-deceit in order to trick our own rules of conduct. We may feel a strong internal prohibition against stealing, for instance. However, we can skirt this prohibition and enjoy the advantage of stealing if we can convince ourselves that what we're doing isn't stealing but, say, "creative accounting."

The common thread among all this thinking is that self-deception, at least in some circumstances, is good—or, at least, in confers benefits on those who practice it. This undoubtedly is true to some degree. Yet the risks of self-deception are also evident. Particularly in our decision making, we may need a harsh assessment of the facts that self-deception only makes more difficult. As we have seen throughout *Liar*, lying has costs and benefits. This turns out to be true whether we are the target of the lies, their teller, or, in the case of self-deception, both.

And just as with the types of deception covered in previous chapters, the first step to living with deception is an awareness of it. This is particularly important with regard to the lies we tell ourselves, since these are the lies we are often least aware of. Carol Tavris is a social psychologist who cowrote a recent book with Elliot Aronson on the dangers of persistent self-justification, *Mistakes Were Made (but Not by Me)*. She summed up the apparently paradoxical need to keep the lies we tell ourselves in mind through a sharp metaphor. "Just as good drivers," she explained to the *Chronicle of Higher Education*, "are aware that they have an optical blind spot, the more we understand our own mental blind spots, the better able we are to compensate for them."

This metaphor is particularly appropriate, of course, because we are all above-average drivers.

CHAPTER 7

Cosmetic Deceit:
Lies to Make Us Seem Richer, Smarter, Better

The town of Gerald, Missouri, population 1,200, has a local police force you can tally on one hand. Unfortunately, Gerald also has a drug problem, specifically with methamphetamines. In this, Gerald is not unique. Meth labs have been popping up in rural areas of Middle America with alarming frequency in recent years. And like Gerald, most towns don't have the resources to deal with the problem. So when a federal agent arrived in Gerald and announced he had been sent to assist local law enforcement officers with their efforts against pushers and users, he was welcomed.

"Sergeant Bill," as he came to be known around town, fit the image of the tough federal drug warrior almost to perfection. He was bulky and clean-cut. He carried a gun and a badge. He drove around town in a Ford Crown Victoria outfitted with sirens and a police radio. And he turned sour when asked to give out his full name, saying it could compromise his investigative work.

Sergeant Bill began participating in an aggressive series of raids not long after arriving in Gerald. He reportedly kicked open doors, ransacked private residences, seized property, and put suspects in handcuffs. He did all this without search warrants, claiming that federal agents weren't required to obtain them. Sergeant Bill's campaign began to attract the attention of local media, in particular his claim that federal agents can act without warrants. (For the record, they can't.)

A reporter for the *Gasconade County Republican*, the local Gerald paper, began digging into Sergeant Bill's story. It didn't take long to uncover that it was all fiction. Sergeant Bill's real name was Bill A. Jakob. He had no affiliation with any federal agency. He had a brief history of small-town law enforcement, and he had also worked, at various times, in the trucking industry, as a wedding minister, and as a security guard. Sergeant Bill, it turned out, was an impostor.

He was certainly a convincing one, though. He fooled the mayor, the police chief, and the town aldermen. Even after Jakob had been revealed as a fraud, for a time some in Gerald clung to the belief that he was a federal agent despite all of it, that the revelations were just an elaborate cover story. There doesn't, however, seem to be any evidence to support this conviction. In the fallout from Jakob's fraud, several police officers lost their jobs, Gerald residents launched multimillion-dollar civil rights lawsuits, and Jakob himself faces a twenty-three-count indictment for impersonating an officer.

In earlier chapters of *Liar*, we have explored how frauds such as Bill A. Jakob can succeed. Liars have a powerful advantage when they seek to fool us. We are in many ways predisposed to trust, and this predisposition is often difficult to overcome. Indeed, it can be argued that it is actually easy to trick other people in the fashion of "Sergeant Bill." But what about the reasons why Bill A. Jakob would engage in such an elaborate ruse? Why would someone want to impersonate a federal drug agent, conduct raids, kick down doors? What is the psychology behind taking on a new identity?

For Bill A. Jakob, the most obvious explanations don't seem to fit. He didn't gain financially from his fraud. He told local authorities that his salary was being paid by the federal government. His services cost the town of Gerald almost nothing in terms of dollars. Nor is there much reason to believe that Bill A. Jakob was simply crazy. He took elaborate steps to hide his true identity, even going so far as to offer a fake phone number for a fake agency, the "multijurisdictional task force," in support of his story. It does not seem, in other words, that Bill A. Jakob really *believed* he was in the employ of the DEA. His deception was deliberate and, at least in terms of how it was pulled off, rational.

Aspiration is a ubiquitous feature of modern life. We live in a society that encourages us to spend whatever it takes in order to make ourselves a little thinner, a little fitter, a little more sophisticated-looking. Perhaps, too, there is some aspect of human nature that resists the complacency of total self-satisfaction—that drives us to expand beyond our present condition and circumstances. Yet regardless of whether it comes from our DNA or our TV, the urge to be *better* is a very real one, and it manifests itself in a huge variety of ways. Some people answer the impulse toward self-enhancement by taking courses to learn a new language, some people buy a new car—and many people resort to deception.

It's ultimately impossible to identify with certainty the underlying motives for Bill A. Jakob's deceit, especially since these motives may have been hazy even to him. Yet if any aspect of his lies stemmed from a wish to be something more than he was—a federal agent instead of small-town cop—then in this regard his actions resemble those of millions of people engaged in what is generally considered normal behavior. Most don't go so far as to impersonate a DEA agent, but almost all of us have taken steps to improve ourselves, and these steps are not always strictly honest.

I call such deception *cosmetic deceit*. This term refers to the broad category of lies we tell to make ourselves appear better—by whatever standard—than we are. The term "cosmetic deceit" may seem to imply something casual—a brief act of minor fabrication, comparable to applying a dab of makeup to hide a blemish. But as the case of Bill A. Jakob shows, cosmetic deceit can encompass substantial fabrication with equally substantial consequences. Indeed, some of the most prominent scandals of recent years stem from lies that can be categorized as cosmetic deceit.

Cosmetic deceit is also among the most common forms of deception. As we have seen throughout *Liar,* lies occur regularly in day-to-day social interactions. These lies can function simply to keep a conversation moving or to avoid hurting the feelings of the target of the lie. Very often, too, the lies that crop up in everyday conversations help service the psychological well-being of the liar. In order to impress someone, or, by the same token, salve nagging insecurities, a person may invent a fact or deceptively soften the edges of an embarrassing event. That is, they may indulge in a cosmetic lie to cast themselves in a better light. A lukewarm performance review is recounted as glowing; a golf score is lowered by a couple shots; the laughter a joke elicited gains a decibel level in the retelling. Such lies are so common because, as we will see later in the chapter, the social and psychological dynamics of interacting with other people can to some extent make cosmetic deceit nearly inevitable.

Yet some argue that interpersonal lies are only one form of a much broader practice of cosmetic deceit. Some psychologists hold that most of Western culture's fundamental activities of ornamentation, such as applying makeup or styling hair, constitute deception. In this view, one's natural appearance has a kind of authenticity. Wearing a shade of lipstick darker than one's natural pigmentation, for instance, thus represents a form of a lie. When our "true" appearance is interfered with, by way of blush or eyeliner or colored contact lenses, the image presented to the world is to some degree false. For the purposes of our discussion, it isn't necessary to plumb the question of whether wearing a wig is the equivalent of lying about the length and color of your hair. It is enough to note that we are accustomed to exercising a great deal of control over our physical appearances. We exercise this control through everything from clothing selection to cosmetics application to trips to the spa. Whether or not we conclude that any of these activities represent deception, it's easy to see how the attitudes that underlie them sometimes take verbal form. A chipped tooth is replaced with a fake; an embarrassingly bad decision is hidden with a lie.

It's not news to anyone that our culture is obsessed with image. What's important to keep in mind is that the idea of "image" is not restricted to the visual realm. Modern society places enormous significance on the perceptions of other people. The explosion in recent years of blogs and reality television demonstrates the great interest people have in scrutinizing other people's lives, as well as in offering up their own lives for scrutiny. Given the centrality of the opinions of others, then, the temptations of cosmetic deceit aren't difficult to understand. When we pay so much attention to what other people think, it's hard to limit the ways we try to influence those thoughts. Representing our true selves can often take a back seat to representing what we perceive to be our "best" selves. And this tendency can be especially pronounced in situations where impressing another person is not just an implicit goal but the entire point of the interaction.

Blind Dates and Other Times You'll Probably Be Lied To

Certain situations seem to lend themselves to horror stories: visits to the dentist; trips to the local Department of Motor Vehicles; and, perhaps most infamously, blind dates. It's likely you've heard more than one story of a disastrous blind date. If you've been single for a while, it's probable you've experienced one, too.

A student of mine once offered me an interesting perspective on the disastrous blind date. He was, he confessed, the initiator of the disaster. He was having dinner with an attractive, intelligent young woman—and suddenly found himself blathering on about a bicycle trip across South America he planned to take the following summer. He discussed the route he would follow, the type of bike he would buy. The problem was, he had no plans to take such a trip. Biking South America was something he'd pondered idly but had no concrete intention of doing. Unfortunately, his date was a cycling enthusiast, and as she pressed him for details, it became increasingly clear that what he'd told her was basically fiction. And so this blind date entered her pantheon of horror stories.

What surprised me about this anecdote was that this student was not habitually dishonest. He was, rather, a forthright, decent person, and one who expressed great embarrassment over his behavior on the date. How was it, then, that he had come to find himself telling a lie about biking across South America?

As we consider the factors underlying cosmetic deceit, the blind date presents an illuminating scenario. These encounters are all about mutual evaluation: assessing a potential partner on a vast array of criteria, from the physical to the financial.

Such a scenario inevitably puts psychological pressure on its participants. When we are being judged, we reflexively want to be judged positively. Even if one of the participants has less than a consuming interest in the date, the interest in maintaining self-esteem remains. The need to come off well, even in the eyes of an unappealing stranger, can be intense.

Yet the process of coming off well is far from simple. In previous chapters, we've examined the psychological mechanism of self-presentation, the way we demonstrate our personality and related traits to other people. As we've discussed, self-presentation is often a question of choice: which impulses to follow or ignore, which opinions to express or withhold, which jokes to tell or save for another occasion. On a blind date, we frequently choose which details in our personal biography to present. The recent promotion is mentioned; the problems securing a car loan are not. Self-presentation represents a kind of packaging of who we are in a form we judge to be appealing and appropriate.

This process of self-presentation is one we enact in every single social encounter we have. Only a pure social incompetent acts the same way in every context, with every group of people. The rest of us weigh such factors as who we're talking to and the situation in which we're interacting as we make decisions regarding how to behave and what to say. A blind date is in some ways only a pressurized version of a circumstance we face all the time. While we may not always be explicitly attempting to woo or impress another person, our encounters with others inevitably involve revealing and concealing, emphasizing and downplaying.

And this brings us back to cosmetic deceit. If we think of self-presentation as a creative process, one in which we tailor ourselves to fit the situation, we can see how there is a very fine line between honest self-presentation and cosmetic deceit. If we feel we lack in some way the *self* a situation demands—if we feel we don't have the intelligence or the wit or the biography the circumstance calls for—we can resort to fiction. Again, even honest self-presentation involves creativity. At some point, we may find ourselves stepping from shading and selection over into distorting and invention.

On a blind date, such temptations can be especially strong. The evaluative pressure of a blind date forces our insecurities to the surface: about appearance, about accomplishments, about status. Cosmetic deceit is a way of answering these insecurities. Further, the stakes on a blind date can be, well, blindingly high. Assuming a person takes a liking to his or her date, he or she might judge the potential rewards of appealing self-presentation to be everything from short-term physical gratification to life-long emotional satisfaction. In other words, a successful blind date can mean snaring Mr. or Ms. Right. In this context, the urge to impress may easily trump the commitment to honesty.

The initially inexplicable deceit of my student regarding his invented bike trip thus becomes more explicable. The barriers against deception in self-presentation are fragile, and the psychological pressures weighing toward cosmetic deceit on a blind date are extreme. My student wanted to impress his date and ended up enhancing his attributes by concocting an athletic adventure.

Certainly, he was not alone in his behavior. Studies have found that cosmetic deceit occurs in a range of romantic contexts. Psychological researchers Wade Rowatt, Michael Cunningham, and Perri Druen of Baylor University conducted a study of the ways people present themselves when they are trying to get a date in the first place. Rowatt and his colleagues were particularly interested in how the strategies for self-presentation might vary depending on the attractiveness of the potential date. In other words, did people change tactics according to whether they were wooing someone more or less attractive?

Rowatt and his colleagues presented volunteers with profiles, featuring photographs and personality descriptions, of members of the other sex. (In this study, the selected participants were all heterosexual.) Some of the profiles featured physically attractive people, some unattractive people. The researchers told the study participants that the profiled individuals would be selecting one participant to go on a date with based on a survey they would fill out. The researchers then analyzed the surveys the participants completed to see how they had presented themselves to what they believed to be potential romantic partners.

The participants were not entirely honest in the surveys. But, given the dynamics of self-presentation, that is not much of a surprise. What is telling, though, is that the participants lied more in the surveys directed to the more attractive individuals. In other words, the greater the attraction, the greater the deception. The nature of the deception Rowatt and his colleagues identified is also instructive. The participants often lied in order to appear more similar to the profiled individual. As opposed to embracing the motto that opposites attract, participants fabricated resemblances to their romantic targets.

Playing up similarities is a conventional tactic in winning the affection of another person. We've all been told to focus on what we "have in common" when meeting someone new. By the same token, having "nothing in common" is usually a damning sentence when it comes to forming a relationship. Cosmetic deceit offers a way to build the bridge of common interests and personality traits, even when it may not exist. When people want to woo an attractive potential mate, Rowatt and his colleagues' study suggests, they lie to present themselves as *just like* him or her.

Cosmetic deceit, then, can serve a variety of functions in the romantic realm. It can be used to build up a suitor's credentials in stereotypically desirable categories, such as achievement, ambition, or status. Further, it can be used in a more psychologically subtle way, to achieve a kind of matching with the romantic target. A man tells his date that he, too, is a devoted family man; a woman tells her date that she, also, is looking for a serious commitment. It should be noted, as well, that these uses are far from mutually exclusive. Indeed, the tweaking of a biography and the fabrication of similarities can overlap in complex ways. For example, as women become increasingly financially successful earlier in life, there is a growing trend among young women to actually pretend to earn *less* than they really do, so as not to threaten the egos of potential male partners. Cosmetic deceit can be used to make yourself seem a little less accomplished, then, when you think it might benefit you or appeal to your date.

The functions of cosmetic deceit are hardly limited to romantic situations, of course. Indeed, they are not limited even to social contexts. The pressures to fit particular criteria can be institutional. Getting and keeping a job necessarily entails matching personal skills and abilities with the specific needs of an employer. And just as people use cosmetic deceit to impress an attractive potential mate with false attributes, so too do they use it to woo potential bosses with degrees they never earned and past experiences they never had.

Being Right for the Job, Even When You're Not

As dean of admissions for the Massachusetts Institute of Technology, Marilee Jones earned a reputation for speaking out against the high-pressure, high-stress culture of the American college admissions system. Jones counseled teens to stop trying to embody the theoretical ideal in the mind of an Ivy League admissions officer and focus more on being themselves. Her publisher's description of the book she cowrote, *Less Stress, More Success: A New Approach to Guiding Your Teen Through College Admissions and Beyond*, promised that it would help applicants in "letting your true, authentic self come through in your paperwork." It's an appealing idea: the truth taking primacy over institutional demands.

Yet however valid Jones's message was, it only rang with irony when application of indiscretions of her own came to light. On her professional résumé, Jones had claimed to hold degrees from three different institutions: Albany Medical College, Union College, and Rensselaer Polytechnic Institute. The truth was that her only degree was from an obscure Catholic college in Albany, New York. In the wake of the ensuing scandal, Jones resigned, ending her twenty-eight-year career at MIT.

The story of Marilee Jones garnered national media attention. The public seemed fascinated by a tale of such glaring fraud at such a renowned educational institution. Yet the fact is that Jones's behavior was far from extraordinary. The practice of embellishing a résumé is fairly common. Exact figures differ, but studies indicate that two-thirds of people exaggerate or simply fabricate their managerial experience. Padding a résumé to a small degree is so common that it often falls into the category of minor crimes dismissed as things "everybody does." In this context, job applicants may even feel at a disadvantage if they *don't* stretch the truth on their résumé, creating another impetus for deceit.

Job interviews, another fundamental element of the job application process, provide an even greater opportunity to lie.

Interviews are conducted orally, so they leave no verifiable record of what occurred. Many people see this as an open invitation to be deceptive. Since statements cannot be vetted later, the checks against exaggerating accomplishments or taking false credit are that much weaker.

If we consider the psychological dynamics of applying or interviewing for a job, perhaps all this cosmetic deceit should not surprise us. In many ways, the factors that induce people to engage in cosmetic deceit on a blind date are the same ones that tempt them to lie when seeking a job. The evaluative intensity of a blind date is paralleled in a job interview. Again, the entire purpose of the interaction is scrutiny, as an interviewer evaluates the candidate on a range of criteria, from business skills to personality. This scrutiny triggers the same impulses to succeed that a blind date does—with the added component of potential financial benefit thrown in. A job interview, like a blind date, is really a high-stakes challenge of self-presentation. Decisions about what to say and what to conceal take on great importance. In this context, self-presentation can easily yield to cosmetic deceit.

As it plays out in the context of job seeking generally, cosmetic deceit is often very specific and very concrete. Employers make clear what they are looking for in a new hire. If a person lacks any of the stated requirements for a job—the experience, the degree—cosmetic deceit allows him or her the opportunity to win the job anyway. As with Marilee Jones, the obstacles to a particular position can be overcome with a few deceptive lines on a résumé.

What's important to understand is that while the form may vary, the underlying psychology of cosmetic deceit remains largely the same. Perceived gaps in *who we are* can be masked through lies. Sometimes the lies involve imaginary bike trips, sometimes college diplomas. Regardless, when we fall short of what we'd like to be—in terms of achievement or personality or experience—cosmetic deceit provides a fix, albeit a temporary one.

In contrast to all this cosmetic deceit in the business world and the dating world is what might be called the Stuart Smalley philosophy of life. Stuart Smalley was a character portrayed by Al Franken on *Saturday Night Live*. A self-help fanatic, Smalley was known for his signature affirmation, which he would repeat while staring at himself in the mirror: "I'm good enough, I'm smart enough, and, doggone it, people like me." Why is cosmetic deceit a part of our lives in the first place? If we don't have the skills for one job, we can learn them, or simply find a job we are suited for. If a romantic partner doesn't like our jokes, surely someone out there will. Why don't we follow Stuart Smalley's lead and simply embrace our own inner sufficiency?

The problem may be that unlike Stuart Smalley, we can't just look in the mirror and be secure in our own greatness. Indeed, our own greatness may not even be the point. We may resort to cosmetic deceit not because we doubt we are good enough, smart enough, and likable enough, but because other people out there are better, smarter, and, doggone it, more likable.

Looking Up and Lying

Wade Rowatt, Michael Cunningham, and Perri Druen conducted another study in conjunction with their research into how people lie to potential romantic partners. They had found that participants were more likely to lie to attractive potential dates than unattractive ones, and they were curious to know whether the participants in their study were aware of this bias. So in a second study, they asked participants directly whether they were more willing to lie to better-looking people. Surprisingly, most of the participants admitted that they were. They said they'd be more apt to lie about everything from their personalities to their income to their past relationships.

These results indicate that cosmetic deceit employed in the course of wooing can be a tactic. It is at times a dishonest method used to ingratiate the liar with the beautiful target of the lie. In other words, a Lothario knows what he's doing when he tells the woman at the bar he's a huge fan of Mariah Carey's music, too.

Yet while cosmetic deceit can be cunning, there does seem to be another side to it. Think again of my student and his invented bike trip. He described being as surprised as anyone by what he was saying. This suggests that cosmetic deceit is not always something we consciously deploy. While its effect may be manipulative, its source may not necessarily be an intent to manipulate.

In order to explore whether cosmetic deceit can occur spontaneously, as my student suggested, I, along with my student James Tyler, conducted a study investigating how people react to threats to their self-esteem. The study worked like this: I told the participants that a large corporation was funding a research project to determine the best way to assess potential employees. The participants would be asked to take a series of tests that would measure their skills and aptitude in particular areas. They would be teamed with a partner in another room, who would be taking the same tests. The participant and the partner would evaluate each other's responses. In fact, the partner was just fiction—another example of employing deceit in psychological research into deceit. But for this experiment to function, it was essential that the participants *believed* there was another person, a lot like them, taking the same tests they were.

The first portion of the test included questions measuring analytic skills. These questions were pulled from old versions of the Graduate Record Exam (GRE). Once the participants had completed this section, it was taken to be "graded." A few minutes later, the participants were given their score on the first section, along with, importantly, the fictional score of their partner.

Again, this was all part of a ruse. There were no partners, and the questions weren't actually graded. The intent was to present the participants with a sharp contrast in performance. The made-up results showed that they had done poorly on the quiz, while their partners had scored well. In other words, a participant looking at her score from part one of the test would see that her partner in the next room had aced it, while she had bombed.

After being presented with these (intentionally unsettling) results, participants were given a questionnaire regarding personal information and told that they would be exchanging the completed questionnaires with their better-scoring partner. The questionnaires asked about grade point average, accomplishments, skills, and so forth.

Once the questionnaires had been completed, participants were informed that the experiment was essentially over. But one more task remained: the participants were asked to review their questionnaire responses and report any exaggerations, discrepancies, or straightforward lies they'd included. It was this evaluation that, in reality, formed the crux of the study. I wanted to see how receiving an inferior score on the analytic questions would shape the way participants presented themselves on the personal questions. How would self-presentation, manifested literally on a survey, be shaped by a blow to self-esteem?

The result showed that participants employed a great deal of cosmetic deceit. In the wake of being told that they had been outscored by their partners, participants responded by inflating their grades, their accomplishments, and their skills. Overall, a quarter of the responses they gave on their surveys were false. (Importantly, also, a group of control participants who were informed that they had outscored their partners lied at much lower rates.)

In considering these results, two facts bear emphasis. First of all, the participants didn't stand to gain anything by their deceit. There was no job on the line, no romantic partner to win over. There was basically no practical benefit to lying on the personal questionnaires at all. Second, the participants never saw their partners and had no reason to believe they would ever meet them. If they were threatened by their partners' scores, if they hoped to impress them with their personal information, these dynamics played out anonymously.

How, then, to account for the high levels of deceit? Psychologists speak of what are called "upward comparisons." These are comparisons individuals make between themselves and people whom they perceive to be superior according to some conventional societal standard—smarter, more famous, more academically successful. A wealth of psychological theory and research, not to mention common sense, tells us what such comparisons can do to our egos. When we engage in an upward comparison, our self-esteem faces damage. No one likes to be reminded that there are people out there who are more successful in their careers, more attractive, more clever. Reflexively, we look for ways to shield ourselves from the threat such comparisons present to our pride.

Cosmetic Deceit

The participants in my study were confronted with a very clear (albeit fictional) comparison: they were told their partners had done better on an analytic test. Their response was often to defend their self-image by *inflating* this image on paper. They used cosmetic deceit to enhance themselves. This deceit was ostensibly targeted toward their partners, who would be reading the fabricated personal questionnaires. But again, these partners were people they had not met, and probably never would. It's not a stretch to conclude that the real focus of the deception was the participants themselves. It was their self-esteem that was threatened by the upward comparison, their own anxieties that demanded some form of comfort.

In this conception, cosmetic deceit acts as a kind of self-administered balm for situations in which our self-esteem is imperiled. It becomes a mechanism for taking the edge off an unflattering upward comparison. This also offers another explanation for why Rowatt and his colleagues found lying to be so frequent in dealings with attractive people. It's not so much that particular individuals are attractive, as that we feel they are *more attractive* than us. And just as in my study, the response to this upward comparison is self-presentation enhanced with cosmetic deceit. We offer a fictional version of ourselves, presenting a person who need not fear the comparison to others. The lie about ourselves may or may not impress or fool its target—but the fiction makes *us* feel better. It's as if the false self-image we create through cosmetic deceit is one we get to admire, too.

The psychological functioning of cosmetic deceit is thus highly varied. Lies about ourselves can function as a tool of callous manipulation or as very personal shields to our fragile self-esteem. Often, these uses run together. Who can say to what extent braggadocio is used to impress another person and to what extent it reassures and comforts the braggart? But there is a particular realm where many of the psychological pressures that trigger cosmetic deceit come together, perhaps in their most concentrated form. It is perhaps not surprising, then, that in this realm so many of the most infamous examples of cosmetic deceit have occurred.

"The Truth Is, I Want Your Vote!"

Hillary Clinton, while campaigning for the Democratic presidential nomination in the spring of 2008, described a memorable trip she made to war-torn Bosnia more than a decade earlier. "I remember landing under sniper fire," she was quoted as saying. "There was supposed to be some kind of a greeting ceremony at the airport, but instead we just ran with our heads down to get into the vehicles to get to our base." News footage, however, told a different story. It showed Clinton strolling calmly with her daughter, Chelsea, upon arriving in Bosnia, and even receiving a present from a young Bosnian girl. It was later revealed that Clinton had been accompanied on the trip not only by her daughter and members of the press but also by the comedian Sinbad. When asked to explain the discrepancy, Clinton asserted that she "did misspeak."

During that same election cycle, Mitt Romney, a candidate for the Republican nomination, claimed that his father, George Romney, a former Michigan governor, had "marched with Martin Luther King." It was soon revealed that the elder Romney had never actually done so. Romney asserted that he had been speaking in a figurative sense, in that his father had *supported* Martin Luther King, not physically *marched* with him.

Such instances of deception (or, more charitably, misunderstandings) are nothing new. In the presidential campaign of 1840, William Henry Harrison played up his "log cabin" roots, even though he was born into a powerful political family and raised on a Virginia plantation. And not an election cycle goes by without some new instance of a candidate claiming to be instrumental in legislation he had little role in, or declaring she supported a cause all along, when in fact she once opposed it. While politicians continue to pay lip service to the importance of honesty, their behavior suggests a very different valuation.

It would be easy to conclude, as many do, that politicians are simply by nature duplicitous. People who run for office, the thinking goes, are the kind of people who lie. It is somehow encoded in their DNA.

Yet keep in mind that, as we have seen throughout *Liar*, people in all walks of life lie. Politicians are not some unusually duplicitous strain within the human race. Rather, their dishonest behavior, and specifically their cosmetic deceit, actually makes them resemble us more than it sets them apart.

To see how this similarity manifests itself, consider the mechanics of a campaign. The demands of self-presentation are acute. Modern campaigning is almost purely a matter of fostering a particular image, one that will appeal to voters (or at least to a majority of them). In a sense, every day on the campaign trail is like an outsized job interview, with a candidate working to fit his or her personal traits to the criteria of a scrutinizing electorate.

The psychological intensity of this is compounded by the pressures of not only the omnipresent media but also omnipresent competitors. For most of us, the competition we face is implicit. A colleague at work with the same title as us may, in theory, stand in the way of our winning a promotion, but the ultimate decision is rarely so dramatic as management making a choice between us and him. Politicians on the campaign trail, on the other hand, face daily, explicit competition, often with rivals who share many of the same skills and attributes.

In short, campaigns combine many of the factors identified as underlying cosmetic deceit. There are high-pressure demands for effective self-presentation; there are ubiquitous comparisons, which frequently can at least be perceived as upward. If psychological research is correct, cosmetic deception is a common response to such conditions. So when Hillary Clinton presents herself as a strong leader based on her dangerous landing in Bosnia, perhaps we should temper our scorn with a measure of identification.

CHAPTER 8

Lies with Intent:
Deceit to Trick or Cheat

Though many would prefer to forget it, during the 1990s, a teen-pop boom swept across the United States. Acts like the Backstreet Boys and 'N Sync were a sensation, filling concert arenas, selling millions of records, and generating vast sums of money. At the eye of this cultural storm was a veteran of the aviation business named Lou Pearlman. Pearlman was responsible for managing the Backstreet Boys and 'N Sync, as well as numerous other, less successful acts. A large, bespectacled man with a soft, doughy face, Pearlman liked to style himself as a father figure to his acts, going so far as to ask group members to call him "Big Poppa."

Pearlman spent lavishly during the height of his success, purchasing cars, homes, and investment real estate. He became a well-known figure in the Florida music scene and was even awarded the key to the city of Orlando. But members of Pearlman's groups began to wonder why all the revenue Pearlman was so clearly enjoying wasn't trickling down to them. Eventually, some concluded that Pearlman was bilking them of their fair share of profits. First the Backstreet Boys sued Pearlman; then 'N Sync followed. Kevin Richardson, a Backstreet Boys member, told *Rolling Stone*, "[Pearlman] totally deceived me." Eventually both the Backstreet Boys and 'N Sync reached settlements that allowed them to break from Pearlman and recover at least some of their earnings.

But the members of his musical acts were hardly the only ones who would come to feel victimized by Pearlman. In the early 1990s, Pearlman had begun selling so-called Employee Investment Savings Accounts (EISA) in a company he controlled, Trans Continental Airlines. Selling often to elderly Floridian retirees, sometimes simply by cold-calling, Pearlman made millions off his EISAs.

The problem was that Trans Continental Airlines did not exist. And, in fact, there was no such thing as an Employee Investment Savings Account. The entire scheme was a paper-based fraud—a Ponzi scheme, in which Pearlman paid out dividends to old investors with money swindled from new ones. Eventually, cheated investors and Florida state officials caught on to Pearlman's massive web of shell companies, bogus accounting firms, and forged documents. After fleeing the country, Pearlman was eventually apprehended at a resort in Bali. In 2008, he was sentenced to twenty-five years in prison and ordered to pay back $300 million in stolen profit.

Up to now, we have focused on some of the surprising motives behind deceit. People lie to benefit others or as an almost unconscious response to threats to their egos. Sometimes, though, the reasons underlying deception don't seem to demand much accounting. You don't need a PhD in psychology to offer a good explanation for why Lou Pearlman sold fake shares in a fake company to vulnerable marks. He did it to *make money*. Whatever other factors contributed to his malfeasance, the immediate goal seems obvious.

In this chapter, we will examine instances where the purpose of deception seems on the surface very straightforward, not to mention baldly unscrupulous. False flattery and lies of social convenience make up the bulk of the lies we encounter in daily life. Yet the lies of swindlers, con men, impostors—to put it simply, the lies like those of Lou Pearlman—have their place in the portrait of deceit, too.

My term for these lies, ones that dupe or con, is *lies with intent*. This phrase helps differentiate them from the more mundane forms of deception we typically encounter in day-to-day life. For example, lies that smooth social interactions blend naturally into the fabric of our relationships. We never find out that our officemate doesn't really like *CSI: Miami*, and, ultimately, it may not be hugely important that we do. Further, as we have seen in many chapters of *Liar*, most of the lies we commonly hear have their roots in the psychological maintenance of the person telling them. The liar herself may not even really understand why she shaved five strokes off her last round of golf. Regardless, the lie has more to do with her own comfort than with fooling us.

Lies with intent, on the other hand, fragment and fray the social fabric of daily life. They undermine trust, and they erode relationships. While we might be content not to sniff out some minor disagreement, not sniffing out a *lie with intent* has serious consequences, most often and most immediately financial. *Lies with intent* are not most relevant to the psychology of the liar (though, as we will see, the psychology of the liar plays a significant role in their origin). Rather, they are most relevant to the person who might be fooled by the lies. Such lies have *intent*: to win misplaced trust, to execute a business fraud, to victimize. In short, lies with intent have the intent to harm.

It's important to keep in mind that while lies with intent have serious, and very worrying, consequences, they are relatively rare. The Lou Pearlmans of the world, those with the capacity and the willingness to execute large-scale deceit with the purpose of victimization, are few and far between. Even more minor lies with intent—say, those told by a plumber who wants to overcharge us for the cost of a repair—are infrequent when compared to the false flattery and insincere social niceties that occur so regularly in daily life.

Yet despite their rarity, lies with intent largely define how we think about lying. We assume that people who lie to us want to gain something tangible through their deception. It's hard to accept the notion that the most common lies we hear yield only psychological benefit, or that this benefit might even be mutual, shared by us and the liar. Yet the fact is that the kind of lie we're most likely to hear is one our spouse tells about the results of our latest home improvement project. We don't want to know that the paint job on the deck looks terrible, and our spouse doesn't want to break it to us, either.

Part of the reason lies with intent dominate our attitudes toward deception generally is that they are so different from such mundane acts of deceit. Unlike domestic false flattery, lies with intent have clear elements of drama: innocent victims, brazen perpetrators, unexpected revelations. When Lou Pearlman's fraud was discovered, it garnered national media attention, as did more recent revelations about the even larger Ponzi scheme of Bernard Madoff. When we discuss and contemplate lying, we focus on the lies we hear about on television or in the newspaper, or those that are worth a recounting from friends. These tend to be lies with intent. More frequent lies just aren't very interesting to those not directly affected.

We need to keep lies with intent in perspective, then. Statistically, few of us will ever be caught up in an elaborate investment scheme or come to realize that our lawyer friend is in fact an impostor. The liars in our life are the ordinary people we interact with day in and day out, people who have no malicious plan to steal from us.

On the other hand, lies with intent are, almost by definition, a very harmful form of deceit. While more frequent, more mundane lies may have an overall corrosive effect on the comfort and honesty of society as a whole, the effects of lies with intent are generally both painfully unambiguous and all too calculable. Further, the concrete goals of lies with intent can obscure a deeper complexity. Although greed may be the primary motive behind lies with intent, it is not necessarily the only motive.

The Joy of Lying

Hakan Yalincak fit an enduring image in popular culture: that of the financial whiz kid. While enrolled at New York University and still in his early twenties, Yalincak ran his own hedge fund, Daedalus Capital Relative Value Fund. The fund attracted millions in investment and, on paper at least, seemed to be booming. By all accounts, Yalincak possessed an excellent mind for numbers and a mastery of the lingo of trading. Apparently happy to share his wealth, he promised NYU a $21 million donation, the first payment of which went toward creating the "Yalincak Family Foundation Lecture Hall."

But things began to unravel when Yalincak attempted to deposit checks of $25 million and close to $18 million. The checks, it turned out, were fakes. In fact, all of Daedalus Capital Relative was fake. The whole operation was a scam, a net of phony numbers and false associations meant to entrap investment capital. For a while it had worked: experienced financial players had dumped millions into Daedalus. But when Yalincak was arrested after trying to pass off the phony checks, investors sued. The gift to NYU never materialized. Eventually, Yalincak was sentenced to three and a half years in prison for his assorted acts of fraud.

The permutations for potential investment have probably never been more dense than they are today, representing a theoretically profitable tangle of securities and derivatives, commodities and futures. As the global fallout from the collapse of the subprime-fueled real estate market shows, even the savviest investors can be enticed into very risky and, ultimately, very bad decisions. In such a financial climate, we might expect a figure like Hakan Yalincak to emerge: someone who could exploit the complexities of the finance system to create the opportunity to invest in something that simply wasn't there. In a sense, it's the logical next step from the storied con of selling a yokel the Brooklyn Bridge. Instead of selling a bridge that wasn't for sale, Yalincak sold a hedge fund that wasn't investing.

From a psychological standpoint, too, Yalincak does not necessarily seem extraordinary. Every day, people break into homes, steal cars, rob at gunpoint. Elaborate fraud does not have to be more psychologically nuanced than "petty" theft. One could even argue that it is simply a difference of the tools of the crime. If we don't wonder much about what's going on in the head of a mugger, is there reason to wonder about Yalincak's mental state? As we discussed with regard to Lou Pearlman's EISA scam, the motive behind lies with intent can seem crystal clear: profit.

Yet construing Yalincak as merely greedy—thinking of him as a mugger armed with false profit statements instead of a knife—would seem to leave something out. We don't need to aggrandize Yalincak to the level of an evil genius to remark that even most paper frauds don't rise to the level of attempting to deposit fake checks for $25 million at a go. Think of it another way: to pull off his fraud, Yalincak needed to fool investors in face-to-face interactions, fabricate a complicated yet sufficiently plausible paper trail, carry on a façade of respectability, and all the while evade the scrutiny of those who enforce the laws he was breaking. At some point, wouldn't it have been simpler just to mug someone? Or, to offer a legal—not to mention potentially more lucrative—spin, why not start a *real* hedge fund?

The apparent contradictions in Yalincak's behavior help underscore the fact that lies with intent are not as simple as they may first appear. All of us, to some degree at least, want to make money. But few of us choose to go about it by engaging in multimillion-dollar fraud. Beyond the ethical objections, there are practical considerations. These considerations generally involve things like the risk of jail time, the possibility of public humiliation, and potential inclusion in a book about liars. What is it that pushes con artists and frauds to disregard these considerations in their pursuit of profit?

In Yalincak's case, fraud seems to have been a kind of family business. His mother, Ayferafet Yalincak, spent nearly two years behind bars for impersonating a doctor in Indiana for six months. She was arrested soon after her son, in connection with his hedge fund scheme, and was eventually sentenced to another two years in prison.

Looking beyond one individual's, or one family's, lies with intent, though, we can identify certain factors that generally drive this form of deceit, despite its inherent risks. To understand more fully why a person might tell a lie with intent, we have to reexamine another one of our preconceived notions about lying. Go back for moment to our discussion of lie detection. The thinking behind most methods of lie detection, and behind polygraph machines specifically, holds that liars experience anxiety when they lie. That is why you might suspect that someone is lying if they avert their gaze and why, in theory, a polygraph machine reveals a lie when it records an elevated heartbeat. Both of these are physiological responses to anxiety, which (again, in theory) is an emotional response to telling a lie.

The problem is that this is *only* theory. The fact is that some people don't get anxious when they lie. Good liars remain remarkably calm, and can exhibit virtually no physiological response that might betray their deceit. This is chiefly why polygraph machines have such a high failure rate, and also why you can't assume someone is telling the truth just because he looks you in the eye.

More to the point in a discussion of lies with intent: not only do some people remain free from anxiety when they tell a lie, but some even experience pleasure. Paul Ekman of the University of California, San Francisco, is one of the leading researchers in the area of nonverbal behavior and deception. He has identified a feeling among liars he calls *duping delight*. This refers to the positive emotional response lying can elicit in certain individuals. In his book *Telling Lies,* he describes the forms duping delight can take: "The lie may be viewed as an accomplishment, which feels good. The liar may feel excitement, either in anticipating the challenge or during the very moment of lying.... Afterward there may be the pleasure that comes with relief, pride in the achievement, or feelings of smug contempt toward the target." We generally think of lying as something difficult, a taxing and anxiety-provoking task. For most of us, it usually is. But just as people will jump out of airplanes and climb mountains precisely because of the physical and mental challenges, so too do people find an almost recreational thrill, as Ekman describes, in deception.

There does seem to be something a bit sinister in the idea

Lies with Intent

of duping delight—in the notion that one might experience pleasure from tricking other people. But think of the concept of bluffing. We've probably all had occasion to bluff, perhaps literally, during a card game or, more figuratively, during a negotiation in our business or private life. For most of us, there is an undeniable thrill in (emptily) threatening to walk away unless the broker shaves a few thousand more off the asking price or, more quaintly, unless the woman at the tag sale takes off another dollar. Whatever the stakes, such deceptive power plays are exciting to make, and exciting to pull off. And a successful bluff is really only a step away from a lie with intent. Indeed, it could be argued that the former is just a milder form of the latter.

Regardless, once we recognize that it is possible to enjoy a lie with intent, this form of deceit becomes at once more understandable and more complex. It is not just the function of the lie that matters. It is the form, too. The act of telling the lie itself brings a kind of profit: an adrenaline rush, a feeling of superiority, a sense of accomplishment. Studies of confidence men, for example, have shown that their interest is less in the money they earn—which they burn through quickly anyway—than in the rush of the con itself. The income is nice; the process of getting it is what really motivates them.

We can see this same phenomenon in an entirely different context in a study conducted by Gideon de Bruin and Hilton Rudnick, researchers at the University of Johannesburg, in South Africa. They were curious about the phenomenon of academic dishonesty; they wanted to know if particular personality types were more prone to cheating on tests. In their research, they found that individuals described as "excitement seeking," those with a tendency to pursue thrills and risk, were more likely to cheat. Academic dishonesty, de Bruin and Rudnick's research suggests, is not strictly about getting better grades. Just as with con men, the thrill of the crime itself is a motivating factor.

Interestingly, duping delight has a parallel in the more mundane forms of deception we normally encounter in everyday life. As was noted above, many lies have more to do with the psychology of the liar than the target of the lie. This is true, again, in many instances of false bravado, such as exaggerating the quality of a golf score, or the size of a paycheck, or what have you. Duping delight suggests that this same phenomenon may be relevant, at least to an extent, for lies with intent. These lies clearly have much to do with their target; specifically, they intend to fleece him or her. Yet perhaps more powerfully, they convey a psychological thrill to their teller. Just like a lie that defends self-esteem, a lie with intent can make the liar *feel good*.

This is not to suggest a moral equivalence between a lie that puffs up self-esteem and a lie that costs the target his or her life savings. Everyday lies don't usually harm us directly, while lies with intent fail if they don't. It's important to realize, though, that the victimization inherent in lies with intent conveys a twofold benefit on the liar: the tangible benefits that come from the scheme (usually money) and the psychological benefit of pulling off the scheme (duping delight). This twofold model of profit (financial and psychological) can help us understand lies with intent that play out on an even larger scale than those of Hakan Yalincak or Lou Pearlman. Sometimes lies with intent create more than a false investment opportunity. Sometimes they are used to create an entirely fabricated person.

Life-Sized Lies

In the late 1880s, a woman by the name of Mrs. Hoover was married to Dr. Leroy S. Chadwick, a high-society Cleveland doctor. She moved into his residence with him on Euclid Avenue, Cleveland's so-called Millionaire's Row, and took his name, becoming Mrs. Cassie L. Chadwick. Mrs. Chadwick did not quite fit in among Cleveland's well-heeled society; she was apparently viewed as something of an eccentric. This prejudice might also have come from the fact that the Chadwicks reportedly met in a brothel, which Mrs. Chadwick may or may not have known was operating out of a boardinghouse she ran.

Mrs. Chadwick's social status took an unexpected turn during a trip she made to New York. She asked an acquaintance of her husband's, a man by the name of Dillon, to take her to Andrew Carnegie's mansion on Fifth Avenue. Mrs. Chadwick was admitted inside while Dillon waited for her. When she emerged, she tripped, accidentally (or so it seemed) dropping a piece of paper, which Dillon saw was a signed promissory note from Andrew Carnegie himself. The amount: $2 million.

When pressed, Mrs. Chadwick explained that she was Andrew Carnegie's illegitimate daughter. He had been giving her promissory notes for years, but she'd been too ashamed of her situation to ever make use of them. She also revealed that when Carnegie died, she stood to inherit $40 million. Dillon offered his assistance, connecting her with numerous Ohio bankers, who were all too eager to give her high-interest loans against the promise of Carnegie's fortune. Mrs. Chadwick spent this money lavishly, on clothing, jewelry, and elaborate parties. She made herself into the self-styled "Queen of Ohio."

Then one of her loans was called in. She couldn't pay, and she was sued. The promissory notes were soon found to be crude forgeries. When the issue was brought to Andrew Carnegie, he stated that he had never heard of Mrs. Chadwick, and certainly had never promised her money. Mrs. Chadwick was put on trial, and her case drew global media attention. Carnegie himself attended the proceedings. It was revealed that Mrs. Chadwick had a long criminal history, about which her husband, Dr. Chadwick, apparently knew nothing. Her real name turned out to be Elizabeth Bigley, and her actual father was a Canadian railway worker. In 1905, Bigley was convicted of conspiracy; she died in prison shortly thereafter.

The lies of Hakan Yalincak, Lou Pearlman, and their predatory ilk are extreme. But figures like Cassie Chadwick/Elizabeth Bigley seem to embody still another level of deception. Bigley didn't just concoct a Ponzi scheme—she concocted an identity. Her lies were ones she lived with day in and day out. Whereas we tend to think of deception as an aberration within a larger practice of honesty, for Bigley, deception was the behavioral norm.

Masquerading of this sort did not end with the nineteenth century, of course. Like Hakan Yalincak's mother, who posed as a doctor for six months, rare individuals continue to blend themselves into ordinary life, posing as people entirely different from who they really are. The popular term for such individuals is impostors. Sometimes, they are motivated merely by necessity. The fugitive Serbian leader Radovan Karadžić posed as a doctor of alternative medicine, hiding his face behind a bushy gray beard, in order to avoid prosecution for war crimes. (He was finally arrested in the summer of 2008.) Others, like Bigley, seem to view impostorism as a way to cash in on a life more privileged than the one they were born to. And for some, there is almost certainly an element of duping delight. This sensation may, in fact, be magnified in impostors, who succeed not just in duping a few people but in fooling more or less everyone with whom they come into contact.

Yet the satisfactions of impostorism are not necessarily limited to the joys of profit and the thrills of manipulation. Ferdinand Waldo Demara is among the most infamous American impostors. At various times, he assumed the role of a lawyer, a college dean, a psychologist, and a sheriff's deputy. For a time during the Korean War he even posed as a medical officer on a Canadian destroyer, going so far as to perform surgeries. It is telling that nearly all the roles Demara took on—surgeon, lawyer, dean, sheriff—are ones society typically holds in high esteem (lawyer jokes notwithstanding). Think, too, of Elizabeth Bigley: she was spurned by Cleveland society until her supposed connection to Andrew Carnegie allowed her to buy her way into the ranks of the elite.

Impostors fully occupy their false role in society. This means that they can reap not only the tangible rewards of that role (such as the salary of a doctor or lawyer), but also all the accompanying social and psychological benefits. Demara was treated with the respect due a surgeon, Bigley with the deference for an upper-class lady. Occupying a place in a particular profession or class can mean gaining the admiration of strangers and the respect of peers, identifying with a wider community, even achieving a sense of self-worth.

Such rewards may be especially tempting for someone who suffers specifically from their lack. Indeed, impostorism, according to the thinking of some who have studied it, is not so much about being another person but, rather, about not being *yourself*. According to this conception, the assumed role fills the gaps the impostor perceives in him- or herself, be it lack of accomplishment, insignificance in the wider world, or just generally low self-esteem. Impostorism can be considered both an embrace of a desired role and a deliverance from an unpleasant one.

From this perspective, impostorism appears, if not more understandable, then at least not necessarily malevolent. All of us have, at one time or another, wished we were different in some way. The idea that we can effect changes to ourselves is an enduring aspect of the national ethos. The American dream is one of willed transformation. Impostorism may be merely a distorted and exaggerated enactment of this dream, one that exchanges deception for effort, while the essential goal remains the same.

Perhaps it is precisely because we can recognize some shadow of our own psychology in impostors that they occupy such an ambiguous place in our culture. Whereas white-collar frauds like Bernie Madoff are pitilessly condemned, society seems to retain some affection for those who push their lies with intent to the level of impersonation. In 1961 Ferdinand Waldo Demara's life was made into a movie, *The Great Impostor,* starring Tony Curtis. More recently, Steven Spielberg directed and Leonardo DiCaprio starred in *Catch Me If You Can,* a movie depicting the many lives and lies of Frank Abagnale, an impostor who posed as a doctor, a lawyer, and, most notoriously, an airline pilot.

Yet even if we admire their guts or identify, to a degree, with their psychology, it's important to keep in mind that the core of what impostors do is exploit the trust and faith of those around them. Lies with intent, by definition, involve manipulation and victimization. While we shouldn't overexaggerate the importance of the profit motive for impostors, we can't ignore it, either. And that profit is stolen from someone. These issues of victimization and loss, which are easy enough to ignore in the Hollywood conception of impostors as lovable rascals, come into clearer focus when we look at the practitioners of another manifestation of lies with intent. If the mental makeup of an impostor is perhaps more sympathetic than we might first assume, the mental makeup of the con artist is probably more sinister.

The Art of Plucking Our Mental Strings

Imagine you are in the mall parking lot, making your way to your car, when you notice an abandoned purse. A young woman happens to see it at the same time, and the two of you chat about what to do about it. The young woman suggests that you open it to look for ID, and when you do, you discover that it is stuffed with cash. There is nothing else in the purse—no identification or other items that might help you track down the owner. It is just a bag of money. The young woman asks what you think you should do next, and after you discuss it, she suggests that she should call the lawyer for whom she works. The lawyer tells her that she should bring the money to him, and he will follow the proper legal procedure to find the bag's owner. If he fails—which, he notes, seems likely—the money will be divided between you and the young woman as its discoverers.

Before heading off to see the lawyer, though, the young woman suggests that the two of you both put some of your own money in the bag; a thousand dollars, she proposes, a minor sum compared to what's in there already, as a show of mutual good faith. She even offers to go first, producing one thousand dollars in cash and putting it in the bag. After that, you feel more at ease, and drive with the young woman to the bank, take out your money, and put it in the bag, too. Next you drive to the lawyer's office. In the lobby of the building, she tells you she needs to use the bathroom. She offers to let you hold the bag while she finds the facilities. After twenty minutes, she hasn't returned, and you start to get worried, but not too worried, since you're the one with the bag of money. After a while, though, you look inside—and see that the bag you're holding is filled with newspaper. Needless to say, you never see the young woman or your "good faith" money again.

This scam is known as a pigeon drop. The "pigeon" in this scenario is you, the one who gets dropped holding a bag of worthless newspaper, out a thousand dollars. There are scores of permutations on this scam, but the core dynamics are always the same: the mark is convinced to add his or her money to some common pool, and then his or her cash and the rest of the pool vanishes. It is a little bit hard to believe that such cons work. What kind of gullible fool would add their own money to a bag of it, just to show "good faith"? But the fact is, pigeon drops and other such confidence games do succeed, which is why they are endlessly recycled and reinvented.

I once saw a con in progress. A man was trying to entice passersby on the sidewalk to play three-card monte with him, at one hundred dollars a hand. I watched as a woman eagerly accepted, plunked down a hundred bucks, picked what was obviously the wrong card, and then chuckled off her misfortune. My first thought was "I can do better than that." My second thought was "This is obviously a con: the woman is a confederate, and it's all a ploy to rope in somebody like me."

From the outside looking in, cons often seem transparent. But even a clumsy scheme like three-card monte, a game synonymous with trickery, induced a moment of minor temptation in me. And it is just this sort of temptation that cons exploit. Con artists—the term is shorthand for those who operate pigeon drops and other such "confidence games"—prey on our own thinking in order to make their otherwise unlikely ruses succeed.

Go back to the pigeon-drop con. It's easy to focus on the foolhardiness of someone who would voluntarily put their own cash in a bag at the suggestion of a stranger. But consider the full context of the con: the mark thinks he or she has just found a huge pile of cash. It's a daydream we've probably all indulged in at one point or another, stumbling upon free money as we go through our daily routine. The possibility of this scenario coming true creates more than just a bias toward cooperating with the young woman who suggests adding "good faith" money; it also creates a bias toward believing in the scenario itself. Skepticism about the young woman and her intentions means skepticism about the unexpected windfall. The mark in the pigeon drop *wants* to believe he or she really just stumbled upon a bag of money—anyone would. It is precisely this desire, conscious or unconscious, to have our dreams fulfilled that the con artist exploits. In a very real sense, a successful con represents a collaboration between the mark and the con artist. The con artist wants the mark to believe something that the mark wants to believe, too. Remember, also, that in any circumstance, people operate under a truth bias. This cognitive rule of thumb means that we are predisposed to believe what we hear and see. (The truth bias was explored in depth in Chapter 2.) While the truth bias usually serves to make our mental processes more efficient, it also aids con men in succeeding in their lies with intent.

The pigeon drop is an example of a generic con. It is targeted not at one specific person but, rather, at whichever person stumbles onto it. Other cons are far more individualized and insidious. A con artist will target a specific person, family, or community to dupe and victimize. Even so, the basic psychological tactics the con artist employs are quite similar to those used in a pigeon drop. He or she exploits the mark's thinking against the mark, identifying and then manipulating the mark's needs or vulnerabilities. These needs might be financial, but they could also be romantic or emotional. Regardless, the con artist casts him- or herself as a solution to the mark's problems.

Charles V. Ford, in his book *Lies! Lies! Lies! The Psychology of Deceit*, explores the relationship between the con and the mark. He writes: "The confidence game appears to be a dynamic relationship built on the needs of the 'mark' as well as those of the exploiter. The con artist has an almost uncanny ability to discover the victim's vulnerable areas and to 'pitch the con' to those areas." The con artist's real skill may not even be telling convincing lies—something, as we have seen throughout *Liar*, many people can do. Rather, the con artist may succeed because of his "uncanny ability" to identify the psychological pressure points of his victims.

The distinctions between the perpetrator of an elaborate paper fraud like Hakan Yalincak, an impostor like Elizabeth Bigley, and a con artist are not hard and fast, of course. Con artists differ from impostors in that they generally engage in more focused, profit-driven schemes—in this they resemble figures like Yalincak and Pearlman. Yet Yalincak did not pretend to be someone he wasn't; he just defrauded investors with a hedge fund that didn't exist. The psychology of the con artist seems to wed the tactics of the impostor to the greed of the fraudster. But, as Ford notes in his book, this greed can extend beyond the desire for money, taking the form of a lust for loyalty, for intimacy, and, naturally, for confidence, thereby filling an emotional void in their own lives. Yet, con artists are often characterized by a pronounced lack of empathy for their victims, and perhaps for others generally.

As we consider this lack of empathy, which can border on the sociopathic, it is useful to return to the broader picture of deception in our society. Again, while lying is common, lies with intent are not. Many of the lies we encounter in our daily lives are actually meant to protect us from hurtful truths, or occur as part of an earnest attempt to strengthen a relationship. As we address the deception in our lives, perhaps we should focus less on an impossible (and probably undesirable) standard of absolute honesty and more on the intentions of the individual telling the lie. Every lie has a price, of course. But not every lie has the intent to harm.

CHAPTER 9

Synthetic Reality:
Media-Manufactured Lies

On August 8th, 2008, at precisely 8:00 P.M. (eight being a lucky number in Chinese culture), the opening ceremonies of the summer Olympics in Beijing began. Around a billion people tuned in to watch the spectacle, which featured fifteen thousand performers and the budget of a Hollywood movie. There were pyrotechnics, dancers, costumes galore, meticulous choreography, and epic pageantry.

Yet for many the focus of the event became a single little girl, in a red dress and pigtails, who sang the patriotic ballad, "Ode to the Motherland." The nine-year-old girl, Lin Miaoke, became an overnight celebrity, and gave interviews in which her performance was lavished with praise. Amid a grand spectacle, she seemed to offer a human face people connected with.

Yet there was nothing human about her performance. Or more precisely, her performance was really the electronic amalgamation of two humans. Lin Miaoke provided the face, but she lip-synched to the recorded voice of another girl, seven-year-old Yang Peiyi. It emerged that quite some time before, Yang Peiyi had been tapped to appear in the opening ceremonies, but during dress rehearsals, a member of the Chinese

Politburo decided she had to go because of imperfect teeth. So Lin Miaoke provided the face, and Yang Peiyi the voice.

The revelation of the fakery caused an uproar, in China and in the United States. People on both sides of the Pacific recoiled at the callous handling of the little girls, who, it seemed, had been accorded all the respect of stage props. Yet the resentment went further than indignation at the treatment of Lin Miaoke and Yang Peiyi. A fellow at the Brookings Institution, Cheng Li, was quoted in the *New York Times* saying, "The people [of China] were so emotionally involved. If you asked them what's the most moving episode [of the ceremonies], I think the majority would tell you that moment, with the little girl in red clothes. Now the Chinese people feel they are fooled. The psychological hurt is enormous." In other words, the people of China, and likely people all over the world, felt duped. They'd formed an emotional bond and discovered that it was based on deceit. And, as people usually do in such a situation, they responded with a combination of anger and embarrassment.

Yet if people the world over had been the victims of deceit, it's worth asking, Who did the deceiving? We can probably let Yang Peiyi off the hook. She seems as much a victim in all of this as anyone, and it's unlikely she had a say in how the recording of her voice was used. Lin Miaoke, of the superior dental work, doesn't seem to warrant much blame, either. She was more the device of the deception, rather than its architect. And if she played along with the deceit in the days that followed, there is some question as to whether she even realized that her voice hadn't been used. It's possible she was duped, too.

The directors of the opening ceremonies, then, the ones who made the switch, might seem to be the liars in this situation. Or maybe it was the member of the Chinese Politburo who decided Yang Peiyi was not the ideal person to represent the People's Republic of China. But these are people none of us have ever met. They never appeared on camera, and, perhaps more importantly, they never assured anyone that the show they were responsible for would be executed in an honest manner. It's worth noting that other parts of the opening ceremony were faked, too. The fireworks that were shown exploding over Beijing were in fact computer-generated. Perhaps the broadcast networks showing the games somehow warranted the truth of the content? Yet it's probably too much to expect Bob Costas and the rest of the NBC sports team to guarantee the veracity of every word and image that occurs during an elaborate stage piece with a cast of thousands.

By now we might expect that deception is more complicated than it first appears. But with most forms of deceit, at least the perpetrator is clear. As we turn to deception in the media—the lies we encounter when we turn on the television or open a book or pick up the newspaper—even this aspect takes on ambiguity. There was clearly some form of deception involved in Lin Maoke's rendition of "Ode to the Motherland." But the responsibility for the fakery is so diffuse it can't be placed on any one individual or even institution. Media lies frequently function this way. We are left with the feelings associated with being deceived, but often without a clear understanding of just who did the deceiving. Perhaps even more frustratingly, we are haunted by a nagging self-recrimination: Why did we trust the media in the first place?

The Reality Bias

A television advertisement for the Gillette Fusion razor brought together some of the world's greatest athletes. Tiger Woods, the legendary golfer, Roger Federer, the legendary tennis player, and Thierry Henry, the legendary soccer player, all ap-

peared in the ad, playing their various sports with a digital version of the earth, then horsing around together, presumably in
celebration of the quality of their shaves. I don't pretend to have
any insight into why Gillette determined that this ad would help
sell razors. For our purposes, what's important is that final shot
in the advertisement, featuring the three superstars all together.

It's important because the three superstars never were all
together, at least not in this razor commercial. Henry and
Federer interacted with a man in a green suit, and Tiger Woods
was added to the shot digitally. It was high-tech sleight of hand,
useful, presumably, in balancing the schedules of three very
busy celebrity athletes.

Most of us like to think of ourselves as fairly shrewd media
consumers. We probably need to be, given the ubiquity of the
media with which we live. It's not enough to turn off the radio,
or the television, or avoid the newspaper or the racks of countless magazines. A lot of us carry all those things in our pocket,
in the form of a BlackBerry or iPhone. So we try to be as savvy
as we can be, sorting out the objective from the tendentious,
the informative from the commercial, the true from the false.
Yet as jaded as we try to make ourselves, it's still news to most
of us that Gillette would employ digital fakery in presenting its
star-athlete money shot. We should know better than to trust
a commercial. We should know a lot better than to trust the
physical reality of a commercial that features people playing
golf, tennis, and soccer with a miniature planet Earth.

In earlier chapters, we've discussed what psychologists call
the truth bias. This is a mental rule of thumb that means, essentially, that we are predisposed to believe what we see and
hear. To doubt the truth, even to scrutinize something fully
for the truth, requires mental energy. The truth bias allows us
to live our lives without expending this energy. It makes our

cognitive life more efficient. But as we've noted, the cost of this efficiency is that we are often predisposed to believe lies, even without being conscious of it.

So far, we've considered the truth bias largely in the context of interpersonal interactions. When the woman at the bookstore tells us that a particular title is on back order, we don't consider the fact that she might be lying, because the truth bias is something we've internalized. It isn't limited to particular interactions, or to particular kinds of information. The truth bias means we're likely to believe the woman at the bookshop, and it also means we're likely to believe that Tiger Woods, Roger Federer, and Thierry Henry all shot a commercial together.

In the context of media, the truth bias forms what I call a *reality bias*. What we see on television is easily manipulated. It's been fifteen years since Cokie Roberts caused a minor media storm when she put on a trench coat and did a report in front of a photographic image of Capitol Hill, claiming she was outside in Washington when in fact she'd never left the ABC News Washington bureau studio. This method of image manipulation is almost crude compared to the possibilities of modern digital technology. Today, it wouldn't take much computer expertise to place Cokie Roberts in Washington, or in Bangkok, or in the middle of the ocean, with a just few clicks of the mouse. Yet when we see a Gillette commercial, our first instinct says that elements of it, at least, are real. This is the reality bias at work. We don't bother questioning and critiquing the parts of every image or piece of information the media delivers. Instead, we assume that they have integrity and save our mental energy for other matters. And again, this is not an assumption we're aware of. The reality bias, extending as it does from the truth bias, operates beneath the level of consciousness.

No one appeared at the start of the Olympic ceremonies

and assured viewers that everything they were about to see and hear was occurring the way it would seem to be. There were no guarantees against lip-synching and digital fireworks. Nor, if we think about it, do we really "trust" television, or the organizers of the Beijing Olympics. The psychological force in play more relevant than trust is the reality bias, which makes us tend to think that what we see is what we get, that Lin Miaoke's voice is the one we hear when she opens her mouth to sing.

Yet our credulity with regard to the media is not exclusively a product of the reality bias. Sometimes our trust flows not from our own mental processes but, rather, from the claims of the media itself. This is the case with so-called reality television, a form of entertainment that is predicated on the promise of the truth, but one that often delivers something very far from it.

Synthetic Reality

The Discovery Channel show *Man vs. Wild* has a very simple premise. A man, Bear Grylls, is placed in some inhospitable tract of the wilderness. Equipped with minimal supplies, Grylls, a lifelong adventurer and a former member of the British special forces, has to employ "localized survival techniques" in order to find his way out. Over the course of different episodes of the show, he's braved everything from hypothermia to desert mountains to a meal of earthworms. Yet the conditions in which Grylls subsisted were not always as harsh as viewers were led to believe. The London *Sunday Times* reported that during the filming of some episodes, Grylls enjoyed the comfort of lodges, rather than sleeping rough. None of this, of course, was shared with viewers.

Since these revelations, the Discovery Channel has made a commitment to be more transparent about the entire filming process of *Man vs. Wild*. But in the broader context of so-called reality television, this is hardly an isolated incident. The mega reality hit *Survivor* confessed to reenacting a key scene using body doubles because the filming of the "real" scene had accidentally included shots of cameras. Then there is "Frankenbiting," a common technique reality show producers use when the facts of an event don't fit the story they want to tell. Frankenbiting involves splicing together lines of recorded dialogue to put words in the mouths of reality-show participants. They may not have actually said what the producers want, but viewers can be fooled into thinking they did. Sometimes, Frankenbiting isn't even bothered with. There have been reports that Paris Hilton was fed specific lines to speak on her show *The Simple Life*.

Even if shows did not resort to reshoots and Frankenbiting, reality television's claim on reality would still be tenuous. After all, what is "real" about a man being flown from dangerous location to dangerous location so he can demonstrate survival techniques? And even the most mundane reality television set-ups inevitably deviate from reality in at least one crucial way: the real people involved are always being tailed by cameramen. The effect being filmed has on people varies, of course, but it's hard to argue that it does not have *any* effect. The presence of a camera shapes its own kind of reality.

What, then, does reality television really show? It's instructive to revisit the amalgamation of Yang Peiyi's voice and Lin Miaoke's face during the Beijing opening ceremonies. Chen Qigang, the music designer for the ceremonies, explained that the girl in the ceremonies had to be, well, perfect. He was quoted as saying, "The child on camera should be flawless in image, internal feelings, and expression." That, obviously, is no small order. In fact, in the end, it seemed impossible for the Beijing organizers to find such a "flawless" girl. Luckily for them, they were able to create one, matching a superior voice with surpassing cuteness.

In a sense, reality television does the same thing. It offers a trumped-up version of events, in the guise of reality. I call this enhanced depiction of life *synthetic reality*. In reality, mountain climbers and other thrill seekers at times run into some dangerous situations, which demand they use some pretty canny survival techniques. But in synthetic reality, such situations are continuous. Indeed, they occur every week, on your television. Arguments and bickering sometimes occur in real life. But in synthetic reality, as offered up on shows like *The Real World* or *Big Brother*, tension and "drama," as it is ubiquitously called in promotional materials for such shows, are both more frequent and more intense. First, the scenarios reality television concocts are usually constructed in order to foster conflict: a dozen or more men or women competing for the affection of a single person; a group of strangers with strong and conflicting personalities trapped on an island or in a house; and *Temptation Island* (which warrants no further explanation). Second, for each episode hundreds of hours of tape are edited down to the most emotionally fraught twenty or so minutes. The result is that in synthetic reality, people are always squabbling, conniving, backstabbing, screaming.

We feel a sense of betrayal, or at least a twinge of surprise, when we learn of reality show producers who Frankenbite to create story lines, who order the reenactment of key events. But we probably shouldn't. Reality television strays so far from the truth in its design that it may be almost inevitable that its execution follows this pattern. After all, if we really wanted reality, devoid of carefully crafted story lines and reliably timed eruptions of discord, we could just turn off the television.

Some might argue, though, that carping about the dishonesty in reality television is a bit superfluous. Among its staunch-est defenders are those who would admit that its reality is more ostensible than genuine: the point is not that it is factual but that it is entertaining. Yet the notion that when we watch re-ality television we should it take it for granted that we're getting synthetic reality itself raises an interesting question: Why call it *reality* television at all? If viewers and producers and partici-pants all accept that there is some level of implicit fakery in-volved in these shows, why append a label suggesting truth in the first place? It seems as if the idea of the truth functions less as a guarantee of authenticity, and more as a selling point.

The Truth Brand

The 1996 movie *Fargo*, created by Joel and Ethan Coen, is set in rural Minnesota and tells the story of a kidnapping gone wrong and the grisly chain of murders that ensue. The crimes are investigated by Marge Gunderson, a very astute and very pregnant local sheriff. Yet as unlikely as this plot may seem, the movie, which was nominated for multiple Oscars and won two, begins with a declaration of its grounding in fact. The opening credits announce: "This is a true story. The events depicted in this film took place in Minnesota in 1987. At the request of the survivors, the names have been changed. Out of respect for the dead, the rest has been told exactly as it occurred."

It's certainly possible to detect some characteristic sly Coen brothers wit in these words. Yet the larger point, evidently, could not be clearer: *what you're about to see really happened.* Except that, it didn't. Journalists couldn't find reports of any events that matched the improbable plot of *Fargo*, and the Coen brothers eventually owned up to the fact that the movie was all fiction. Their explanation for why they sought to dupe their viewers, though, is telling. "We felt the audience would have certain expectations if they were told it was a true story that would allow us to do things that we wouldn't be allowed to do if they thought it was fiction," Joel Coen, *Fargo*'s director, explained.

Audience members, then, according to Joel Coen, assess material differently if they believe it is factual. They accept greater stretches of logic and more implausible plot developments, he suggests, than they would from "pure" fiction. This gives those creating the material greater latitude in what they produce.

Labeling something as true, or "based on true events," or even just "inspired by true events," thus has its benefits. For those in the media, it is not simply a matter of accurately conveying where their movie or book or television show came from. The truth represents a kind of brand, a source we credit more, it seems, than the imaginations of directors, writers, or producers.

Indeed, in some ways the truth—or, more precisely, "the truth"—has never been more popular. Reality television continues to be a ratings juggernaut. Nonfiction book sales easily outpace fiction. Politicians offer dueling "truth squads" to point out the lies of the other side. Again, though, this is not a matter of the media adhering to objective fact. A cursory nod toward the truth is what the media offers us, but they present this truth with all the bells and whistles of fiction. It's like when a brand of cookies claims to be a healthy alternative because it offers 10 percent less fat than its competitors. The greatest substantive difference is not in the content but in the packaging.

Consider again reality television. All the tools of a fictional television show are employed. Lines are constructed via Frankenbiting, or simply given to the performers. Plots are edited to present an artificially coherent story line. And sometimes scenes are simply staged, as in the case of *Survivor*. Yet as Joel Coen suggested was the case with regard to *Fargo*, reality television's use of the truth brand allows it to get away with things that would otherwise seem ludicrous. Most would demand more of a fictional show than twenty minutes of people screaming at one another between commercials. The truth brand exploits our credulity—or perhaps we allow ourselves to be taken in by it—and we accept even the most preposterous of dramatic events because "it really happened that way."

Beyond eliciting a greater willingness to suspend disbelief, the truth brand also seems to have an emotional component. We can see this in one of those infamous cases of truth branding, that of James Frey's book *A Million Little Pieces*. The memoir tells the story of Frey's struggles with drug abuse and his long road to recovery. The book became a hit after Oprah Winfrey selected it for her book club in 2005. She pointed to the inspirational qualities of the book's tale of one man's fight against his own demons. It's fair to assume that a large share of this inspiration stemmed from the fact the tale was *true*. The battle with addiction played out not in the mind of a writer but, rather, in the real world, and this gave *A Million Little Pieces* a particular emotional piquancy.

When it infamously emerged that portions of the memoir were fabricated, however, the fallout had an emotional piquancy, too. There are reports that Frey initially shopped *A Million Little Pieces* as a novel but it found a publisher only when given the truth brand and repackaged as a memoir. Readers seemed to take personally the revelations of invented details and scenes. Oprah herself told Frey she felt "really duped" by his actions, and subjected him to a ritualistic on-air grilling. The book's publisher, Random House, took the unusual step of offering a refund to readers who had bought the book and felt defrauded by its claims of veracity.

To be fair, one should never read a memoir thinking that every detail is reported exactly as it occurred. More to the point, one would never *want* to read such a memoir. We get enough of the inevitable boring episodes in life outside of books. While it seems apparent that Frey crossed a line from truth to deception, damaging his own reputation and triggering genuine feelings of betrayal among some of his readers, most memoirists employ many of the tactics of fiction. Pulling a story from the density and ambiguity of real life would probably be impossible otherwise.

Yet it's clear that the application of the truth brand can have a transformative affect on a book, both in terms of its sales and in its emotional impact for readers. The initial success of Frey's fabrication of parts of his life shows again how effective the media's exploitation of the idea of honesty can be. And what we also see, again and again, is how tolerant we as media consumers are of this exploitation. Reality television's synthetic reality is apparent to the critical eye, yet its success endures. And there is an important caveat to Frey's story, as well: in 2007, he signed a three-book, seven-figure deal with HarperCollins, and his latest work, *Bright Shiny Morning*, was a best seller.

The use and abuse of the truth brand is not the limit of media dishonesty. Works that use the label "reality" or "based on true events" generally retain at least some link, albeit tenuous, to real occurrences, but recent years have seen numerous instances of outright deception. Indeed, some in the media have deceived the public to such a degree that James Frey seems by comparison like a paragon of honesty.

False Stories, Fake Authors

Initially, the critical reception of *A Million Little Pieces* was somewhat mixed. The book's notoriety came when it made

Synthetic Reality

Oprah's Book Club—and its infamy when its many fabrications were revealed. *Love and Consequences*, on the other hand, a memoir by Margaret B. Jones, garnered immediate critical praise. The *New York Times* hailed it as "humane and deeply affecting." The book tells the story of Jones's youth as a foster child in South-Central Los Angeles, navigating gang violence and making money running drugs. She writes with a keen sense for the telling anecdote, recounting how she prepared crack to pay her family's bills, how she received a handgun for a birthday. As mentioned above, memoirists typically exaggerate certain details in their works, and some reviewers noted that *Love and Consequences* had passages that seemed to border on the novelistic. Still, this was forgiven in the context of the book's larger emotional impact. But it turned out that Jones's work didn't just borrow some of the methods of fiction. It was all fiction, right down to the author.

Margaret B. Jones was the pen name for Margaret Seltzer. Margaret Seltzer did not grow up as a foster child in South-Central Los Angeles, or anywhere. She was raised by her biological family in Sherman Oaks, an upscale section of the San Fernando Valley, and she had no affiliation with gangs or with selling illegal drugs. In admitting her deceit, Seltzer claimed that *Love and Consequences* was in fact based on the experiences of friends she'd known growing up. "For whatever reason, I was really torn and I thought it was my opportunity to put a voice to people who people don't listen to," she told the *New York Times*.

However altruistic her motives, Jones's deception is of a different order than what you would get from a night of reality television. In fact, despite her defense, it's probably reasonable to compare Seltzer's act with some of the more insidious forms of deceit we've discussed, such as lies with intent. After all, she gained both literary fame and fortune through her deceit.

Yet what is even more surprising than Seltzer's deceit is the fact that it was hardly an isolated incident. *Misha: A Mémoire of the Holocaust Years,* by Misha Defonseca, is ostensibly the true story of how Defonseca, as a young girl, escaped the Holocaust by trekking across Europe. The book, first published in 1997, was translated into eighteen languages and was made into an opera and then a French feature film before it was revealed to be fiction, in 2008. Misha Defonseca was in fact Monique De Wael, a Catholic who'd spent her girlhood during the war in Belgium. *Fragments,* by a man calling himself Binjamin Wilkomirski became an acclaimed Holocaust memoir but was in fact written by a gentile called Bruno Doessekker who was later found not to have intentionally sought to deceive the public. And then there is the writer J. T. LeRoy, who published several books before being revealed to be an entirely fabricated persona of the writer Laura Albert. Albert even used a stand-in to act as LeRoy for public appearances.

The invention of J. T. LeRoy is clearly an extreme example. But memoir fabrication is nothing new. Indeed, it is a practice older than America. John Smith's seventeenth-century accounts of his adventures in the early colony of Jamestown, Virginia, including his stories about his relationship with Pocahontas, have long had their veracity questioned by scholars. Ours is hardly the first generation of authors to recognize the potential profits in the exaggerated or simply made-up life story.

Yet while it's fair to point out that deceptive memoirists benefit financially from their lies, it's probably an oversimplification to assume that money is the only relevant motivator. The impostors we discussed in Chapter 8 carried out a similar type of fraud in their assumption of new, and often improved, identities. Faking an account of one's life is really only a kind of retroactive impostorism: instead of pretending to be someone in the present, individuals like Margaret Seltzer and Monique De Wael pretended to have been someone in the past. The psychology of those who write up a fake life and those who live a fake life is likely similar. We can assume there is at least some element of duping delight, the pleasure liars feel in fooling their targets. For fake memoirists, this feeling may be compounded by the fact that they fool not only those they know but literally tens of thousands of others. There can also be a similar element of wish fulfillment at play, allowing the author to assume a life that is more dramatic, and elicits more sympathy or esteem, than their own might warrant.

Another factor underlying memoir falsification is that, in many ways, it is easier to pull off than we might think. After all, only the author really knows what he or she did or did not experience. When memoirists write about an event that no one else witnessed—*Misha* includes multiple encounters in the woods with wolves, for instance—their claims can be all but impossible to contradict. And when their tales stretch to the improbable, they have a ready, and essentially bulletproof, excuse: *That's how I remember it.*

On the other hand, Margaret B. Jones/Margaret Seltzer was not recounting events that took place in the forests of a war-torn continent more than a half century ago. Even granting the inherent difficulties in disproving the autobiographical assertions of another person, we might hope one of Seltzer's editors would have caught on to the fact that she had never even been a foster child, let alone one who ran drugs. Yet in looking to the editors or publishers of a memoir to verify its accuracy, we find that they frequently pass the buck on verification, too. Most editors would say that it is the author of a book who guarantees its truth. Generally, newspaper and magazine pieces are rigorously fact-checked (not that this is necessarily a surefire way to prevent deceit, as we will see), but most books are not so strictly vetted. When it's revealed that a memoir has been falsified, editors often claim to be victims of the deception as much as readers are. And, indeed, editors do sometimes form personal relationships with their writers, and so experience a double sting of personal betrayal and professional humiliation when authorial duplicity comes to light.

Still, we as readers are probably right in feeling a bit hung out to dry by this system. We generally take it on faith that when a book announces an "Incredible True Story," the story will actually be true, and not just incredible. Yet the fact is that this claim of truth sometimes may be based on no more than the word of the author, someone who stands to gain financially by making the assertion, whether it is factual or not. Perhaps we'd be wise to take the stunning details in the memoirs we read with a grain of salt—just another example of how deceit can dampen the experience of ordinary life, even when it does not victimize us directly, or in the ways we usually assume it might.

It's simple enough to take a critical attitude when browsing the autobiography section of Barnes & Noble. Media deception makes its way into formats that we look to for more than recreational reading. When we pick up a newspaper or a newsmagazine, we assume we are getting the facts about what is happening in the world around us. Unfortunately, several recent incidents have shown that this conjecture might be flawed.

News That Isn't Worthy

During the 1990s, I was a subscriber to the *New Republic*, a respected weekly magazine of political commentary. I was regularly struck by the articles that appeared near the beginning of the magazine, narrative pieces focused on particular events or trends. Often they included extraordinary details; I still remember a piece about a group of absurdly virulent anti-Clinton conservatives. I never noticed that all these remarkable pieces were written by the same author: Stephen Glass.

In May 1998, Glass published another piece in the *New Republic*, "Hack Heaven." It described how a fifteen-year-old computer hacker named Ian Restil was being courted to work at a software company called Jukt Micronics. According to the story, Restil demanded everything from an *X-Men* No. 1 comic to a Miata, and Jukt was happy to oblige. The article caught the eye of a reporter at *Forbes.com*, but when he followed up on the story, he couldn't confirm any of its details. It turned out there was no Ian Restil, and no Jukt Micronics. Glass had fabricated the entire story. In fact, Glass had fabricated some or all of more than two dozen stories—including ones I had noticed for being so astonishing. Glass had fooled his editors at the *New Republic* and thousands of readers just like me.

As mentioned above, magazines like the *New Republic* employ fact-checkers to verify the accuracy of what they print. Glass was able to fool the fact-checkers by crediting his own notes and anonymous sources for his reporting. Perhaps the *New Republic*'s fact-checking standards were not rigorous enough (they were strengthened in the wake of the Glass debacle), but fact-checking can perhaps never be so rigorous as to prevent journalistic deceit. Reporters write about things they have seen or been told. That's why they're called "reporters." As with a memoirist, ultimately only the journalist really knows what he or she has experienced in investigating a story.

Perhaps this is why incidents of journalistic duplicity have become, if not commonplace, than at least less exceptional. The *New York Times* prides itself on its role as "the paper of record," printing corrections to stories sometimes decades after the fact to maintain its reputation for accuracy. Hence the sensation when it was revealed that Jayson Blair, a *Times* reporter, had fabricated or plagiarized material for dozens of national news stories. He'd offered reporting from places he had never been, he'd given quotes from people he had never interviewed or met, he'd misstated facts, and he'd made up details. *USA Today* reported Jack Kelley was a finalist for the Pulitzer Prize before it was revealed, in 2004, that he had invented material, including portions of the story that had earned him a Pulitzer nomination. In a front-page article, *USA Today* admitted that "Kelley fabricated substantial portions of at least eight major stories, lifted nearly two dozen quotes or other material from competing publications, lied in speeches he gave for the newspaper and conspired to mislead those investigating his work."

A distinction can be made between the deceit of people like Stephen Glass and Jayson Blair and the deceit perpetrated in formats like reality television. In the former cases, the lies are an aberration. Glass and Blair broke the institutional rules of their media employers, violating very clear ethical guidelines that all reporters follow (or at least are supposed to). When their deception was uncovered, it was punished: both reporters were fired. The synthetic reality we see on television is not the work of a few duplicitous individuals. Rather, it is the intended product of all involved. Synthetic reality is not the punished exception but the rule.

So it may seem something of an oversimplification to place, say, *Survivor* and Stephen Glass in the same media-deception category. Yet in a crucial way they resemble each other: they both erode our trust in the media. Whether I feel deceived when I learn that certain articles in the *New Republic* were fiction or whether I feel deceived when I learn that sometimes lines have been fed to the subjects of a reality television show, in either case, I am duped. If I am reassured that the *New Republic* is at least vigilant to prevent such deception in its pages, I am probably also more worried by the fact that the *New Republic* is the sort of media organ I depend on to stay informed about the world. Losing trust in reality television is one thing. Losing trust in the *New York Times* is quite another.

Whichever news outlet we prefer, be it one in print, on television, or online, we depend on journalists to convey information about local and world events to us. Given the abundance of news options in modern society, it's unlikely that we'll be wholly deceived about something for very long. *Forbes.com* formed an effective check on the *New Republic*, for example. Yet Stephen Glass was able to pass off outrageous stories as fact for years before anyone, at the *New Republic* or elsewhere in the media, caught on. Further, while it's easy enough for a newspaper to go back and recheck the articles of a mendacious reporter, our opinions aren't so easily vetted. If it's possible that some of the facts that underlie our judgments are untrue, can we be sure we've supported the right candidate, advocated the right decision?

These hypothetical questions played out in reality in the wake of the Iraq War. When it was learned that Iraq did not, in contrast to media reports and government assurances, possess weapons of mass destruction, the entire rationale for the war came into question. In this case, it didn't take a Jayson Blair to compromise the veracity of respected news outlets. The *New York Times,* for example, admitted that some of its reporting on Iraq's weapons had been flawed. And when it came to assigning responsibility for the misinformation that had been parroted and reported, a game of pass the buck ensued, sadly reminiscent of what occurs when a memoir turns out to be fake.

Reporters blamed the government, the government blamed the CIA, the CIA blamed its sources—and, as with a false memoir, the public was left to sort out how we'd been misled and why.

As individuals, of course, we can't find out the news of the world for ourselves. In the end, we have to rely on journalists to bring us news, much as we rely on friends or coworkers to tell us the weather or if our tie is crooked. We can't function as informed citizens without some degree of trust, any more than we could function as neighbors or community members without it. It seems clear, though, that healthy skepticism is in order. Even the most trusted media outlets are, in the end, staffed by individuals, and some individuals, as we have seen throughout *Liar*, simply can't be trusted at all. But as we have also seen, these individuals are the exception. It's reasonable to hope that the bulk of people who commit themselves to ethical and objective reporting have every intention of upholding that commitment.

CHAPTER 10

Career Lies:
Deception in the Workplace

I n 1999, a major drugstore chain paid $1.5 million in a settlement over allegations by a California district attorney that it had sold expired goods, including baby formula and contraceptives, at dozens of its stores. Eight years later, the New York State attorney general announced plans to sue this same drugstore chain for selling expired food and drugs at, according to his investigation, 43 percent of its locations.

MetLife, among the largest life insurance companies in the United States, settled a class action lawsuit for $1.7 billion. Among the allegations in the suit was that MetLife had engaged in a variety of deceptive sales practices. These included portraying policies as investment opportunities with exaggerated promises of returns and selling policies on the promise that the premiums would at some point "vanish"—though, of course, they never did.

When *PRWeek*, a public relations trade magazine, conducted a survey of 1,700 public relations executives, 25 percent of them admitted lying on the job, 39 percent confessed to exaggerations of the truth, and 62 percent felt their honesty had been compromised by being lied to by a client or by being told only a partial truth.

Dr. Seymour I. Schlager served as an executive scientist at Becton, Dickinson, a major medical technology company. He was a published author, his book *Clinical Management of Infectious Diseases* having been released by Williams & Wilkins. And he served on the board of a New Jersey drug company. What Dr. Schlager did not tell Becton, Dickinson, or his publisher, or the drug company, was that in 1991 he had been convicted of attempting to smother his wife with a pillow, had spent years in prison for the crime, and had had his medical license revoked.

There is probably no single anecdote or story that epitomizes the deception that occurs in the business world. As the examples above suggest, lying in the workplace can take myriad forms. Sometimes the lies occur through an institutional practice, such as a pharmacy selling expired drugs in nearly half of its stores. Sometimes the institutional lies are perpetrated by a sales force and directed at customers, employed as enticements to get them to buy life insurance or a used car or a "Rolex" watch. Workplace lies can be told in the context of job performance, as when a public relations officer assures a financial reporter that a company's earnings will be good news for stockholders, when in fact they will be anything but. And workplace lies can victimize companies, as when an employee adds something false to—or, as in the case of Seymour Schlager, leaves something very important off—a résumé.

Just as it is varied, lying in the business world is also widespread. It is not limited by industry or market, by size of company or structure, by culture or geography. Even industries that place an emphasis on honesty can be hit with scandals over deceit. Perhaps no place of work holds honesty more sacrosanct than academia. Scholarship depends on truthfulness in the reporting of experimental results, on the supremacy of fact over self-interest and prejudice. Yet recent years have seen numerous examples of outright fabrication on campuses. Joseph Ellis, a history professor at Mount Holyoke College and the winner of the Pulitzer Prize for his book *Founding Brothers*, was temporarily suspended from teaching after it was revealed that his claims of having fought in Vietnam were false. A scientist at Purdue University, Rusi Taleyarkhan, attracted national attention when he reported in *Science* that he had achieved nuclear fusion through the manipulation of bubbles. The results came into question when others could not duplicate the experiment, and a Purdue panel eventually concluded that Taleyarkhan had falsely claimed independent verification of his work. Instances of plagiarism in academia are becoming so common that their revelations sometimes seem mundane. And again, this is in a realm where honesty is a necessity—if not in practice, then at least in theory.

Businesses in which a strict adherence to the truth is not even given the benefit of lip service often have even higher incidences of deception. This helps explain the statistics reported in the *PRWeek* survey. The nature of the work done in public relations involves shading and tailoring to present facts in a particular form. It's essentially the same thing a salesperson does when glowingly describing a car or vacuum cleaner or piece of real estate. The law defines this sort of embellishment and exaggeration as "puffing," and makes a distinction between it and outright fraud. But the line between deceit and puffing can be easily crossed and, indeed, can sometimes be difficult to identify.

Beyond instances when the legitimate work of a job blends easily into deceit, there seems to be another prominent motive underlying workplace deception: money. Since money is the common element in the many forms of human employment, it makes sense to consider it the common element in the many forms of deception related to that employment. Indeed, some of the most prominent business scandals of recent years seem driven almost solely by the lust for profit. Names like Enron and WorldCom have become synonymous with greed that outstrips good sense and sound ethics. Yet it would be a mistake to consider workplace deception as merely a means to a few more dollars. The complexities of lying on the job resist a simple, singular explanation.

It may be more instructive to focus not on what a job gets you but on what a job can mean. After all, money is only one reason people seek the jobs they do. Jobs can also convey a certain status within society, a sense of purpose and belonging. Perhaps this is why workplace deception often begins before people have even found a job.

Lying to Get in the Door

As competitive as the American college application process can seem, it is probably still far less stressful than the education system in South Korea. From an early age, South Korean children begin preparing for college entrance exams in intense cram sessions. Admission to the right school means qualification for top jobs and social benefits that extend as far as marriage prospects. Not getting into an elite school, though, can close career and societal doors permanently.

It was against this backdrop that it emerged that Shin Jeong-ah, a top art historian, had falsified her educational experience. Fired from her position at the elite Dongguk University, she left South Korea for the United States. Yet the revelations of Shin Jeong-ah's false credentials turned out to be only the first in a series of résumé scandals. A well-known monk, the Venerable Jigwang, the head of a temple with 250,000 members, confessed that he did not, as he had claimed, hold a degree from Seoul National University, South Korea's top school. Lee Chang-ha, a popular architect, was forced out of Kimcheon Science College after disclosures that he claimed to hold a degree in fine arts from a Los Angeles university that does not give degrees in fine arts. A movie director, a celebrity chef, a radio host, a comic-book artist—more and more well-respected and well-known South Koreans were added to the list of academic pretenders.

It would be wrongheaded to conclude that the South Korean intelligentsia is composed largely of frauds, or of those ruthless enough to fabricate credentials. The nationwide scandals, sweeping up individuals in so many walks of life—religious, intellectual, artistic—would seem to point instead to the stakes of educational success. Or, to put the issue more bluntly, the scandals point to the stakes of *superficial* academic success. After all, as in the United States, the question is not so much what an individual learns at a university as the reputation of that university. The line on the résumé is what opens doors, not the content of the education.

Again, this is true not only of South Korea; many American companies screen résumés for particular degrees. Without that degree, an applicant will not even be considered, regardless of skills, knowledge, experience, or any other sort of qualification. This helps explain why so often the lies on American résumés relate to education. Generally, all résumés are prone to deceit. A low estimate is that a quarter of résumés contain lies. But with educational background in particular, job seekers are apt to invent the facts.

Jude M. Werra, the head of a headhunting firm in Wisconsin, conducts a biannual review of the high-powered résumés his firm receives. He checks the educational backgrounds of CEOs and vice presidents, then compiles what he calls the

Liars Index: a statistic that represents the number of résumés with inaccuracies divided by the total number of résumés he has checked. In 2008, the Liars Index was nearly 16 percent. That's down from the high of 23.3 percent, reached in 2000. Applicants claimed degrees they had never earned, honors they had never received. And again, these are not the résumés of inexperienced college graduates (or nongraduates, as it were), ready to lie in order to launch their careers. Werra's index describes executive résumés, those of individuals already established in the business world—though, it seems, not established enough.

Examples of degree falsification by highly successful people abound. Ronald Zarrella, the former chairman of Bausch & Lomb, admitted that he did not, as he had claimed, hold an MBA from New York University. The new head football coach of Notre Dame, George O'Leary, resigned after holding the job for only five days when it was revealed that he did not, as claimed on his résumé, hold a master's degree from New York University (apparently a college holding a certain attraction to those falsifying their résumés). The CEO of RadioShack, David J. Edmondson, resigned after it was revealed that he'd added to his résumé degrees in psychology and theology that he didn't have. A former president of the U.S. Olympic Committee falsely claimed to have a doctorate in American literature. And Chapter 7 detailed the story of an MIT dean who claimed to hold three degrees, when in fact she held only one, from an obscure college.

It may be tempting to conclude, as with the South Korean résumé scandals, that the people who make it to the top are the ones who are unscrupulous enough (and maybe bold enough) to lie about their degrees. But a less morally charged explanation is also possible. To make it to the top requires a foot in the door. A lie on a résumé may be the means to start a career that, through skill, luck, determination, or some combination thereof, ends up in a chair or a presidency. In other words, highly successful people may not be more prone to faking their educational background; rather, it may be that those initial lies enable people to become successful in the first place.

If applicants for high-profile positions engage in deception on their résumés, we might expect that people applying for more mundane jobs might feel even less encumbered by the truth. Certainly, it seems remote that one's application for a job at the corner dry cleaners would be subject to stringent fact-checking.

Furthermore, as mentioned earlier, the other major form of information gathering—the job interview—offers opportunities to stretch the truth even beyond what one might be tempted to list on a résumé. Conducted in face-to-face settings, job interviews typically yield no written record that can later be used to check against reality.

In fact, one of my own research studies, conducted with Brent Weiss, found that job applicants are more than ready to bend the truth to obtain an attractive position. In the study, we offered college students the opportunity to apply for a job that paid $15 an hour—an enticing amount to impoverished undergraduates. The job ostensibly involved tutoring high school students, but the specific nature of the position varied in one of two ways. Some of the potential tutors were the told that the job required technical skills such as managing student data files and some statistical analysis; the job description focused on mathematical prowess. In contrast, other job applicants were told that the position required strong interpersonal skills, with high sociability and enthusiasm central requirements.

After learning about the job requirements, applicants filled out an application form and then participated in a job interview. Both the application form and the interview asked a wide range of questions but also focused on applicants' math and social skills—key components of the job requirements.

After the interviews, we let applicants know that in reality there was no job and that the entire situation had been designed to study the interview process. (We worked very hard to explain the rationale for the study and to make participants understand why our own brand of deception was necessary.) We then had participants view a videotape of their responses during the job interview, and we asked them to identify any deviations from the truth.

The results were quite consistent with our other studies of the frequency of deception in everyday life. Just over 80 percent of the participants admitted telling at least one lie in the interview. The average number of lies was 2.2 during the interviews, which lasted from ten to fifteen minutes. Furthermore, the nature of the lies was consistent with the job requirements. Applicants applying for a position involving math skills were more likely to boast about their mathematical prowess. In contrast, applicants applying for the job where social skills were paramount were more apt to lie about their adeptness in socializing with others.

Perhaps it's predictable to find such a high level of deception when people are seeking to obtain a job. After all, many people consider résumés and job interviews to be sales opportunities, ones whose purpose is to put the best possible gloss on past experience and accomplishments. In this view, it is standard practice for an afternoon digging through files for a lost invoice to become "extensive research experience." Embellishment can easily lose its grounding in the facts, if it ever had one in the first place.

What's particularly surprising, though, is the degree to

which even facts that can be easily checked, such as educational background, appear to be fair game for self-promotion. After all, a degree was either conferred or it wasn't. Further, while it may be difficult to check or to ascertain what "extensive research experience" constitutes, a degree can be verified with a single phone call, or even a single Web search.

Perhaps the fact that educational background remains so frequently fudged points to a certain attitude toward such credentials. Again, the importance of such degrees can certainly be viewed as only surface deep. A master's degree might help you land an interview for an executive-level job, but the extent to which that degree will benefit you in doing that job is debatable. By that same token, individuals may feel a certain frustration if they consider themselves qualified for a certain job in terms of experience but disqualified from even pursuing it because they lack a higher degree or a degree from a brand-name college.

This ambivalence regarding the practical benefits of a degree, as opposed to the surface benefits, may actually be echoed among employers. Given how easy it is to check educational background, it is surprising how many companies don't. The proof of job worthiness may ultimately lie in job performance. This is not to argue that companies don't care when applicants falsify their educational experience. Rather, it is to state that their interest in finding a person to fill important job vacancies is very strong, as well. Employers don't benefit from losing good employees in résumé scandals any more than the fired employees do. This may be another reason why the Liars Index never approaches 0 percent. After it was revealed that Ronald Zarrella did not have an MBA from NYU after all, he was docked his $1.1 million bonus. However, he continued serving as Bausch & Lomb's CEO for another five years.

Of course, faked education credentials may be among the more benign forms of workplace deceit. Other practices can be far more insidious. Sometimes the lies in a résumé, especially lies of omission, can cover over a past of deception that no company would—or, more importantly, could—tolerate. This was the case with one of the most infamous CEOs of the booming '90s: Chainsaw Al.

Why Apples Turn Bad

Albert J. Dunlap seemed to enjoy his reputation as a CEO who took no prisoners. He made his name on Wall Street at Scott Paper, a struggling company that Dunlap rejuvenated to the tune of a $6.3 billion increase in market value. One way he achieved this was by the cutting thousands of jobs. But Dunlap was unapologetic over his hardball tactics. He titled his autobiography *Mean Business: How I Save Bad Companies and Make Good Companies Great.* The book, with its titular wordplay suggesting both seriousness and toughness, became a best seller. When Sunbeam Corporation, a maker of small consumer appliances, named him CEO, its shares surged 60 percent. Dunlap reportedly declared, "The old Sunbeam is over," and oversaw a restructuring plan that would eliminate 87 percent of Sunbeam products and about half of its jobs.

At first, Dunlap's black-hat tactics seemed to work, and Sunbeam reported big gains in earnings. But the apparent boom at Sunbeam didn't last. Its stock tanked, and as the company started to fall apart, Dunlap was fired. Accusations of fraud emerged. The Securities and Exchange Commission alleged that Sunbeam had overstated its profits during Dunlap's tenure, and the Justice Department soon opened its own investigation. Dunlap eventually settled with the SEC, admitting no wrongdoing but paying a $500,000 fine. Sunbeam went bankrupt, and Dunlap had to pay a further $15 million to settle a lawsuit by disgruntled shareholders.

Sunbeam executives thought they were hiring a ruthlessly effective CEO who would stop at nothing to make their company profitable. Instead, their company collapsed amid allegations of fictitious accounting. What Sunbeam didn't know when they hired Dunlap—and, indeed, what it seems few of Chainsaw Al's admirers knew—was that Dunlap had once been the president of a company called Nitec Paper. And Dunlap's leadership of Nitec had played out in a remarkably similar fashion to his tenure with Sunbeam.

Dunlap's omission of Nitec from his employment history meant that Sunbeam didn't know Dunlap had been fired from Nitec. Nor did Dunlap disclose that the reported profits during his leadership of Nitec had vanished after he left amid, once again, allegations of accounting fraud, reportedly perpetrated at his direction. Dunlap and Nitec became embroiled in lawsuits, but Nitec went bankrupt and the case never went to trial. By leaving Nitec off his résumé and, of course, out of his memoir, Dunlap was able to escape the odor of fraud and become a Wall Street star—at least for a while.

Most immediately, Dunlap's story points to the dangers of résumé fraud, not to mention the urgency companies should give to employee résumé verification. If a fabricated degree can be rationalized as unimportant in the context of job performance, hidden stories of disastrous, or even criminal, work history obviously can't. Jude Werra, the creator and compiler of the Liars Index, warns of a "halo effect" surrounding the hiring of high-level executives. These executives can be so impressive by reputation and bearing that they don't receive the scrutiny in the hiring process they should. The story of Chainsaw Al, and those of the other fabricated résumés of prominent people recounted in this chapter, should demonstrate that a complete and truthful employment history can never be taken for granted.

More broadly, Chainsaw Al's downfall points to issues of workplace deceit beyond those that show up on a résumé. Résumé fabrication is, in theory, isolated to a single employee. Accounting fraud or other such crimes can bring down entire companies, with effects that ripple across the economy. No better example of the dangers of deceitful business practices can be found than the fallout from the subprime mortgage collapse, which threatened to send the entire global economy into a tailspin.

Psychologists have sought to understand the dynamics that underlie cooking the books, fixing markets, and the other forms of fraudulent business dealings. One possible explanation is among the most obvious: the key to white-collar crime lies with the individuals who perpetrate it. Unethical or simply criminal businesspeople deviate from accepted procedures for their own benefit. This conception might be called the Bad Apple Theory of White Collar Crime. Indeed, it was just this metaphor former President George W. Bush used in discussing the fall of Enron. A few bad apples, aberrations in their companies and in the business world generally, brought down a profitable and respectable business.

One reason the Bad Apple Theory makes sense is that individuals, particularly high-level individuals within a company, have so much to gain personally by cheating the system. This is born out by a study concluding that CEOs were responsible, either through direct action or through attitude, for nearly three-quarters of corporate accounting fraud. As stated above, the incentives to cheat go beyond mere dollars and sense—though, of course, money usually plays a role, too. CEOs can directly benefit from overinflated profits through performance bonuses and the value of stock options they hold. Beyond financial gain, though, company heads have other motivations to engage in business deceit, ones that are more psychological than tangible.

We've seen throughout *Liar* how deception is frequently a response to a threatened ego. When we're faced with a comparison that we feel reflects badly on us or a social situation that brings withering scrutiny, lying can be an almost knee-jerk response. To a degree, CEOs may employ this same defense mechanism, though in a more intense form. CEOs, with their positions of power and their track records of achievement, often have outsized egos. Yet an inflated ego often comes with inflated feelings of anxiety and vulnerability, as well. This combination can make the prospect of bad results extremely threatening and, indeed, more threatening than an outside observer might consider rational. In any case, under pressure of this ego threat, CEOs may respond by sanctioning or even creating a more palatable fiction.

What bears emphasis is that this fiction may also be one CEOs believe in themselves. Those outside the business world (and I certainly consider myself a member of this group) too often think of profit statements as simple reportage: income minus costs equals profits, or some such simple formulation. The reality of accounting is, of course, far, far more complicated, and to a degree it is even subjective. The heads of companies have a good deal of flexibility in how they present their results to the world and, more importantly, to themselves. Given this wiggle room, we can imagine how numbers can be crunched past the point of honesty, but in such a way that it resembles honesty even to the person doing the crunching. Rather than accept failure, some CEOs may find it easier to accept "creative accounting," or, as most of us call it, fraud.

What's interesting is that while many people lie to protect their self-esteem, they usually enact these lies personally. That is, they will verbalize a lie about their own talents, their own accomplishments. The conception of CEOs defending their egos through business deceit has them enacting the defensive lie through a secondary mechanism such as an earnings report. This points to another reason company leaders may cook the books rather than accept disappointing results. For many high-level executives, work can become all-consuming. They spend far more hours on the job than with family or friends, and form an attachment to their business that may be unrivaled outside it. This bond can be especially strong for businesspeople who helped found a company. J. Richard Anderson and Michael E. Tirrell, professors of business administration and psychology, respectively, at Stonehill College, cowrote an insightful article on CEO deceit titled "Too Good to Be True: CEOs and Financial Reporting Fraud." In the article, they describe the link between executive and company in vivid terms. They write: "It is very natural for the firm's success or survival to be visualized by the founding CEO as *personal* success or survival.... For individuals who have built their sense of self-esteem around the business, the possibility of a publicly announced failure represents a direct threat that necessitates protective actions." The identification between leader and company becomes so strong as to be nearly indivisible. Company failure becomes the CEO's personal failure, and lies that protect the former also protect the latter.

Anderson and Tirrell also point out another reason, related to identification, why CEOs might engage in deceit to keep their companies looking strong. The collapse of a business does more than bruise the ego of its leaders. It throws into some degree of turmoil the professional lives of every person the business employs. A CEO who cares about his company, or who just cares about people in general, might find the prospect of every person who works under him losing their job extremely troubling. If the alternative to duplicity is bankruptcy, a CEO might resort to business lies out of something akin to compassion.

It should be remembered that these motives rarely operate independently. The issues of greed and pride, identification and compassion often blend in subtle ways. Further, since self-deception can easily come into play, CEOs who believe themselves to be acting out of compassion might actually be using this as a kind of mental excuse for essentially selfish behavior. In any case, duplicity can sustain a business for only so long. At some point, even the most cleverly executed or best-intentioned lies give way to economic realities.

It's clear, though, that business leaders have a range of incentives, some apparent and some subtle, to engage in deceit related to their companies. But the Bad Apple Theory of business deceit, which holds that crooked business practices are ultimately the doing of unethical individuals within the business, has a serious flaw. Perhaps in some cases a CEO or a small group of executives can execute significant fraud without the awareness of anyone else in the company. In general, though, it would be difficult without the complicity, or at least the knowledge, of others within the company bureaucracy.

In fact, in some cases it seems that malfeasance cannot be traced to a particular individual or group but is, instead, endemic to the entire company hierarchy. In such cases, the problem of business deceit cannot be put down to a few bad apples. The whole barrel seems to be bad.

Bad Barrel Theory

The story of Enron and its principle villains is by now a familiar one. Kenneth Lay, the founder of Enron, Jeffrey K.

Skilling, the CEO, and Andrew Fastow, the chief financial officer, conspired to prop up Enron through fraudulent accounting and outright deceit. In September 2001, Lay assured his employees that Enron stock was a smart investment and that "the third quarter is looking great." Three weeks later, Enron disclosed a $600 million loss. By the end of the next year, the company was bankrupt. Fastow pleaded guilty to conspiracy charges, and Skilling and Lay were convicted of conspiracy and fraud. Lay died of a heart attack before he was sentenced.

According to the Bad Apple Theory, Enron was undone by ruthless and reckless leadership. Lay, Skilling, Fastow, and perhaps a few others brought down what would otherwise have been a successful, or at least a reputable, company. The problem with this conception of Enron's demise, though, is that deceit at Enron was widespread. Even aside from the massive accounting scandal that was its undoing, Enron's business practices were often duplicitous. For instance, Enron traders reportedly took steps to fuel the California energy crisis, since the demand for energy drove up Enron's stock price.

Michael Shermer, an author and a regular columnist for *Scientific American*, wrote an article analyzing Enron's corporate culture entitled "Do All Companies Have to Be Evil?" He describes how when Jeffrey Skilling came to Enron in 1996, he instituted a policy that became known as "Rank and Yank." Under this system, every employee was ranked by his or her peers on a scale of 1 to 5. Any employee who got a 5 was fired. Results of the review were posted on the Enron Web page, along with employee photographs. Rank and Yank meant that every six months, between 10 and 20 percent of Enron employees lost their jobs. More to the point, according to Shermer, Rank and Yank "established an environment that brought out the worst in Enron's employees: selfishness, competitiveness and greed."

It was this atmosphere that fostered the widespread duplicity at Enron, in the accountants to executives to traders.

This explanation for what occurred at Enron might be called the Bad Barrel Theory of corporate deception. It isn't so much that the people who engage in workplace deception are prone to duplicity. Rather, they are encouraged to duplicitous acts by the culture in which they find themselves. It is a triumph of environment over character.

In considering the roots of infidelity, we discussed the idea of social norms. Social norms are the informal rules a society holds that govern behavior. There is no written law against sitting down in an elevator or cutting to the head of a line, but social norms dictate that these are things you don't do. You stand up in the elevator; you start out at the back of the line.

As we noted in our discussion of adultery, social norms generally discourage duplicitous behavior. However, if social norms within a specific group—say, a company—are strong enough, they can counteract the broader societal prohibitions against lying and cheating. In other words, if everyone in your office is telling lies, you might feel it is okay to do the same. Indeed, the power of social norms is such that you might actually feel you *should* act in a deceitful manner, in order to align your behavior with that of your colleagues. If everyone in your department were fudging their sales numbers, you would likely feel professionally handicapped and personally isolated by being honest. The Bad Barrel Theory posits that corporations that engage in business deceit can function in precisely this way. Lying is the norm, a norm encouraging everyone in the organization toward duplicity.

Yet social norms characterized by deceit are not the only way in which lying can be fostered within an organization. Bad barrels can be composed of many types of wood. There was nothing in Rank and Yank, for example, that explicitly encouraged deceit. Yet the atmosphere Rank and Yank helped create at Enron was one in which deceit easily took root. Researchers into business deceit have found that stressful work environments are conducive to deception. This makes intuitive sense. Constant pressure to meet difficult goals can erode a commitment to honesty if deception presents itself as a way to alleviate that pressure. Lying can be a way simply to keep one's head above water. So, an employee tells his or her supervisor that a report is finished when it isn't, that sales in his or her district are strong when they're not.

Further, in looking at the Bad Barrel Theory, it's important to keep in mind that dishonesty can be fostered throughout the chain of command. A supervisor who pushes her subordinates to get the job done *no matter what* may in effect be pushing them to lie to her. These subordinates may (correctly) conclude that a lie, of whatever scope, may benefit them more professionally than a disappointing truth; and, moreover, that a hard-driving manager would rather they cheat than fail, even if this is never explicitly stated. At high-pressure companies, lying can become systemic: managerial expectations are met through dishonesty, those expectations, even if unrealistic, endure; and then they must be fulfilled through further dishonesty. This can occur at every level of a corporate structure, pressure from supervisors manifesting itself as pressure on those supervised, from the CEO on down.

Stressful work environments can thus herd employees into business deceit. But there is also the matter of who such environments attract in the first place. Undoubtedly, there are honest people who thrive on the adrenaline and mental stimulation of a high-pressure job. But cut-throat evaluation systems and hard-driving managers can also appeal to individuals with less rigorous ethics, those more interested in profit and career success than strict honesty. It's almost as if bad barrels can draw in bad apples.

Paul Babiak is an industrial and organizational psychologist who has done extensive research on the topic of psychopaths in the workplace. The term "psychopath" usually evokes thoughts of serial killers, or at least vengeful exes. Yet psychopaths, or at least those with psychopathic traits, need not appear crazed, much less be murderous. Indeed, psychopaths can often be charming and articulate—as well as ruthless, manipulative, and cruel. Babiak believes that psychopaths are over-represented in the business world, and are particularly drawn to high-pressure, fast-moving organizations, where their cunning and impulsiveness is rewarded. He argues that companies need to be far more aware of the danger of psychopaths in their ranks.

Implicit in the idea that companies can protect themselves from psychopaths, and implicit in the Bad Barrel Theory generally, is the belief that there are steps companies can take to prevent business deceit from occurring. Lying is not inevitable in business. It is the result of bad business practices or bad business culture. The Bad Apple Theory largely concurs on this point: business deceit can be chalked up to the behavior of duplicitous individuals. Yet not everyone agrees with this premise. Some researchers believe that business deceit occurs because of the very structure of business itself.

Work and the Need to Deceive

Throughout *Liar*, we have explored how fully intertwined deception is with ordinary social interactions. Standards of tact and politeness, the demands of context, and expectations can make deception, to some degree, almost inevitable. This is why researchers have found that so many lies occur every day. The way we usually interact with one another makes it very difficult to be completely honest. Unless we decide we want to know that our new haircut is a mess, that our child is a terrible Little Leaguer, that our colleague is not happy to run into us at the gym—and, indeed, unless we are prepared to tell other people this sort of thing—deception is here to stay.

It's helpful to keep the functioning of interpersonal deception in mind as we consider the thinking of David Shulman. In his book *From Liar to Hire*, Shulman, a professor of anthropology and sociology at Lafayette College, presents a picture of the modern workplace that in many ways resembles the picture of modern social interactions presented above. In Shulman's view, business deception is not a question of bad apples or a bad barrel. It is, rather, a normal aspect of everyday working life. Shulman writes: "Workplaces generate social pressures and situations that help people to overcome proscriptions against lying, just as everyday social niceties encourage 'white lies' to help people preserve the peace in routine interactions with family and friends."

What are the pressures and situations that trump the tendency toward honesty? To some degree, they are simply part of the package of attitudes and behaviors we might equate with functioning in a workplace. An employee must defer to his or her boss; treat customers with respect and courtesy; put aside personal dislikes or envies in order to cooperate with colleagues. In effect, in order to be what we normally call a "professional," one must put up a front. No one is *always* eager to perform the roll a job demands—but this is often precisely what work requires. It goes back to the issue of self-presentation. The context of work has certain clear demands for personal conduct. In matching these demands, we sometimes need to lie about how we really feel about an idea, a coworker, a customer's request.

Beyond fake on-the-job personal attitudes, Shulman argues, the organizational dynamics of a company also often necessitate deceit. For instance, anyone who has worked in an office has had the experience of being told by a supervisor to do something one way, while knowing there is a better, faster alternative. Frequently, too, officially mandated channels for certain tasks are cumbersome—the demands of a bureaucracy can make it all but impossible for an individual to do his or her assigned tasks. In such cases, most people will simply ignore the prescribed method and do their job the way they believe (and often know) is best. That breaking the rules in this way often requires varying levels of deception seems secondary to the larger goal of *doing one's job.* Shulman's larger point is that offices inevitably lend themselves to such situations: deception becomes a more effective means of work than honesty. This can be true even at companies where the work is not stressful and where management is not duplicitous.

It's perhaps easy to be sanguine about this sort of deception. After all, if a lie is told in service of job performance, is it really so terrible? The problem with this reasoning is that, as with the arguably benign forms of interpersonal deception, there are no clear limits. Outside of work, there's no easy way to signal the times and situations in which we want the cold, harsh truth and the times we'd rather hear a comforting lie. At work, the situation is parallel. There are times when a business might indeed benefit from an employee stepping beyond official policies to accomplish a task. On the other hand, such policies are in place for a reason. Shulman makes the point that employees who commit "illicit acts" will often utilize deceit in order to hide these acts from managers inside the company or monitors of conduct outside the company. Even if these acts are well-intentioned, hiding conduct is obviously a start down a slippery slope.

If it's true, though, that the very structure of business lends itself to deceit, is there any way to avoid this slippery slope? Fortunately, the answer is probably yes. While some deceit will always occur in the workplace, just as it will in every aspect of modern life, there are ways to try to minimize this deceit so that it won't escalate into an Enron-sized debacle.

The Bad Apple Theory and the Bad Barrel Theory may at first seem to stand in total opposition, but in fact there is significant overlap. The Bad Apple Theory posits that business deceit is the work of individuals. But the business culture that the Bad Barrel Theory holds up as the root of business deceit does not come out of a vacuum. The expectations and attitudes of a company are signaled, if not formally codified, by those at the top of the company, and are echoed and reinforced by those beneath them. In other words, both the Bad Apple Theory and the Bad Barrel Theory hold that business deception can be shaped, if not eliminated, by those within a company. If we are serious about reducing the lies in the business world, the place to start might be with ourselves. Even if Shulman is right, and lying at work is unavoidable, the lies we tell and the lies we accept or choose to overlook are something we retain control over. We also retain control over where we work in the first place. Business lies can't get out of hand if there is no one at the business to tell them.

CHAPTER 11

Web of Deceit:
The Brave New World
of Internet Dishonesty

The history of the Internet is short enough that, as late as 2001, what we know as blogs were still called, quaintly, "Weblogs." One early Weblog that garnered a great deal of interest was Living Colours, the online journal of a Kansas teenager named Kaycee Nicole Swenson. Kaycee was an attractive, athletic girl battling leukemia, and she used Living Colours to narrate her struggles with the disease. Thousands read Kaycee's Weblog, many drawing inspiration from both Kaycee's courage and her sunny optimism in the face of her illness. Some readers even got to know Kaycee via instant messaging and phone calls.

Then, on May 15, 2001, a posting on Living Colours announced that Kaycee Swenson had died. A note thanked her readers for the love and support they had shown her. A huge outpouring of grief followed. Though none (and I mean *none*) of the readers of Kaycee's Weblog had met her face-to-face, many in the digital community that had sprung up around her seemed to have formed a real emotional connection with the brave teenager, albeit a one-sided one. Kaycee's death hit these people hard.

Yet it was not long before some in that community also became suspicious. Certain aspects of Kaycee's death seemed odd. Debbie Swenson, Kaycee's mother, claimed that Kaycee's memorial service had been completed only two days after her death. She also offered no address where mourners could send cards or flowers. Online snooping by the Living Colours readership revealed further eyebrow-raising details, such as the lack of any mention of Kaycee's death in local newspapers and the absence of medical records at local hospitals.

Eventually, the chorus of skepticism grew to a roar, and Debbie Swenson was forced to admit the truth. There was no Kaycee Swenson. Debbie had made her up, writing Living Colours, even posing as her online and on the phone. Quite simply, Kaycee was a digital illusion, a fiction Debbie Swenson had invented in order, she said, to do something "positive."

When we assess the honesty of our cultural institutions, we tend to embrace the notion of a more innocent past. Journalists used to be more ethical; newspapers used to be more reliable; George Washington and Abe Lincoln never lied; a handshake used to count for something in business. Some of this is simply naïveté, of course, nostalgia for a time we can at least tell ourselves was more virtuous than our own. Yet it's revealing that we don't think of business or journalism or even politics as necessarily dishonest. They only *became* that way, or so many often claim.

When it comes to the Internet, on the other hand, one rarely hears such an assertion. Debbie Swenson's invention of Kaycee was one of the first examples of large-scale blog fraud, and it occurred just as the form was emerging in the popular mind. We may be right to think that there never was an antediluvian era of digital honesty—not even an imagined one.

We have become so familiar with the Internet that it is easy to forget what a revolutionary form of communication it represents. The power to send information instantly, to anywhere in the world, entirely collapses the strictures of physical space that had governed communication for tens of thousands of years. Interacting with another person no longer requires enough physical proximity to hold a conversation. It does not even require the time or effort necessary to move some physical object, like a letter, between two distant parties. Geography and time are no longer limiting factors to interpersonal communication.

The new possibilities for interaction the Internet allows have yielded tremendous benefits. Yet when the requirements of physical space are lost, the advantages of face-to-face communication are lost, as well. When we greet our neighbor over the fence, to choose an aptly old-fashioned example, we at least know it's our neighbor we are talking to. We can't know, though, who is responsible for the text we read in an e-mail or an instant message or a forum posting. We may not be able to conclude in a personal conversation whether our interlocutor is telling the truth, but via the Internet we can't even be sure whether our interlocutor *exists*. Digital communication is vast and limitless, but it is also generally completely unverifiable as to its source. Further, the people we interact with over the Internet aren't just neighbors, members of the local community, or fellow employees. We can't make any assumptions based on a common home or working life about their values or standards of behavior. All we can assume is that they have an Internet connection.

Yet perhaps because the Internet remains such a new form of communication, we tend to approach it with the same assumptions we bring to the more traditional means of interaction. In other words, we generally assume that those we communicate with on the Internet are telling us the truth. To a degree, of course, we have to, just as we have to assume that our neighbor over the fence is telling the truth when he says he heard the town sewer tax is going to rise. Community and communication aren't possible without some level of trust. Further, our minds are to some extent wired for credulity. We all operate with a truth bias, the cognitive rule of thumb that makes us predisposed to believe others (as we discussed in Chapter 2). The problem is that our standards for trust, whether cultural or cognitive, weren't formed based on a still new technology that cloaks identity and makes proximity irrelevant.

It's almost paradoxical that we feel betrayed by incidents like the fabrication of Kaycee Swenson, or any of the countless similar cases of Internet-driven deceit. The Internet ensures anonymity, makes identity flexible. Indeed, that is one of its appeals. Who doesn't enjoy inventing a screen name or tailoring a user profile so that it presents just the right image? Yet although we acknowledge and even embrace the elements of the Internet that enable deception, we feel no less stung when a hoax is revealed. Our expectations for honesty don't seem to be entirely consistent when it comes to the Internet (though, to be fair, they may not be very consistent in any other arena, either). Perhaps in a forum where any detail can be changed with the click of a button, it's almost inevitable that our trust will be violated.

The 1's and 0's of Internet Lies

One of the administrative editors of the online encyclopedia Wikipedia, Essjay, as he was known to Wikipedia users, reported that he sometimes spent fourteen hours a day on the site. He edited thousands of Wikipedia articles, checked accuracy, and settled disputes between authors. Wikipedia is a collectively written encyclopedia. Its premise is that knowledge can be conveyed not just by experts but also by groups of nonexperts working collaboratively. Still, in such a project knowledgeable editors remain essential, and it certainly helped Essjay's reputation as an editor that he held multiple doctoral degrees and worked as a tenured professor at a private university. His credentials lent Wikipedia credibility, too, as a source of accurate information and sophisticated discussion.

But Wikipedia eventually lost the credibility it gained from its association with Essjay—and then some. After being featured in a July 2006 article about Wikipedia in the *New Yorker*, Essjay confessed that his credentials were false. He was not a professor; in fact, he was a twenty-four-year-old who lacked any higher degrees. After initially defending Essjay, whose real name was revealed to be Ryan Jordan, those who run Wikipedia eventually asked him to resign from his "positions of trust within the community."

What the story of Essjay/Ryan Jordan highlights is how simple even sustained and egregious lies are to execute online. Jordan fooled not only the fact-checkers at the *New Yorker* but also the community of people, in regular Wikipedia users, with the greatest familiarity with his work. This was also a community, moreover, held together by the common mission of maintaining accuracy and credibility on the Wikipedia Web site. And yet under these scrutinizing noses, Jordan was able to assume the identity of a professor with multiple degrees.

The reasons electronic deception is generally so easy to pull off aren't difficult to apprehend. As mentioned above, the Internet encourages anonymity, or at least its possibility. Users choose their own screen names, write their own bios for forums or Web sites, pick the pictures that are associated with their profiles. This information is as easy to falsify as it is to post online. Further, checking the veracity of user-provided biographical data is often made difficult by the safeguards that ensure user privacy. Obviously, we all hope that at least some of the details of our lives will be protected online. Indeed, Essjay claimed that he concocted his phony identity only in order to keep would-be electronic harassers (perhaps bitter due to his editorial decisions?) off his trail. And the checks that guarantee such privacy function as checks against verification, too. It's not easy to confirm whether the blogger whose journal you are reading really has cancer and lives in Kansas because such off-line investigation is not supposed to be easy. Finally, there is the simple fact that lies are hard to detect in any context. As we discussed in Chapter 2, even trained professionals such as police officers and polygraph administrators aren't very good at spotting lies. Most ordinary people are no better at detecting deception than they'd be if they flipped a coin. Obviously, the task of separating honesty from duplicity is made all the more difficult when one has only the digital text of an e-mail to go on.

The ease of executing an Internet lie helps explain, in part at least, the ubiquity of online deception. Thus far, we have focused on digital impersonation, such as Essjay's or Debbie Swenson's. Yet this is far from the only form of online fraud. Most of us are exposed to lies every time we check our e-mail. In-boxes are regularly flooded with news of inheritances we've won or pleas for help accessing a frozen Nigerian bank account. Such fraudulent spam suggests another dynamic of the Internet that allows for a great deal of deceit: it gives those willing to lie—through a phishing scheme or a fictional blog—easy access to millions of people. Online, lies can travel quickly and widely.

We should not overlook, either, our own role in spreading Internet lies in this regard. During the 2008 presidential election, I received from friends my fair share of forwarded e-mails about the candidates—some serious, many ridiculous. In sending these e-mails on to other friends, I admit, my focus may have been more on entertainment than on disseminating accurate political information. With a click of a button we can become party to dishonesty about this or that candidate's beliefs, background, or personal life. And while we may not take such forwards seriously, there is no guarantee that everyone on an exponentially expanding chain of recipients shares this view. Just because we don't write an Internet falsehood does not mean we don't participate in it.

Deception on the Internet does not have to be exclusively textual, either. In 2008, sports fans were captivated by a YouTube video of Los Angeles Lakers star Kobe Bryant apparently leaping over a speeding Aston Martin. Only later did viewers learn that the clip was created digitally as part of a viral marketing campaign for a new brand of Nike shoes. The deception was twofold: the clip itself was a digital fake, and its ostensible source as a home movie made by Kobe Bryant was fake, too. This sort of viral video marketing is becoming more and more popular with advertisers, as they turn to deceit to capture the attention of increasingly savvy consumers.

Nike's motives in creating a deceptive YouTube video are clear enough: the company wants to sell shoes. Behavior such as Debbie Swenson's in inventing—and then killing—a fake daughter may seem harder to figure. Why concoct a digital tragedy? Adam Joinson of the Open University in England and Beth Dietz-Uhler of Miami University conducted a case study of an incident very similar to the invention of Kaycee Swenson. This act of digital deceit occurred on the AnandTech forums. These forums were used primarily by those in the information technology industry to discuss issues of software and memory and so forth, but as with most online forums, there was also an "Off Topic" section, where members could post messages unrelated to the tech industry. It was primarily in the Off Topic section that a user named Nowheremom began to post. She quickly formed a relationship with another Anand-Tech member, DF, and they soon entered into a forum-based public flirtation.

A few months after Nowheremom joined AnandTech, though, DF shared some shocking news in a posting with the pithy heading: "NOWHEREMOM's dead…" Reporting that he was "so focking sad," DF said he'd received a call from Nowheremom's father, informing him that Nowheremom had been killed in a car accident. The AnandTech community was grief-stricken; Joinson and Dietz-Uhler describe the sincere efforts users made to honor and memorialize a woman they had known only through her posts. It was nearly a year and a half before the other shoe dropped. After AnandTech users could find no record of Nowheremom's life or death, DF finally confessed. He had invented the "cyberpersona called NO-WHEREMOM," he wrote in a post. "I had never expected the grief that overcame this community. It even overcame me and I sobbed for three days as if she had been real."

When seeking to understand Internet deception, it's perhaps too easy to become overly focused on the Internet itself. We may start to look at online forums and e-mail and such as somehow the source of the deceptive impulse. Joinson and Dietz-Uhler caution against such a narrow view. They point, rather, to an interaction between online and off-line values, online and off-line identities in analyzing the causes of Internet deceit. Remember that the Internet provides only the packaging and transmission system for deception; the content of lies is generated in the minds of those who use it. The question of why people lie online is inextricably linked, Joinson and Dietz-Uhler suggest, to why they lie off-line.

Inventing a fake tragedy, as DF and Debbie Swenson did, is often an attempt to win attention and sympathy that the perpetrator of the deceit feels he or she would otherwise lack. The Internet allows the deception to victimize more people, more quickly, but its fundamental motivation may be no different online or off. Ryan Jordan's impersonation of a professor on Wikipedia fits a model we discussed in Chapter 8 when regarding impostors. Such individuals often assume the role of someone with societal standing. This allows them to reap the psychological benefits of being treated with respect and admiration by their peers, something that is often particularly tempting for those who suffer from feelings of insignificance or societal contempt. Just as the Internet did not fundamentally change how and why we trust other people, it did not fundamentally change the psychological underpinnings of deceit—underpinnings that have been discussed throughout *Liar*.

Yet by the same token, while the dynamics of the Internet may not provide a comprehensive explanation for online deceit, those dynamics clearly have some influence. Internet users may not lie *because* they're online. But being online just might make deception more likely.

Deterrence versus Deindividuation

When people meet for the first time face-to-face, lies are frequent. As the study I conducted of unacquainted strangers (described in detail in Chapter 1) shows, an individual sitting down and getting to know another person will lie to him or her about three times in ten minutes. The pressure to impress another person and to come off a particular way, even if we aren't consciously aware of it, often takes precedence over an adherence to the truth.

A more recent study of mine (conducted with Mattitiyahu

Zimbler) framed the unacquainted-strangers scenario differently. What if the two people get to know each other not by sitting at a table but by sitting at computers? I was curious about what the effect the Internet had on interpersonal honesty.

The setup for the study was very simple. I had pairs of participants get to know each other in one of three ways: either in a face-to-face conversation in a room together, via a fifteen-minute e-mail exchange, or through a fifteen-minute instant-messaging session. Only the face-to-face pairs were in the same room; those using e-mail or IM were physically separated and never saw each other. Also, in all three conditions, the interactions were recorded. I used a hidden video camera to document the face-to-face conversations, and a computer record was generated of the e-mails and instant messages. After the interactions were completed, I asked the participants to review the video or transcript of the conversation, and to note any instances in which they deviated from the truth.

As I approached this investigation into Internet deceit, I mulled over two alternative explanations for what I might find. The first was what might be called the Deterrent Hypothesis. We all know that e-mail, by definition, creates a record of an interaction; the same is also true for an exchange of instant messages. The Deterrent Hypothesis holds that Internet users, aware of the digital record their interaction generates, will be less likely to lie. The record and the possibility that it could be checked later for accuracy will make people be more truthful than they'd be in a casual, face-to-face interaction, which generally involves no permanent documentation. (Remember, the participants did not know that their face-to-face chat was being videotaped.)

The second, competing explanation for how Internet use would shape interpersonal honesty involved a concept known as "deindividuation." The term, coined in the early 1950s, refers to the tendency of individuals to act with less social restraint in situations from which they are physically or psychologically detached. For instance, when an individual enjoys a degree of anonymity, the concept of deindividuation suggests, his or her behavior can become more spontaneous, less regulated by conventional norms.

The Deindividuation Hypothesis for this study holds that Internet users lie more online because their communication is conveyed not personally but by way of electronics. The digital filter creates a level of personal detachment, and so makes users more likely to ignore conventional restraints against deceit. The Deindividuation Hypothesis would also suggest that lies would be most common on e-mail. E-mail creates a barrier of time as well as one of space: individuals have to wait longer between replies than in an instant-messaging or face-to-face interaction. This further layer of deindividuation should make the prohibitions against dishonesty even weaker, and hence lying more likely.

The results of the study showed, as one might guess by now, that participants in every situation lied to each other. Whether conversing in the same room or chatting online or trading e-mails, the vast majority of participants strayed from the truth. Again, though, the question was not whether the participants would lie. The crucial element of the study was *how* they would lie in the different situations. The Deterrent Hypothesis suggests that those interacting via the Internet would lie less than those interacting face-to-face, because the creation of a permanent record would encourage them to stick more closely to the truth. The Deindividuation Hypothesis suggests the opposite: those using the Internet to converse would lie more because of the depersonalizing aspects of computer-driven communication.

The results of my study show that when it comes to using the Internet, the dynamics of deindividuation trump the deterrence of the digital record. Participants told significantly more lies when communicating via computer than they did face-to-face. Further, they told the most lies when communicating through e-mail. This lends further credence to the Deindividuation Hypothesis, since, again, e-mail involves the greatest level of personal detachment of the three forms of communication employed. Moreover, the fact that the most lies were told via e-mail shows just how powerful deindividuation is. When we send e-mail, we don't just worry that someone might be recording what we write—we *create* that record, and send it on to another person. Yet even given this possibility that an untrue statement could be checked and discovered to be false, participants lied on e-mail again and again.

Examining the content of the participants' lies sheds some light as to why they ignored the permanent record of their deceit. It may be that, in fact, they did *not* wholly ignore this record. In the face-to-face situation, the participants usually lied about their plans, or about other factual information. The lies told on the Internet more often related to the participants' inner lives. The deception involved what the liar thought or felt. It's possible that the participants sending the e-mails or instant messages did feel deterred from lying by the permanence of the communication—but only about matters that could easily be verified. In other words, a participant would not send an e-mail discussing a planned safari in Kenya, since such a statement could be checked for its veracity. On the other hand, a statement about whether or not the participant loves wild animals is much more difficult to verify, regardless of the form it takes. There may be a digital record of an e-mail exchange, but there is none of the inside of the liar's head.

Regardless of the particular content of the lies, though, my study suggests that when we use a computer, our standards for honesty are weakened. Bear in mind, too, that they are probably not all that strong to begin with. But the deindividuation that computer-mediated communication creates seems to lower the bar for deception that much further. If looking someone in the eye doesn't do much to discourage deceit, looking into a computer monitor does even less.

There is another aspect of deindividuation that is also relevant to a discussion of Internet deceit. As we've noted throughout *Liar*, there are no reliable cues that divulge deception. Many people believe that an averted gaze reveals a dishonest intent, but an averted gaze can simply signal anxiety or, just as easily, interest in something across the room. Yet this (mistaken) belief that averted gazes or sweaty palms or tapping fingers signal lies is itself crucial to recognize. If people believe that something they do physically will announce their deception, they may be less likely to engage in that deception. A computer, though, protects people from these theoretically telltale tics. You can avert your gaze all you want when you write an e-mail, secure in the knowledge that its recipient will have no idea you ever did. So the deindividuation Internet communication not only has the psychological effect of making users feel that they have more freedom to lie, it also has a practical element. Communicating via the Internet weakens a crucial barrier against lying: the fear of getting caught.

It would seem, then, that the anonymity engendered by the physical and temporal distance of Internet communication results in a greater likelihood of online deceit. Yet there is a crucial assumption inherent in this line of thinking that, admittedly, may not be accurate. When we consider deceit in terms of deindividuation, we start with the idea that lying is prohibited. We then posit that the dynamics of being online encourage people to ignore this prohibition. Yet the situation may not be so simple. It may be that people don't ignore a prohibition against online deceit so much as they do not feel that prohibition in the first place. In other words, lying online might not be a matter of breaking the rules. In fact, it's possible that for some it's a matter of following them.

eHonesty

Imagine you pick up a copy of the *Wall Street Journal* and on the cover is a lengthy article about a huge scandal in the United States Department of the Interior. It states that federal employees responsible for giving out oil contracts for years accepted gifts from those in the oil industry. The article goes on to detail a tawdry web of corruption, sex, and even drug use. Now imagine you read the same article, word for word, in the *National Enquirer*. It's probable your reaction to the two articles would be very, very different.

Just about all of us judge the truth of what we read or hear based on its source. And, of course, not all sources are created equal. The standards for reporting at the *Enquirer* are very different from those at the *Journal*, just as they're different for movie gossip Web sites and network news, for blogs and for talk radio. In our evaluations of what is true and what is not, we account for context.

To see how this relates to Internet dishonesty, consider a study by Holtjona Galanxhi and Fiona Fui-Hoon Nah of the University of Nebraska, Lincoln. The two researchers had participants, in pairs, interact with each other through two different methods of Internet communication. Some pairs conversed via a simple, text-based instant-messaging program. Other pairs conversed through a program that used avatars, graphic representations of the participants. These anthropomorphic avatars might resemble the participants or they might not; that was left up to the participants.

In my study of Internet deception, I instructed the participants simply to get to know each other; I then reviewed the records of their conversations with them to identify the lies they'd spontaneously told. Galanxhi and Nah were more direct in their instructions: they told some of the participants to lie. They were curious to see how using the different forms of Internet communication—text-based chat or avatar-based chat—might affect the responses of the participants as they tried to deceive their partners. What Galanxhi and Nah found has important implications for an understanding of online deception generally.

Participants in Galanxhi and Nah's study reported feeling anxiety when they lied to their partners via the text-based chat. It seems that even being physically hidden did not completely salve the participants' unease about engaging in deceit. What is surprising, though, is that the participants who lied using the avatar-based program did not feel this same anxiety. Participants who employed a graphic representation of themselves were calmer when they lied—as calm, in fact, as participants in a control group who were instructed to use the avatar program to engage in honest communication. Somehow, the deceit came more naturally to those using an avatar.

We've examined online deception in the context of deindividuation, noting how the physical and psychological detachment of computer-driven communication can lead to a loosening of the strictures against dishonesty. Yet something more than deindividuation seems to be at work in Galanxhi and Nah's study. As we consider their results, one other finding from their study bears particular emphasis: participants instructed to lie were more likely to select an avatar that did not resemble them than those in the control sample who were instructed to be honest. In other words, those who intended to lie adopted a kind of digital mask.

On the surface, it seems that this finding can be wholly explained by the concept of deindividuation. If communicating with instant messages provides one level of psychological remove, donning graphic camouflage would likely provide another. Hence, it shouldn't be surprising that participants in Galanxhi and Nah's study who lied using an avatar were not very nervous.

Yet recall our earlier discussion about the experience of reading an article in the *Wall Street Journal* or the *National Enquirer*. As we noted, the context for the information we receive matters a great deal in how we evaluate it. We consider some sources reliable; others, a forum for unsubstantiated rumor and gossip.

The notion of varying standards for reporting is not exclusively applicable to journalism. And when we present ourselves online—offer names and biographical details, voice opinions and sentiments, present images that ostensibly have some relation to how we look—the standard we use may be much more *National Enquirer* than *Wall Street Journal*. In other words, we don't hold ourselves to a high standard of honesty online because, well, *we're online*. And online, as in the pages of the *National Enquirer*, the truth is mutable, the facts are unreliable, and everybody knows it.

My name for this conception of online deceit is *eHonesty*. The term refers to the idea that we apply a different standard for the truth when we're communicating using a computer than we do when we're in a boardroom or having dinner with friends or in any other real-world situation. In real life, we have one standard of honesty. In the digital world, we follow the weaker standard of eHonesty.

In previous chapters of *Liar*, we've discussed the power of social norms. These are the unwritten rules that govern behavior in a society. In China, for instance, if you don't hand someone a business card with two hands, you are breaking an important rule of etiquette. There is no law against handing over a business card with one hand, but social norms stand against such behavior. Social norms are, of course, an important element of the reasons why people do (or do not) lie. It isn't illegal to cheat on a girlfriend or to invent an excuse to avoid helping a sibling move, but social norms encourage a certain level of honesty in our actions.

Online, though, the social norms are very different. Picking a new name (or online "handle," to employ some modest insider lingo) is the first thing one does in nearly every new online activity, be it creating an e-mail address or launching a blog or joining a forum. Occasionally online users stick to a firstname. lastname formulation, but very often they do not. Indeed, the mutability of identity in the digital realm is part of its appeal. We *could* set up a firstname.lastname handle, but what would be the fun in that? The freedom to be another person online—or, at least, to present the person we are in a new way—can be thrilling. For some users, identity play is the entire purpose of going online in the first place.

There is nothing wrong, really, with identity play, with embracing the opportunity digital media afford to take on a new name, a new biography, even a new gender or race. The issue is that such behavior helps establish a social norm more tolerant of deception. The more permissive standard of eHonesty may inevitably lead to incidents in which lies spill over from the realm of the accepted to the realm of the hurtful and condemned.

Adam Joinson and Beth Dietz-Uhler discuss in their case study on the invention of Nowheremom this balance between online lies that are tolerated and those that are scorned. When DF revealed to the AnandTech forums that he had invented Nowheremom, the reaction was not as homogeneous as one might imagine. Many AnandTech users expressed outrage at what DF had done, shocked by what they saw as his callous emotional manipulation. Others, though, saw DF's behavior as consistent with what always occurs online. Joinson and Dietz-Uhler quote one user as writing, "This is the net and lots of people use it to escape from their jobs or life for a second." They quote another as telling DF, "I don't blame you at all for the part about creating Nowheremom, it's so easy and tempting to do something of that sort especially in a forum like this one where so much kidding goes on." DF's actions, then, as Joinson and Dietz-Uhler point out, were to an extent seen as consistent with online social norms. Yet the genuine emotional distress DF caused clearly was regarded as a violation of these norms, as the angry comments of many Anand-Tech users reflect.

The problem, it seems, is that while some deception is generally accepted online, other acts of deceit are generally condemned. There are no clear boundaries between harmless online identity play and hurtful manipulation. As the split in the AnandTech forum over DF's actions shows, too, these boundaries exist in different places for different people. What is par for the digital course for one user is emotional cruelty to another. In some ways, this situation parallels the one in our off-line lives. Some level of deceit is part of everyone's daily life, but in some areas we prefer honesty—though no one can say with certainty how the divisions should be made.

These issues are often all the more intense online, though, both because deceit is so much easier to perpetrate and because the online world is so new. The social norms of the Internet are only decades old, at most. Avatar-based communication is even younger. When compared with one old-fashioned way humans communicate—we've been talking face-to-face for tens of thousands of years—it's not hard to see why online social norms can sometimes be ambiguous. To a large extent, they are still being created. It may take generations of DFs and Nowheremoms and Essjays and Kaycee Swensons before the rules of online deception are clear. And it's worth noting, again, that even after all this time, off-line standards of deceit are often contradictory (hence this book).

Another element of the digital dishonesty puzzle is that the Internet does not exist in a vacuum. Our off-line and online lives intersect with increasing frequency. When it comes to deceit, then, this raises a crucial question: Do we apply off-line standards of honesty or online standards of eHonesty? As many prominent incidents of Internet deception have shown, there may not be a right answer, but it's certainly possible to get this question wrong.

The CEO and the Sock Puppet

During the early 2000s, the user posting on the Yahoo message boards under the name Rahodeb was known as a staunch defender of the organic grocery store chain Whole Foods. Rahodeb would promote Whole Foods' financial prospects and disparage the company's major rival, Wild Oats. He had particular praise for Whole Foods' CEO, John Mackey, once writing: "I like Mackey's haircut. I think he looks cute!" Between 1999 and 2006, Rahodeb made well over a thousands posts.

Then, in 2007, a footnote in a legal filing by the Federal Trade Commission revealed something curious. Rahodeb was not just a fan of Whole Foods and its CEO, John Mackey. Rahodeb *was* John Mackey. For years, the Fortune 500 CEO had hidden his identity to insert his thoughts into the digital discussions of his company.

Mackey's actions were not unique. His use of an online alias to promote a company he ran is an example of what's known as "sock-puppeting." Sock-puppeting can involve assuming a digital disguise to support any sort of company or cause or product. The key element is an insider, like Mackey, voicing his or her opinions through an anonymous Internet "puppet." Recent years have seen numerous prominent cases of sock-puppeting: by CEOs praising their own companies, by congressional staff members praising their own bosses, by journalists praising their own stories. Often, the puppeteers' excuse is similar to the one Mackey offered for the Rahodeb incident (Rahodeb is an anagram of Deborah, the name of Mackey's wife.) He explained, "I posted on Yahoo! under a pseudonym because I had fun doing it."

CEOs of major companies don't have many opportunities to speak off-the-cuff. Even when they want us to think they're speaking off-the-cuff, what they're saying has usually been filtered through a public relations staff or, worse, vetted by lawyers. Given the media and shareholder scrutiny that accompanies a CEO's comments, it's not hard to imagine that for them, yes, anonymously unloading on an Internet site probably would be a lot of fun. The fun stops, of course, when the deceit is uncovered. Then the consequences can range from embarrassment to career implosion. For example, a staffer for a Republican congressman lost his job when it was revealed that he had been acting as a digital agent provocateur on Democratic Web sites.

Sock-puppeting provides a good example of the conflict between eHonesty and conventional off-line standards for conduct. By the rules of eHonesty, there was nothing wrong with Mackey hiding his identity in order to post messages on a public forum. Such messages are almost always posted anonymously. Yet his off-line identity (that is, his *real* identity) as CEO of Whole Foods demanded that his public comments on his own company, if not those about his haircut, be attributable to him. The online rules say Mackey can hide his identity. The off-line rules say Mackey is accountable for what he says about his business.

Similar contradictions have to be negotiated in Internet environments such as Second Life. This online, multiplayer game allows users to create three-dimensional avatars who populate a world eerily similar (in some ways, at least) to our own. Avatars have jobs, earn money, make friends, go to parties—in short, engage in many of the same activities we do off-line. Avatars can also get married and have sex. This raises some predictably thorny issues with regard to what is and is not permissible within a marriage. For instance, to what degree is cybersex really sex? Can digital infidelity be grounds for an off-line breakup?

The answers to such questions quite simply don't exist yet. The Internet is both the frontier of technology and the frontier of a new kind of social interaction. Standards for honesty will emerge only as individuals play out scenarios along the online/ off-line divide again and again and again.

Until Internet culture stabilizes, if such an event is even possible, the best course of action is to proceed with doubled skepticism about what we read and who we know online. We may be willing to live with the general principles of eHonesty, accepting false names and deceptive biographical details. But there is no filter for the lie that would harm us or hurt us. We have to raise our own firewalls to protect our digital trust.

Living with Lies

Think about the last time you were lied to.

This was the proposition with which we began this book, and it seems useful to revisit it now. Before reading *Liar*, you probably thought of the last lie you heard in the context of some nefarious ex, some customer service representative who misled you, some deliveryman who promised a speedy delivery that simply never arrived. By this point, though, it should be clear that the liars in our lives aren't just the unsavory characters we're unlucky enough to encounter every now and again. The truth is that there is no one who is strictly, exclusively honest with us, and the lies we hear are as common as the interactions we have on a daily basis.

To put it simply, the liars in our lives are *everyone* in our lives.

The notion that deception is rare, something that stands out in our minds because it is so unpleasant, is actually a comforting one. It reassures us that the lies we encounter are to some degree compartmentalized. Yet the true extent of our relationship with deceit can be found simply by picturing our lives without it. Imagine turning on the television and seeing a celebrity announce, "I was paid a lot of money to appear in this commercial." Imagine if a job applicant admitted, as you were interviewing her, "I don't really have the skills to do this job, but I want you to hire me anyway." Or imagine being told by your spouse, "Your new hair color makes you look absolutely ridiculous." Regardless of whether this honesty might be refreshing, it would certainly be wholly unfamiliar.

The fact is that lies are woven into our most intimate relationships and our most casual ones; they are essential to how we think of ourselves and how we present ourselves to others; they play a role in how we elect our leaders and how we make our money. Dishonesty is everywhere in modern life. And there is little reason to think this will change any time soon.

The challenge for us is how we deal with deception. We may have no choice as to whether or not we encounter lies. But there are certainly attitudes and tools we can adopt to help us function more healthily, not to mention more honestly, as we navigate the deception we face every day.

Understanding Why People Lie to Us

Every lie entails some degree of harm and victimization. Granted, some lies exact a steeper cost, be it emotional or tangible, than others. But even the smallest act of deceit necessarily means manipulating the opinions or intentions of another person. Lying, to put it plainly, just isn't very nice.

Perhaps for this reason, it's tempting to idealize a world of total honesty. We can imagine an alternate reality in which politicians would always tell us exactly what they would do if elected, we would always get accurate-to-the-penny estimates on repair work, and if a date promised to call, he or she would call. We could trust everyone we met, they could be confident in trusting us, and this mutual trust would be the foundation for fuller, more intimate relationships.

While this scenario is undoubtedly appealing, it reflects a misunderstanding as to why people deviate from the truth in the first place. Again, lying isn't very nice. But we shouldn't assume that the reason most people tell lies is that *they* are not very nice, either.

To understand better what motivates a good deal of deception, let's consider what a purely honest society might actually look like. Brad Blanton, a Virginia psychotherapist, is the founder of a movement known as Radical Honesty. According to the tenets of Radical Honesty, one should never, under any circumstances, lie in a personal relationship, nor accept the lies of others. Instead, adherents to Radical Honesty are taught to express every underlying thought and emotion, even anger, resentment, and outright loathing.

While proponents of Radical Honesty do not argue that people should go out of their way to be confrontational, they do suggest that total honesty is the precursor of psychological health and happiness. According to Radical Honesty, if someone asks you how you like their new spouse and you find her obnoxious and unattractive, you should say so. If a friend is worried that his troubled child might not be okay, you have no right to reassure him unless you really think the child will be okay. Radical Honesty—or, for that matter, any system of total honesty—does not allow for any tailoring of opinion, any well-intentioned shadings of the truth. If the truth is brutal, you need to be brutal, too.

Radical Honesty pokes holes in our idealization of total honesty. No, lying is not very nice. But the *truth* is not necessarily very nice, either. Would we really want to live in a society in which every foible, every flaw, every bad haircut, and every needless purchase would be made nakedly apparent to us? Just as importantly, would we want the responsibility of making such information apparent to our closest friends and family members? And are we always sufficiently in touch with our true feelings to ensure that we can always be truthful, even if we wished to be honest all the time?

For most of us, the answer to such questions is a firm no. A key element of dealing with lies is understanding that a great deal of deception is well-intentioned. People lie to us to protect our feelings. They lie to us out of loyalty to the bonds we share with them. And very often, they lie to us because they realize that we actually want to be lied to.

This is not to suggest that we should be passive in seeking the truth. Nor should we be unthinking in telling well-intentioned lies to others. But coping with deceit means understanding deceit, both how it occurs and why it occurs. The liars in our lives might be everyone we know. Crucially, however, this does not mean that everyone we know is mean-spirited or disreputable or even necessarily untrustworthy. It may be sincere affection that leads other people to tell us lies.

In other cases, the emotional stakes behind a lie can be very low. Some lies serve merely to keep a conversation moving, such as when a colleague falsely tells you she has heard of the restaurant you ate at, simply to keep your anecdote moving forward. Other deception has much more to do with the teller than the recipient of the lie. Lying can be an almost spontaneous response to what psychologists call an upward comparison, a situation in which an individual feels compared to someone smarter, or prettier, or just plain better by whatever the criterion might be. In such circumstances many people turn to deceit, offering false bravado as an automatic, sometimes even nearly subconscious defense to their threatened sense of self-worth. Finally, a good deal of lying occurs in the normal course of self-presentation, the process whereby we select which of our reactions and impulses to express to other people. Socially sensitive people will often hide, say, their loathing of a boss at her birthday celebration because basic civility, not to mention professional considerations, weighs against fully honest expression.

To deal with dishonesty we need to recognize that its ubiquity is tied less to society's lapsed morals and instead has more to do with the great *utility* of deceit. Where honesty would interrupt a conversation, fray a relationship, or make a social situation uncomfortable, deception (sometimes, at least) can help a conversation continue naturally, keep a relationship warm, and relax a social situation.

Again, though, while it's important to understand the more benign uses of deception, we shouldn't become convinced of deception's ultimate harmlessness. Even when lying is convenient, even when it is kinder than the truth, it can exact a toll. Social psychologist Bella DePaulo, who has carried out extensive research on deception, has identified in her work the "twinge of distress" lying can cause. This occurs not necessarily for the target of the lie, who might not notice the deception. Rather, the person who experiences the twinge is the *teller* of the lie. Putting one over on a friend, on a loved one, even on a new acquaintance can make the liar feel at least somewhat guilty, at least to some degree less connected to the person he or she deceives. DePaulo's twinge of distress means that liars can be victims of deceit as much as those they target.

Examining protective or well-intentioned lies from the perspective of the person they fool reveals another of their hazards. It might preserve our self-esteem to be told, falsely, that our suit is flattering when it isn't, that our renovated kitchen looks great when it doesn't. But at some point, we may want to know the truth that is apparent to the rest of the world. The compassion that prompts friends, for instance, to let us persist in the idea that we have real singing talent doesn't do us much good when we are getting booed off stage during the local open-mic night. Yet we can't easily signal to others the truths we want to know and the truths from which we want to be shielded. Indeed, this distinction may not even be clear to us.

Hence, it remains important, for practical as well as ethical reasons, to be vigilant in seeking out the truth. Lying may serve many functions, but so too does recognizing honesty. In many ways, when we try to sort out the truth from lies, the deck is stacked against us. Nonetheless, there are tactics we can employ to make ourselves better equipped to grapple with lies.

Defensive Driving in Our Social Lives: Active Honesty Assessment

Most adults in the United States know how to drive. But there are also those special few among us who describe themselves as *defensive drivers*. These drivers are masters of more than just the rules of the road. Like the rest of us, they follow the speed limit and signal their turns. But they take their mastery of driving a step further. They employ tactics and watch for cues that make them even less likely than an ordinary driver to be caught up in an accident. They gauge the distance between their car and the car ahead so that even if it stops suddenly, they will have time to break. They decelerate with practiced slowness at stop signs. They look left, right, then left again before entering an intersection. Of course, even defensive drivers have accidents. There are some things even the savviest drivers can't control. But defensive drivers take all the extra precautions they can to keep themselves, and their fellow motorists, safe.

People are not very good at detecting lies. Study after study has shown that the average person has barely a 50 percent chance of telling if a statement is true or false. Even such trained professionals as FBI agents and police officers typically don't perform any better than the rest of us. Further, there are no universal clues that tip a liar's hand. If a person averts his gaze or fidgets in his seat, he might be lying, or he might be nervous, or he might have to use the bathroom. There is just no reliable connection between behavior and deception.

In other words, it is not easy to tell when we are being lied to. Even beyond what's described above, there are numerous other components of the Liar's Advantage, the edge that liars have in fooling us. We might be able to mitigate some of these factors, but ultimately it's impossible to level the lying playing field between ourselves and those who seek to fool us. The fact of the matter is, sooner or later someone is going to successfully deceive us.

Yet just as with defensive drivers who know that, while they might not be able to escape every accident, they can at least minimize their risk of accidents, so too can we, while still being susceptible to lies, minimize the Liar's Advantage and make ourselves harder (if not necessarily hard) to fool. There are tactics we can employ and attitudes we can adopt that will make lying to us more difficult—less likely to be attempted and, if attempted, less likely to succeed. I call this posture toward deceit Active Honesty Assessment, or AHA—or, more familiarly, Aha!, the cry that celebrates discovered truth. We are not destined to be the victim of every lie and liar. By employing Active Honesty Assessment, we have the power to lessen the deception we live with.

The first essential piece of Active Honesty Assessment is one we're already familiar with. To determine when someone is lying, we need to know *why* people usually lie. Conventional wisdom holds that people lie when they want to cheat us out of money or hide something they've done. The reality of the motivations behind deceit is, again, far more complex. Lies can, and do, occur in nearly every social situation, serving to calm insecurities, move a conversation along, follow rules of tact, and so forth.

Knowing that lies commonly occur in so many contexts means that we need to be consistently vigilant in searching for them. We can't, for example, let down our guard in conversations in which there is nothing tangible or important at stake. Lies aren't limited to negotiations or arguments about money, nor to serious conversations about what someone might or might not have done. Even the most mundane interactions usually contain lies. Admittedly, some lies really may not be worth ferreting out. Is it really important, for example, to determine that our friend in the office actually doesn't remember the guy from accounting who got fired the year before? Just as some conversations contain only trivial content, so too do some falsehoods. Yet the comparison between defensive driving and Active Honesty Assessment is again useful. It may seem tedious to refrain from passing on the right in certain situations. But the idea of defensive driving and the idea of AHA both involve a commitment to certain practices that, while at times seemingly unnecessary, in the long run reduce the likelihood of our falling victim to accidents and lies, respectively.

Related to this tactic of constant vigilance in looking out for lies is another important element of AHA. The Liar's Advantage has a range of components. One of its most stubborn is the fact that all of us operate with the cognitive rule of thumb known as the truth bias. The truth bias means that we don't judge the information we receive objectively. Instead, we assume that what we hear or read or see is true. The benefit of the truth bias is that it makes our cognitive workings more efficient:

we don't spend our mental energy critiquing new information; instead, we employ our brains in other ways. The downside of the truth bias, of course, is that sometimes we *should* critique what we hear, because very often people lie to us.

The truth bias, though, is not something we can turn on or off. It is an unconscious element of how we think. In a sense, our default prejudice is toward belief, and it is not a prejudice we can rid ourselves of. The best way to counteract the truth bias is to employ what can be thought of as a *falsehood bias*. This does not mean that you should assume that everything you are told is a lie. Instead, maintain an awareness that everything you are told *could* be a lie. Rather than just passively trusting, try to enact a process of verification. This active scrutiny will help you counteract the workings of the truth bias.

Again, though, even if you do your best to assess whether a statement is true or false, research suggests that you won't necessarily have much success. It is just very hard to tell when someone is lying, particularly with regard to a person you don't know well. And even if you can identify a particular tic or clue to an individual's deceit, if that individual learns of that tic, it will likely disappear quickly, or even be used against you.

Rather than focusing, then, on determining if information you receive is a lie based on the mannerisms of the person who offers it, employ other, more reliable forms of verification. The falsehood bias suggests that we should independently verify everything we are told. After all, if we assume that what we hear could be a lie, shouldn't we try to find out for certain? Naturally, there are practical limits to this approach. We have neither the time nor the cognitive capacity to research the veracity of every slice of information. Doing so would not even be the equivalent in defensive driving of sticking to the slow lane. It would be the equivalent of never starting your car. We may worry about deception, but we should not allow this worry to cripple our social interactions past the point of recognition.

A useful rule of thumb is this: If we care enough about a piece information to verify it, then verify it. If we don't, then, well, don't. It's possible that the man who sells us our morning cup of coffee might be lying when he says it's his wife's birthday, but really, who cares? On the other hand, if we hear a rumor that affects our working life or a surprising detail about a presidential candidate's past, it's probably worth finding out for ourselves—as best we can—if the story is true.

A key to AHA is becoming more comfortable with uncertainty. If we want to face the ubiquity of deception in modern life, we simply have to stop believing, without consideration, everything we hear. To put it another way, we have to accustom our palates to the proverbial grain of salt.

AHA goes beyond how we assess information from others, though. It also involves changing our own relationship to lies. Perhaps the most powerful aspect of the Liar's Advantage is that there are many times when we not only don't notice lies but we don't even want to notice them. We are frequently all too susceptible to the reassuring lie, the false compliment. When we ask a colleague how our presentation went, when we ask our spouse how we look in the morning, it's not necessarily the truth we are seeking. It can be emotional comfort; it can be a balm for our imperiled ego. Regardless of the specifics, in such situations lies are something we actually embrace. The liar wants to fool us, and we want to be fooled.

Obviously, in order to deal with daily deception, we need to end our reliance on reassuring falsehoods. Or if not end it, then at least be aware of it. For all of us, there are situations in which what we want is not an objective evaluation but, rather, the support of friends or loved ones. We need to make a distinction in our minds as to which category our ostensibly truth-seeking behavior falls. The best course may be to find the support all of us need from time to time in an honest way. This will spare us exposure to lies, and will spare those we care about having to deceive us.

There is no sure way to control whether or not someone lies to us. But we can do our best to make clear the times when we truly desire to hear the truth, painful though it may be. Simple phrases like "I won't be offended if you don't like this" or "It's important to me that I look good today, so please tell the truth" can be very effective ways of laying the groundwork for honesty. We also need to be aware that, even despite these phrases, sometimes people in our lives will spare themselves the cognitive effort and emotional risk the truth demands and just give us an offhand lie. Again, the key is to employ Active Honesty Assessment. Be sensitive to the times when others might be tempted to spare your feelings—or their own—via deceit.

As I mentioned earlier, even the most defensive drivers can get in car wrecks. And even the most careful and consistent application of AHA won't stop us from being deceived. Unfortunately, AHA can't make us immune to the kinds of lies we most fear: the lies that betray us, the lies that break our hearts and take advantage of our trust. It's not inevitable that we will be hurt in this way. But if we are, it's worth asking: If we can't escape lies, can we at least recover from them?

Learning to Trust Again

There is probably no way to overstate the emotional and psychological pain that accompanies a major violation of trust. Couples therapists have increasingly come to understand that the reaction to major betrayals of trust such as infidelity is often similar in degree to the psychological pain that follows war traumas, the death of a partner, or rape. And perhaps the worst consequence is that this pain is not limited to the context of the particular lie or lies. We often speak of "shattered" or "broken" trust. This language suggests something that anyone who has suffered significant betrayal knows well: the damage of a lie impairs our ability to trust anyone, in just about any context. It's as if a lie breaks our internal trust mechanism.

Hence, recovering from a lie is not just a matter of filing a police report or challenging a credit card charge, of going through with a divorce or explaining to the children why Mommy or Daddy has moved out. These are necessary, painful steps, but beyond the practical requirements of dealing with a lie, recovering means recovering our ability to trust. And this, unfortunately, is often the hardest step.

One key to regaining the ability to trust involves coming to a better understanding of what trust really represents. We too often think of trust as a kind of inner divining rod, pointing us toward more honest people and more honest relationships. Then, when we are betrayed, we spend far too much mental and emotional energy berating ourselves for our "flawed" sense of who is trustworthy. But trust does not lead us to honest people—it is, rather, the faith we have in other people's honesty. We need to accept that we *can't* know who is telling us the truth. Trust is the act of believing in other people despite this knowledge.

If we think of trust as a form of faith, the challenges toward restoring it become clearer. The issue is not finding someone who can convince us (again) that they would never lie to us. Rather, it is taking the leap to believe that there is anyone out there who would not lie to us in a significant way.

Taking this leap after we have been duped or wronged requires a lot of courage. Whereas before a major betrayal trust might have been a visceral, natural impulse, we may find that following such betrayal, trust is more of a conscious choice. But if the later acts of trust are less romantic, they are also by definition more realistic. We may not be able to trust like a child anymore—but once we enter adulthood, we probably shouldn't anyway.

For couples who have worked through, or are trying to work through, the pain of infidelity, the restored trust has a very specific object. The wronged party has to find a way to believe in, and simply believe, his or her partner. Trust is a necessary part of any healthy relationship. But it may be unwise for couples to try to trust each other "the way they did before." For one thing, this is often impossible. More importantly, though, *renewed* trust—trust that is the result of a choice and effort as opposed to an impulse—can in some ways be stronger than the former variety. If both partners understand that trust is not permanent, that it comes from labor and commitment, they might very well value this trust more than they did their previous version. Thus it is possible, in some cases, for betrayal to acutally strengthen a relationship.

For those who choose to continue their post-betrayal life without their betrayer, the challenges of restoring trust are somewhat different. These individuals don't need to trust someone else *again*—they need to be able to offer trust in the first place. For them, there is no apologetic partner to ease this process. They must find a way to make the leap of trust on their own. The path of each individual toward restored trust is very different. Perhaps even the leap metaphor itself is misleading. Sometimes, trust is restored slowly, incrementally—day by day, perhaps even truth by truth. For others, it *can* be a leap: a decision to risk betrayal in the name of a fully engaged relationship.

The essential thing to realize is that betrayal is not a life sentence. Trust can be restored, with time and effort. This effort may be formal, inculding therapy or marital counseling, or informal and idiosynchratic. But no one should begin the process of repairing their ability to trust feeling that the exercise is futile. Our faith in other people may at times seem fragile—but it has also proved resilient.

The recovery from betrayal and the preventative tactics of AHA both represent only one side of the coin of dealing with deception. There is another, more sensitive side to this coin, as well. We not only encounter lies—we *tell* lies. If we want to fully address the liars in our lives, we need to acknowledge the one staring at us in the mirror.

Being Honest About Being Honest

There's a dirty secret I've been trying to avoid emphasizing in this book, but it's about time we faced it. All of us are liars. Yes, that means you. And yes, it means me, too. Our lies may not be significant or intentionally hurtful, but all of us, even the most dedicated practitioners of Radical Honesty, indulge in deceit to some degree.

In many ways, this is socially appropriate. As we know, deception forms a common part of ordinary social interactions. It is embedded in the idea of tact and helps protect other people from upsetting truths. If we didn't lie, we would probably be considered socially awkward, not to mention something of jerk.

On the other hand, we can't forget the potential damage to relationships that lies can create, the twinge of regret that comes from even the most minor deception, or simply the guilt that can come from lying. And, quite apart from the social utility of lying, there is the moral value of truthfulness that we teach our children and about which philosophers have argued for centuries.

Moreover, it's impossible to anticipate the consequences a lie can have, even the best-intentioned one. We may be lying for good-hearted reasons when we tell a friend he's an excellent dancer. When he humiliates himself at the office holiday party, though, we are culpable.

We need to strike a balance when we seek to reduce the deception we perpetrate. Though extremes may be tempting, they are best avoided. We can't maintain anything like a normally functioning relationship with other people if we lie to them whenever it is convenient or rub a harsh truth in their faces simply because we have decided never to lie.

The principles of AHA encourage attention to when others might be lying to us. Perhaps we ought to apply a parallel strategy to our own discourse. Too often, lying is something we do automatically, unthinkingly. When a friend asks how we're doing, we offer the same, essentially automated response, regardless of our mood: "I'm great." A coworker asks if she should be worried about her job, and rather than explain the latest complications of office politics, we answer in a way that saves us time and falsely reassures her: "Nah, you're okay."

Though we seem to have built its neglect into our society, the truth has value. The surest way to respect that value is not through an obsessive scrutiny of every single thing we hear but, rather, through a careful scrutiny of every single thing we *say*. Again, this does not mean Radical Honesty. It does mean choosing our lies as carefully as we choose the moments when we are fully, unreservedly honest.

Frequently, we may tell ourselves we are lying to protect the feelings of another person. As in the example of the worried coworker, though, this protection cuts both ways. What saves the target of the lie emotional pain just about always saves its teller social inconvenience. In other words, there is very often a selfish aspect to the lies we tell. If we're going to use altruism as an excuse for manipulation (and, again, that's what lying is), it seems appropriate that we be sure that altruism, and not its opposite, really is the motive.

We need lies—at least, for the foreseeable future. We can't rebuild society using a purely honest model (and probably wouldn't want to). But rebuilding society using a *more* honest model can begin with a commitment of each individual to do something very simple: try to lie less. The truth can be inconvenient; it can be awkward and even hurtful. But there is also an undeniable satisfaction to telling the truth, not to mention to hearing it. Further, the truth has practical benefits. We and those around us can judge our opinions and our behaviors not by a convenient (or nefarious) fiction but by the clear light of fact.

Honesty may not be a perfect, universally applicable policy—but it is still the *best* policy.

Acknowledgments

The research I describe in this book would not have been possible without the hard work, ideas, ingenuity, and intelligence of a group of superb students with whom I've been lucky enough to work over the last three decades. They include John Blanchette, Erik Coats, Richard Chesley, Robert Custrini, Joel Feinman, James Forrest, Naomi Goldstein, Benjamin Happ, Daniel Hrubes, Sarah Levine, Pierre Philippot, Christopher Poirier, Darren Spielman, James Tyler, Brent Weiss, John White, and Mattitiyahu Zimbler. I thank each of them for going way beyond the call of duty and turning work into play.

I'd also like to thank my colleagues in the field of psychology who have, with brilliance and great insight, sought to understand why people lie, and who have shared their insights in numerous articles, books, and e-mails. I'm thankful, as well, to my friends, colleagues, and acquaintances who have shared stories of personal deception with me. Although I have disguised your identities within the pages of this book—thank me later—your personal stores have brought to life the topic of lying.

I've also been the beneficiary of advice, suggestions, and intellectual stimulation from many colleagues at the University of

Massachusetts, Amherst, most of all my office neighbors (past and present) on the sixth floor of Tobin Hall. These include Icek Aizen, Jim Averill, Nilanjan Dasgupta, Sy Epstein, Susan Fiske, Linda Isbell, George Levinger, Ronnie Janoff-Bulman, Paula Pietromonaco, and Ervin Staub. I'm enormously grateful to Janet Rifkin, who, despite luring me away from Tobin, provided support and encouragement and gave me the opportunity to write this book. I could not have asked for better colleagues or friends.

Jonathan Karp, my editor at Twelve, offered thoughtful and insightful feedback, and his constant flow of ideas was a source of great inspiration. He is not only a tremendous editor but a very smart and funny guy. And my fine agent, Gillian MacKenzie, provided encouragement, direction, and just the right amount of prodding. Her finely tuned sense of what works and what doesn't helped turn a vague, unformed idea into a book.

My editorial assistants, Tolley Jones and John Graiff, provided the research support that made it possible for me to complete this book, tracking down obscure articles and statistics. I am grateful for their unflagging enthusiasm in the face of unreasonable demands.

Several individuals taught me about good writing, and their tutelage remains reflected in every word of this book. I'm grateful to Rhona Robbin and Judith Kromm, my all-time favorite developmental editors. Furthermore, I'm thankful to Joshua Feldman, whose brilliant writing skills continue to astonish me and who has taught me so much about the craft and art of fine writing. Their fingerprints can be found on every page of this book.

Finally, my wife, Katherine Vorwerk, deserves the ultimate thanks. Her love, encouragement, and patience mean everything to me, and she knows that I'm not lying when I say that.

SOURCES

CHAPTER 1. Everyday Inventions of Everyday Life

Campbell, J. 2001. *The Liar's Tale: A History of Falsehood*. New York: Norton.

DePaulo, B. M., and D. A. Kashy. 1998. "Everyday Lies in Close and Casual Relationships." *Journal of Personality and Social Psychology* 74: 63–79.

DePaulo, B. M., D. A. Kashy, S. E. Kirkendol, M. M. Wyer, and J. A. Epstein. 1996. "Lying in Everyday Life." *Journal of Personality and Social Psychology* 70: 979–95.

Ekman, P. 2001. *Telling Lies: Clues to Deceit in the Marketplace, Politics, and Marriage*. New York: Norton.

Feldman, R. S., J. A. Forrest, and B. R. Happ. 2002. "Self-Presentation and Verbal Deception: Do Self-Presenters Lie More?" *Basic and Applied Social Psychology* 24: 163–70.

Gozna, L. F., A. Vrij, and R. Bull. 2001. "The Impact of Individual Differences on Perceptions of Lying in Everyday Life and in a High Stake Situation." *Personality and Individual Differences* 31: 1203–16.

Kaplar, M. E., and A. K. Gordon. 2004. "The Enigma of Altruistic Lying: Perspective Differences in What Motivates and Justifies Lie Telling Within Romantic Relationships." *Personal Relationships* 11: 489–507.

Robinson, W. P. 1996. *Deceit, Delusion, and Detection.* London: Sage Publications.

Smith, E. A. 2007. "'It's interesting how few people die from smoking': Tobacco industry efforts to minimize risk and discredit health promotion." *European Journal of Public Health* 17: 162–70.

Vrij, A., M. Floyd, and E. Ennis. 2003. "Telling Lies to Strangers or Close Friends: Its Relationship with Attachment Style." In *Advances in Psychology Research*, ed. S. P. Shohov, pp. 61–73. Hauppauge, N.Y.: Noca Science Publishers.

CHAPTER 2. The Liar's Advantage

Barron, J., and M. A. Farber. 1991. "Tracing a Devious Path to the Ivy League." *New York Times.* March 4. B1.

Bond, C. F., Jr., and B. M. DePaulo. 2006. "Accuracy of Deception Judgements." *Personality and Social Psychology Review.* 10: 214–34.

———. 2008. "Individual Differences in Judging Deception: Accuracy and Bias." *Psychological Bulletin* 134: 477–92.

Cherkashin, Victor, and Gregory Feifer. 2005. *Spy Handler: Memoir of a KGB Officer; The True Story of the Man Who Recruited Robert Hanssen and Aldrich Ames.* New York: Basic Books.

Cohen, L. P. 2008. "The Polygraph Paradox." *Wall Street Journal.* March 22. A1.

Committee to Review the Scientific Evidence on the Polygraph, National Research Council. 2003. *The Polygraph and Lie Detection.* Washington, D.C.: National Academies Press.

Ekman, E. P., M. O'Sullivan, and M. C. Frank. 1999. "A Few Can Catch a Liar." *Psychological Science* 10: 263–66.

Goode, E. 1999. "To Tell the Truth, It's Awfully Hard to Spot a Liar." *New York Times.* May 11. F1.

Kawagoe, T., and H. Takizawa. 2005. "Why Lying Pays: Truth Bias in the Communication with Conflicting Interests." January 15. Available at SSRN: http://ssrn.com/abstract=691641.

Keppel, Robert. 2004. *The Riverman: Ted Bundy and I Hunt for the Green River Killer.* New York: Pocket.

Sources

Levine, T. R., H. S. Park, and S. A. McCornack. 1999. "Accuracy in Detecting Truths and Lies: Documenting the 'Veracity Effect.'" *Communication Monographs* 66: 125–44.

Masip, J., E. Garrido, and C. Herrero. 2006. "Observers' Decision Moment in Deception Detection Experiments: Its Impact on Judgement, Accuracy, and Confidence." *International Journal of Psychology* 41: 304–19. Special issue: "The Indigenous Psychologies."

O'Sullivan, M., and P. Ekman. 2004. "The Wizards of Deception Detection." In *The Detection of Deception in Forensic Contexts*, ed. P. Granhag and L. Stromwall, pp. 269–86. New York: Cambridge University Press.

Samuels, D. 2001. "Profiles: The Runner." *New Yorker*. September 3. 72.

Schaivo, C. 2004. "Nurse Set to Plead Guilty Today to 3 Warren County Murders." *Philadelphia Enquirer*. May 19. B01.

Stiff, J. B., H. J. Kim, and C. N. Ramesh. 1992. "Truth Biases and Aroused Suspicion in Relational Deception." *Communication Research* 19: 326–45.

Suro, R. 1997. "Justice Department: FBI May Have Violated Jewell's Rights." *Washington Post*. July 29. A03.

Talbot, M. 2007. "Duped: Can Brain Scans Uncover Lies?" *New Yorker*. July 2. 52.

Temple-Raston, D. 2007. "Neuroscientist Uses Brain Scan to See Lies Form." *Morning Edition*, National Public Radio. October 30.

Vonk, R. 2002. "Self-serving Interpretations of Flattery: Why Ingratiation Works." *Journal of Personality and Social Psychology* 82: 515–26.

CHAPTER 3. Deception 101: How Children Learn to Lie

Bronson, P. 2008. "Learning to Lie." *New York Magazine*. February 10.

Clowes, G. A. 2004. "Survey Results: Student Attitudes Toward Cheating." *School Reform News*. February.

Custrini, R. S., and R. S. Feldman. 1989. "Children's Social Competence and Nonverbal Encoding and Decoding of Emotion." *Journal of Clinical Child Psychology* 18: 336–42.

Feldman, R. S., L. Jenkins, and O. Popoola. 1979. "Detection of Deception in Adults and Children via Facial Expressions." *Child Development* 50: 350–55.

Fu, G., and K. Lee. 2007. "Social Grooming in the Kindergarten: The Emergence of Flattery Behavior." *Developmental Science* 10: 255–65.

Fur, G., A. D. Evans, L. Wang, and K. Lee. 2008. "Lying in the Name of the Collective Good: A Developmental Study." *Developmental Science* 11: 495–503.

Josephson Institute of Ethics. 2006. "Josephson Institute Report Card on the Ethics of American Youth. Part One, Integrity: Summary of Data." Retrieved November 13, 2008 from http://josephson-institute.org/pdf/ReportCard_press-release_2006-1013.pdf.

McCabe, D., L. K. Trevino, and K. D. Butterfield. 2004. "Academic Integrity: How Widespread Are Cheating and Plagiarism?" In *Restorative Justice on the College Campus: Promoting Student Growth and Responsibility, and Reawakening the Spirit of Campus Community,* ed. D. R. Karp and T. Allena. Springfield, Ill.: Charles C. Thomas.

Philippot, P., and R. S. Feldman. 1990. "Age and Social Competence in Preschoolers' Decoding of Facial Expression." *British Journal of Social Psychology* 29: 43–54.

Price, M. 2008. "Liar, Liar, Neurons Fire." *Monitor on Psychology* 39: 30.

Reddy, V. 2005. "Feeling Shy and Showing-off: Self-conscious Emotions Must Regulate Self-awareness. In *Emotional Development: Recent Research Advances,* ed. J. Nadel and D. Muir, pp. 183–204. New York: Oxford University Press.

Rousseau, Jean-Jacques. 1762. *Emile, or On Education.* Trans. Allan Bloom. New York: Basic Books, 1979.

Talwar, V., and K. Lee. 2008. "Social and Cognitive Correlates of Children's Lying Behavior." *Child Development* 79: 866–81.

Sources

Tyre, P. 2007. "To Catch a Cheat." *Newsweek*. October 15. 41.

Wang, S., and S. Aamodt, 2008. "Your Brain Lies to You." *New York Times*. June 27. A19.

CHAPTER 4. The Evolution of Deceit: Are We Born to Lie?

Adenzato, M. 2001. "The Approach of Evolutionary Psychology to the Study of Human Cognitive Architecture: The Case of Deception." *Sistemi Intelligenti* 13: 53–76.

Andrews, P. W. 2001. "The Psychology of Social Chess and the Evolution of Attribution Mechanisms: Explaining the Fundamental Attribution Error." *Evolution and Human Behavior* 22: 11–29.

Brockway, R. 2003. "Evolving to Be Mentalists: The 'Mind-Reading Mums' Hypothesis." In *From Mating to Mentality: Evaluating Evolutionary Psychology*, ed. K. Sterelny, Kim and J. Fitness, pp. 95–123. New York: Psychology Press.

Byrne, R. 2002. "Social and Technical Forms of Primate Intelligence." In *Tree of Origin: What Primate Behavior Can Tell Us About Human Social Evolution*, ed. F. B. M. de Waal, pp. 145–72. Cambridge: Harvard University Press.

Byrne, R. W., and A. Whiten. 1992. "Cognitive Evolution in Primates: Evidence from Tactical Deception." *Man* 27: 609–27.

CBS News. 2005. "Lottery Scam Targets Elderly." *60 Minutes*. June 12.

Darwin, C. 1884. *On the Origin of the Species*. New York: D. Appleton.

McKay, R., R. Langdon, and M. Coltheart. 2005. "'Sleights of Mind': Delusions, Defences, and Self-deception." *Cognitive Neuropsychiatry* 10: 305–26.

Platek, S., and S. L. Levin. 2005. "Only the Mean Survive?" *Cortex* 41: 705–07. Special issue: "Consciousness, Mind and Brain."

Platek, S. M., and T. K. Shackelford, eds. 2006. *Female Infidelity and Paternal Uncertainty: Evolutionary Perspectives on Male Anti-cuckoldry Tactics*. New York: Cambridge University Press.

Plooij, F. X. 1984. "The Behavioral Development of Free-Living Chimpanzee Babies and Infants." *Monographs on Infancy*. 207.

Rosas, A. 2004. "Mind Reading, Deception and the Evolution of Kantian Moral Agents." *Journal for the Theory of Social Behaviour* 34: 127–39.

Searcy, W. A. and S. Nowicki. 2005. *The Evolution of Animal Communication: Reliability and Deception in Signaling Systems.* Princeton: Princeton University Press.

Smith, D. L. 2004. "Why We Lie. The Evolutionary Roots of Deception and the Unconscious Mind." *Psychoanalytic Psychotherapy* 19: 330–32.

Spinney, L. 1998. "Liar! Liar!" *New Scientists.* February 14. 22–26.

Trivers, R. 2000. "The Elements of a Scientific Theory of Self-deception: Evolutionary Perspectives on Human Reproductive Behavior." *Annals of the New York Academy of Sciences* 907: 114–31.

Van Leeuwen, D. S. N. 2007. "The Spandrels of Self-deception: Prospects for a Biological Theory of a Mental Phenomenon." *Philosophical Psychology* 20: 329–48.

Zimmer, C. 2006. "Devious Butterflies, Full-Throated Frogs, and Other Liars." *New York Times.* December 26. F1.

CHAPTER 5. Broken Trust: Loving a Liar

Alan, R. 2006. *First Aid for the Betrayed.* Victoria, B.C.: Trafford Publishing.

Borash, David P., Quoted in N. Angier. 2008. "In Most Species, Faithfulness Is a Fantasy." *New York Times,* March 18. F1.

Blow, A. J., and K. Hartnett. 2005. "Infidelity in Committed Relationships, I and II: A Substantive Review." *Journal of Marital and Family Therapy* 31: 217–33.

Boon, S. D. and B. A. McLeod. 2001. "Deception in Romantic Relationships: Subjective Estimates of Success at Deceiving and Attitudes Toward Deception." *Journal of Social and Personal Relationships* 18: 463–76.

Cole, T. 2001. "Lying to the One You Love: The Use of Deception in Romantic Relationships." *Journal of Social and Personal Relationships* 18:107–29.

Sources

Cole, Tim. 2005. "Deception Confidence in Romantic Relationships: Confidently Lying to the One You Love." *Advances in Psychology Research*. 34: 127–39.

Drigotas, S. M., and W. Barta. 2001. "The Cheating Heart: Scientific Explorations of Infidelity." *Directions in Psychological Science*. 10: 177–80.

———, C. A. Safstrom, and T. Gentilia. 1999. "An Investment Model Prediction of Dating Infidelity." *Journal of Personality and Social Psychology* 77: 509–24.

Duncombe, J. K. Harrison, G. Allan, and D. Marsden. 2004. "The State of Affairs: Explorations in Infidelity and Commitment. In *LEA's Series on Personal Relationships*, ed. J. Duncombe., K. Harrison., G. Allan., and D. Marsden. Mahwah, N.J.: Lawrence Erlbaum Associates.

Fife, S. T., G. R. Weeks, and N. Gambecia. 2008. "Treating Infidelity: An Integrative Aproach." *Family Journal* 15: 316–23.

Gillespie, M. 2001. "Americans Consider Infidelity Wrong, but Acknowledge Its Prevalence in Society." Gallup News Service. July 10.

Jones, W.H., D. S. Moore, A. Schratter, and L. A. Negel. 2001. "Interpersonal Transgressions and Betrayals." In *Behaving Badly: Aversive Behaviors in Interpersonal Relationships*, ed. R. M. Kowalski, pp. 233–56. Washington, D.C.: American Psychological Association.

Kowalski, R. M., S. Walker, R. Wilkinson, A. Queen, and B. Sharpe. 2003. "Lying, Cheating, Complaining, and Other Aversive Interpersonal Behaviors: A Narrative Examination of the Darker Side of Relationships." *Journal of Social and Personal Relationships*, 20: 471–90.

Lusterman, D. 2001. "Treating Betrayal Issues After the Discovery of Marital Infidelity." *NYS Psychologist* 13: 13–16.

Schlessinger, L. Quoted in Stanley, A. 2008. "Mars and Venus Dissect the Spitzer Scandal on TV Talk Shows. *New York Times*. March 12. E1.

Schmitt, D. P., and T. K. Shackelford. 2003. "Nifty Ways to Leave

Your Lover: The Tactics People Use to Entice and Disguise the Process of Human Mate Poaching." *Personality and Social Psychology Bulletin* 29: 1018–35.

VanderVoot, L., and S. Duck. 2004. "Sex, Lies, and…Transformation." In *The State of Affairs: Explorations in Infidelity and Commitment*, ed. J. Duncombe, K. Harrison, G. Allan, and D. Marsden, pp. 1–13. Mahwah, N.J.: Lawrence Erlbaum Associates.

Vangelisti, A. L. 2006. "Lying and Deception in Close Relationships." In *The Cambridge Handbook of Personal Relationships*, ed. M. Knapp and D. Perlman, pp. 517–32. New York: Cambridge University Press.

Warren, J.A., M. M. Morgan, S. L. Williams, and T. L. Mansfield. 2008. "The Poisoned Tree: Infidelity as Opportunity for Transformation." *Family Journal* 16: 351–58.

Wenner, M. 2008. "The Merry Band of Wrigglers: Men, Women, Passion, and Sperm." *Slate*. February 13. Retrieved on November 14, 2008 from http://www.slate.com/id/2184363/.

Williams, S. S., and G. H. Payne. 2002. "Perceptions of Own Sexual Lies Influenced by Characteristics of Liar, Sex Partner, and Lie Itself." *Journal of Sex and Marital Therapy* 28: 257–67.

CHAPTER 6. Self-Deception: The Lies We Tell Ourselves

Baumeister, R. F. 1993. "Lying to Yourself: The Enigma of Self-Deception." In *Lying and Deception in Everyday Life*, ed. M. Lewis and C. Saarni, pp. 166–83. New York: Guilford Press.

———. 2007. "Denial Makes the World Go Round." *New York Times*. November 20. F1.

Carey, B. 2008. "I'm Not Lying, I'm Telling a Future Truth. Really." *New York Times*. May 6. F5.

Chronicle Review. 2007. "Lying to Ourselves." *Chronicle of Higher Education*. August 10. B2.

Erber, R., and U. DePaul. 2002. "Perpetrators with a Clear Conscience: Lying Self-deception and Belief Change." In *Understand-*

ing Genocide: The Social Psychology of the Holocaust, ed. L. S. Newman and R. Erber, New York: Oxford University Press.

Fairbanks, R. A. 1991. "Belief, Deception, and Self-deception." *Dissertation Abstracts International* 51(8-A): 2770.

Festinger, L., and J. M. Carlsmith. 1959. "Cognitive Consequences of Forced Compliance." *Journal of Abnormal and Social Psychology* 58: 203–11.

Ford, C. V. 1996. *"Lies! Lies! Lies!: The Psychology of Deceit."* Washington, D.C.: American Psychiatric Association.

Gramzow, R. H., and G. Willard. 2006. "Exaggerating Current and Past Performance: Motivated Self-enhancement Versus Reconstructive Memory." *Personality and Social Psychology Bulletin* 32: 1114–25.

———. W. B. Mendes. 2008. "Big Tales and Cool Heads: Academic Exaggeration Is Related to Cardiac Vagal Reactivity." *Emotion* 8: 138–44.

Grubin, D. 2005. "Commentary: Getting at the Truth About Pathological Lying." *Journal of the American Academy of Psychiatry and the Law* 33: 350–53.

Hirstein, W. 2005. *Brain Fiction: Self-Deception and the Riddle of Confabulation.* Cambridge: MIT Press.

Jacobson, A. S. 2005. "The Effect of Fluctuating Asymmetry and Attractiveness on Self-perception, Self-deception and Preferences for Others in Rural Jamaica." *Dissertation Abstracts International Section A: Humanities and Social Sciences* 66(5-A): 1839.

Johnson, K. 2006. "Suspect Cleared in Ramsey Case After DNA Tests." *New York Times.* August 29. 1.

Kassin, S., and K. Kiechel. 1996. "The Social Psychology of False Confessions: Compliance, Internalization, and Confabulation." *Psychological Science* 7: 125–28.

Kruger J., and D. Dunning. 1999. "Unskilled and Unaware of It: How Difficulties in Recognizing One's Own Incompetence Lead to Inflated Self-Assessments." *Journal of Personality and Social Psychology* 77: 1121–34.

Larrabee, G. J. 1998. "How We Deceive Ourselves and Others." *PsycCRITIQUES* 43: 439.

Mar, R. A., C. G. DeYoung, D. M. Higgins, and J. B. Peterson. 2006. "Self-Liking and Self-Competence Separate Self-Evaluation from Self-Deception: Associations with Personality, Ability, and Achievement." *Journal of Personality* 74: 1047–78.

Rosenthal, R. J. 1986. "The Pathological Gambler's System for Self-deception." *Journal of Gambling Behavior* 2: 108–20.

Sackeim, H. A., and R. C. Gur. 1979. "Self-deception, Other-deception, and Self-reported Psychopathology." *Journal of Consulting and Clinical Psychology* 47: 213–15.

Safer, M.A., and D. J. Keuler. 2002. "Individual Differences in Misremembering Pre-psychotherapy Distress: Personality and Memory Distortion." *Emotion* 2: 162–78.

Sigmon, S. T., and C. R. Snyder. 1993. "Looking at Oneself in a Rose-colored Mirror: The Role of Excuses in the Negotiation of a Personal Reality." In *Deception and Lying in Everyday Life*, ed. M. Lewis and C. Saarni, pp. 271–86. New York: Guilford Press.

Solomon, R. C. 1993. "What a Tangled Web: Deception and Self-deception in Philosophy." In *Lying and Deception in Everyday Life*, ed. M. Lewis and C. Saarni, pp. 30–58. New York: Guilford Press.

Tavris, C., and E. Aronson. 2007. *Mistakes Were Made (but Not by Me): Why We Justify Foolish Beliefs, Bad Decisions, Hurtful Acts*. Orlando: Harcourt.

Tigner, J. A. 1996. "A Social Conception of Self-deception." *Dissertation Abstracts International Section A: Humanities and Social Sciences* 57(2-A): 0719.

Tyler, J. M., and R. S. Feldman. 2005. "Deflecting Threat to One's Image: Dissembling Personal Information as a Self-presentation Strategy." *Basic and Applied Social Psychology* 27: 371–78.

Vrij, A., K. Edward, and R. Bull. 2001. "People's Insight into Their Own Behaviour and Speech Content While Lying." *British Journal of Psychology*, 92: 373–89.

Sources

CHAPTER 7. Cosmetic Deceit: Lies to Make Us Seem Richer, Smarter, Better

Callander, S., and S. Wilkie. 2007. "Lies, Damned Lies, and Political Campaigns." *Games and Economic Behavior* 60: 262–86.

Davey, M. 2008. "Drug Arrests Were Real; the Badge was Fake." *New York Times.* July 1. A1.

de Bruin, G. P., and H. Rudnick. 2007. "Examining the Cheats: The Role of Conscientiousness and Excitement Seeking in Academic Dishonesty." *South African Journal of Psychology* 37: 153–64.

DePaulo, B. M., J. A. Epstein, and M. M. Wyer. 1993. "Sex Differences in Lying: How Women and Men Deal with the Dilemma of Deceit." *In Lying and Deception in Everyday Life*, ed. M. Lewis and C. Saarni, pp. 126–47. New York: Guilford Press.

Ennis, E., A. Vrij, and C. Chance. 2008. "Individual Differences and Lying in Everyday Life. *Journal of Social and Personal Relationships* 25: 105–18.

Goldman, V. 2007. "Résumés: The Gatekeepers' Gate. *New York Times.* July 29. 4A, p. 4.

Herzog, D. 2006. *Cunning.* Princeton: Princeton University Press.

Hodgin, H. S., E. Liebeskind, and W. Schwartz. 1996. "Getting Out of Hot Water: Facework in Social Predicaments." *Journal of Personality and Social Psychology* 71: 300–14.

Hussain, M. S., and E. Langer. 2003. "A Cost of Pretending." *Journal of Adult Development* 10: 261–70.

Levenson, M. 2007. "Romney Never Saw Father on King March." *Boston Globe.* December 21. A1.

Muscatine, L., and M. Verveer. 2008. "Straight Shooting from Tuzla." *New York Times.* April 1. A23.

Rowatt, W. C., M. R. Cunningham, and P. B. Druen. 1998. "Deception to Get a Date." *Personality and Social Psychology Bulletin* 24: 1228–42.

———. 1999. "Lying to Get a Date: The Effect of Facial Physical Attractiveness on the Willingness to Deceive Prospective Dating Partners." *Journal of Social and Personal Relationships* 16: 211–25.

Seiter, J. S., J. Bruschke, and C. Bai. 2002. "The Acceptability of Deception as a Function of Perceivers' Culture, Deceiver's Intention, and Deceiver-Deceived Relationship." *Western Journal of Communication* 66: 158–80.

Winstein, K. J., and D. Golden. 2007. "MIT Admissions Dean Lied on Résumé in 1979, Quits." *Wall Street Journal.* April 27. B1.

Wortham, S., and M. Locher. 1999. "Embedded Metapragmatic and Lying Politicians." *Language & Communication* 19: 109–25.

CHAPTER 8. Lies with Intent: Deceit to Trick or Cheat

Burrough, B. 2007. "Mad About the Boys." *Vanity Fair.* November. Retrieved November 14, 2008, from http://www.vanityfair.com/fame/features/2007/11/pearlman200711.

Crichton, R. 1960. *The Great Imposter.* New York: Random House.

Crosbie, J. S. 1975. *The Incredible Mrs. Chadwick: The Most Notorious Woman of Her Age.* Toronto: McGraw-Hill Ryerson.

De Bruin, G. P., and H. Rudnick. 2007. "Examining the Cheats: The Role of Conscientiousness and Excitement Seeking in Academic Dishonesty." *Sabinet* 37: 153–64.

Ekman, P. 2001. *Telling Lies: Clues to Deceit in the Marketplace, Politics, and Marriage.* New York. Norton.

Fishman, S. 2005. "Mommy's Little Con Man." *New York Magazine.* June 18. Retrieved November 14, 2008, from http://nymag.com/nymetro/news/people/features/12070/.

Ford, C. V. 1996. *Lies! Lies! Lies! The Psychology of Deceit.* Washington, D.C.: American Psychiatric Association.

Keyes, R. 2004. *The Post-Truth Era: Dishonesty and Deception in Contemporary Life.* New York: St. Martin's Press.

Kropp, R., and R. Rogers. 1993. "Understanding Malingering: Motivation, Method, and Detection." In *Lying and Deception in Everyday Life,* ed. M. Lewis and C. Saarni. New York: Guilford Press.

Sources

CHAPTER 9. Synthetic Reality: Media-Manufactured Lies

Beam, C. 2008. "The Fake Memoirist's Survival Guide: How to Embellish Your Life Story Without Getting Caught." *Slate.* March 6. Retrieved November 14, 2008, from http://www.slate.com/id/2185918/.

Booth, R. 2007. "TV 'Survival King' Stayed in Hotels." *Sunday Times.* July 22. 5.

Eskin, B. 2008. "Crying Wolf." *Slate.* February 29. Retrieved November 14, 2008, from http://www.slate.com/id/2185493/.

Ford, P. 2008. "Faking It." *Christian Science Monitor.* August 12. Retrieved November 14, 2008, from http://features.csmonitor.com/olympics08/2008/08/12/faking-it/.

Feuer, A. 2007. "Trial of Writer Reveals a Life as Strange as Fiction. *New York Times.* June 16. 2.

Morrison, B. 2004. "Ex–*USA Today* Reporter Faked Major Stories." *USA Today.* March 19. 1A.

Penenberg, A. 2008. "Lies, Damn Lies, and Fiction." *Forbes.* May 11. Retrieved November 14, 2008, from http://www.forbes.com/1998/05/11/otw3.html.

Poniewozik, J. 2006. "How Reality TV Fakes It." *Time.* January 29. Retrieved November 14, 2008, from http://www.time.com/time/magazine/article/0,9171,1154194,00.html?internalid=AOT_h_01-29-2006_how_reality_tv.

Qigang, C., quoted in O'Connor, A., and J. MacArtney. 2008. "The Counterfeit Games: Designed to Look Good from Every Angle." *The Times (London),* August 13. p. 18.

Rich, M. 2008. "Frey Defends His Memoir." *New York Times.* April 29. E 2.

———. 2008. "Gang Memoir, Turning Page Is Pure Fiction." *New York Times.* March 4. A1.

———. 2008. "Lies and Consequences: Tracking the Fallout of (Another) Literary Fraud." *New York Times.* March 5. E1.

Roberts, S. 2007. "It's Time to Welcome a Symbol of Substance." *New York Times.* August 12. SP7.

CHAPTER 10. Career Lies: Deception in the Workplace

Abbott, W. A. 2001. "Negative Nonverbal Communication: Retaliation, Sabotage, Theft, and Violence in the Workplace." *Dissertation Abstracts International Section A: Humanities and Social Sciences* 62(5-A): 1637.

Aguilera, R. V., and A. K. Vadera. 2008. "The Dark Side of Authority: Antecedents, Mechanisms, and Outcomes of Organizational Corruption." *Journal of Business Ethics* 77: 431–49.

Anderson, J. R., and M. E. Tirrell. 2004. "Too Good to Be True: CEOs and Financial Reporting Fraud." *Consulting Psychology Journal: Practice and Research* 56(1): 35–43.

Aquino, K., and T. E. Becker. 2005. "Lying in Negotiations: How Individual and Situational Factors Influence the Use of Neutralization Strategies." *Journal of Organizational Behavior* 26: 661–79.

Babiak, P. 1996. "Psychopathic Manipulation in Organizations: Pawns, Patrons and Patsies." In *International Perspectives and Psychopathy*, ed. A. Cooke., A. Forth., J. Newman, and R. Hare, pp. 12–17. Leicester, U.K.: British Psychological Society.

Braynov, S., and T. Sandholm. 2002. "Contracting with Uncertain Level of Trust." *Computational Intelligence* 19: 501–14.

Bringman, M. A. 2004. *Swapping Lies! Deception in the Workplace*. Victoria, B.C.: Trafford Publishing

Business Wire. 2002. "CEOs Held Primarily Responsible for Recent Accounting Scndals According to Special Edition TEC Index. *Business Wire*. July 17, 2002. Stamford, CT: Gale/Cengage Learning.

Byrne, J. A. 1999. *Chainsaw: The Notorious Career of Al Dunlap in the Era of Profit-at-Any-Price*. New York: HarperCollins.

Carrell, R. C. 2005. "The Use of Verbal Precision: The Impact of Potential Gain, Potential Loss, Verification, Likelihood, and Truthfulness." *Dissertation Abstracts International: Section B: The Sciences and Engineering* 65(8B): 4336.

Cohen, P. 2007. "Tough Guy Faces Stern Reality." *New York Times*. July 25. E2.

Sources

Davis, J. L., G. T. Payne, and G. C. McMahan. 2007. "A Few Bad Apples? Scandalous Behavior of Mutual Fund Managers." *Journal of Business Ethics* 76: 319–34.

DePaulo, P. J., B. M. DePaulo, J. Tank, and G. W. Swaim. 1989. "Lying and Detecting Lies in Organizations." In *Impression Management in the Organization*, ed. R. A. Giacalone and P. Rosenfeld, pp. 377–93. Hillsdale, N. J.: Lawrence Erlbaum Associates.

Foldes, H. L. J. 2007. "Ethical Misconduct of Senior Leaders: Counterproductive Work Behaviors at the Top." *Dissertation Abstracts International: Section B: The Sciences and Engineering* 67(9-B): 5453.

Giacalone, R. A., and P. Rosenfeld. 1987. "Reasons for Employee Sabotage in the Workplace." *Journal of Business and Psychology* 1: 367–78.

Greene, A. S. 1999. "Honesty in Organizations: Perceptions of the Corporate Environment and Their Impact on Individual Behavior." *Dissertation Abstracts International: Section B: The Sciences and Engineering* 60(4-B): 1914.

Grover, S. L. 1993. "Lying, Deceit, and Subterfuge: A Model of Dishonesty in the Workplace." *Organization Science* 4: 478–95.

Jehn, K. A., and E. D. Scott, 2008. "Perceptions of Deception: Making Sense of Responses to Employee Deceit." *Journal of Business Ethics* 80: 327–47.

Jones, D. 1996. "Recruiting: People Lie on Résumés—Even on Facts That Can Be Checked." *Detroit News*. September, 16.

Jones, J. W., and M. W. Boye. 1994. "Job Stress, Predisposition to Steal, and Employee Theft." *American Journal of Health Promotion* 8:331–33.

Keep, W. 2003. "Adam Smith's Imperfect Invisible Hand: Motivations to Mislead." *Business Ethics: A European Review*, 12: 343–53. Special issue: "EBEN-UK Conference April 2003."

Knights, D., and M. O'Leary. 2005. "Reflecting on Corporate Scandals: The Failure of Ethical Leadership." *Business Ethics: A European Review* 14: 359–66.

Kuczynski, A. 2000. "In Public Relations, 25% Admit Lying." *New York Times.* May 8. C20.

Lee, S. H. 2007. "Revelations of False Credentials Shake South Korea." *New York Times.* September 1. A3.

Lerer, L. 2007. "Did you Lie on Your Résumé?" *Forbes.* February 7. Retrieved November 14, 2008, from http://www.forbes.com/2007/02/07/leadership-resume-jobs-lead-career scx110207resume.html.

Levashna, J., and M. A. Campion. 2007. "Measuring Faking in the Employment Interview: Development and Validation of an Interview Faking Behavior Scale." *Journal of Applied Psychology* 92: 1638–56.

Lewicki, R. J., T. Poland, J. W. Minton, and B. H. Sheppard. 1997. "Dishonesty as Deviance: A Typology of Workplace Dishonesty and Contributing Factors." In *Research on Negotiation in Organizations* Vol. 6, ed. R. J. Lewicki., R. J. Bies, and B. H. Sheppard, pp. 53–86. New York: Elsevier Science/JAI Press.

McBarnet, D. 2006. "After Enron Will 'Whiter Than White Collar Crime' Still Wash? *British Journal of Criminology* 46: 1092–1109. Special issue: "Markets, Risk and 'White-Collar' Crimes: Moral Economies from Victorian Times to Enron."

McCool, J. D. 2007. "Executives: Making It by Faking It." *BusinessWeek.* October 4. Retrieved November 14, 2008 from http://www.businessweek.com/managing/content/oct2007/ca 2007104_799274.htm?campaign_id=rss_null.

McGee, R. W. 2008. "Applying Ethics to Insider Trading." *Journal of Business Ethics* 77: 205–17.

Micewski, E. R., and C. Troy. 2007. "Business Ethics—Deontologically Revisited." *Journal of Business Ethics* 72: 17–25.

Minkel, J. R. 2008. "Bubble Fusion Researcher Charged with Misconduct." *Scientific American.* July 21. Retrieved November 14, 2008, from http://www.sciam.com/article.cfm?id=taleyarkhan-bubble-fusion-misconduct.

Murphy, K. R. 1993. *Honesty in the Workplace.* Belmont, Calif.: Thomson Brooks/Cole Publishing.

Sources

Neese, W. T., L. Ferrell, and O. C. Ferrell. 2005. "An Analysis of Federal Mail and Wire Fraud Cases Related to Marketing." *Journal of Business Research* 58: 910–18.

Petersen, M. 2001. "A Résumé Distinguished by What It Didn't Mention." *New York Times.* September 6. A1.

Robinson, W. P., A. Shepherd, and J. Heywood. 1998. "Truth, Equivocation/Concealment, and Lies in Job Applications and Doctor-Patient Communication." *Journal of Language and Social Psychology* 17: 149–64. Special issue: "The Language of Equivocation, Part II."

Ryan, A. M., M. J. Schmit, D. L. Daum, S. Brutus, S. A. McCormick, and M. H. Brodke. 1997. "Workplace Integrity: Differences in Perceptions of Behaviors and Situational Factors." *Journal of Business and Psychology* 12: 67–83.

Schein, E. H. 2004. "Learning When and How to Lie: A Neglected Aspect of Organizational and Occupational Socialization." *Human Relations* 57: 260–73.

Shermer, M. 2008. "Do All Companies Have to Be Evil?" *Scientific American Mind and Brain,* January.

Shulman, D. 2006. *From Liar to Hire: The Role of Deception in the Workplace.* New York: Cornell University Press.

Theisen, T. 2002. "It's Easy to See Through Resume Lies." *Orlando Sentinel.* May 12.

Weisman, R. 2007. "The Fine Art of Negotiating (with Liars)." *Boston Globe.* August 19. D1.

Weiss, B., and R. S. Feldman, 2006. "Looking Good and Lying to Do It: Deception as an Impression Management Strategy in Job Interviews." *Journal of Applied Social Psychology* 36: 1070–86.

Williams, M. 2001. "Why Do They Lie?" *Washington Post.* June 20. A27.

Wokutch, R. E., and T. L. Carson. 1999. "The Ethics and Profitability of Bluffing in Business." In *Negotiation: Readings, Exercises, and Cases,* 3rd ed., ed. R. J. Lewicki, D. M. Saunders, and J. W. Minton, pp. 225–33. Boston: Irwin/McGraw-Hill.

Wood, J. L., J. M. Schmidtke, and D. L. Decker. 2007. "Lying on Job Applications: The Effects of Job Relevance, Commission, and Human Resource Management Experience." *Journal of Business and Psychology* 22: 1–9.

Xu, Y., and D. E. Ziegenfuss. 2008. "Reward Systems, Moral Reasoning, and Internal Auditors' Reporting Wrongdoing." *Journal of Business and Psychology* 22: 323–31.

CHAPTER 11: Web of Deceit: The Brave New World of Internet Dishonesty

After, A. 2007. "Is This Man Cheating on His Wife?" *Wall Street Journal.* August 10. W1.

Caldwell, C. 2007. "Not Being There." *New York Times Magazine.* August 12. 11.

Cohen, N. 2007. "A Contributer to Wikipedia Has His Fictional Side." *New York Times.* March 5. C5.

Galanxhi, H., and F. Fui-Hoon Nah. 2007. "Deception in Cyberspace: A Comparison of Text-Only vs. Avatar-Supported Medium." *International Journal of Human-Computer Studies* 65: 770–83.

Hafner, K. 2001. "A Beautiful Life, an Early Death, a Fraud Exposed." *New York Times.* May 31. G1.

Joinson, A. N., and B. Dietz-Uhler. "Explanations for the Perpetration of and Reactions to Deception in a Virtual Community." *Social Science Computer Review* 20:275–89.

Martin, A. 2007. "Whole Foods Executive Used Alias." *New York Times.* July 12. C1.

Stone, B., and M. Richtel. 2007. "The Hand That Controls the Sock Puppet Could Get Slapped." *New York Times.* July 16. C1.

Whitty, M. T., and S. E. Carville. 2008. "Would I Lie to You? Self-serving Lies and Other-Oriented Lies Told Across Different Media." *Computers in Human Behavior* 24: 1021–31.

Sources

CONCLUSION: Living with Lies

Blanton, B. 1996. *Radical Honesty: How to Transform Your Life by Telling the Truth.* New York: Dell Publishing.

Druckerman, P. 2008. "After the End of the Affair." *New York Times.* March 21. A23.

Fife, S. T., G. R. Weeks, and N. Gambecia. 2008. "Treating Infidelity: An Integrative Approach." *Family Journal* 15: 316–23.

Glass, S. P., and J. C. Staeheli. 2003. *Not "Just Friends": Rebuilding Trust and Recovering Your Sanity After Infidelity.* New York: Free Press.

Jacobs, A. J. 2007. "I Think You're Fat." *Esquire.* Retrieved November 14, 2008, from http://www.esquire.com/features/honesty0707.

INDEX

Abagnale, Frank, 176
About a Boy (movie), 16–17
Active Honesty Assessment
        (AHA), 251–55
adaptation, 83–84, 94
advantages of liars. *See* Liar's
        Advantage
advertising, 6, 183–85, 229
Alan, Richard, 117–18
Albert, Laura (a.k.a. J.T. LeRoy),
        194
altruism, 259–60
Ames, Aldrich, 39, 41
A Million Little Pieces (Frey),
        191–93
AnandTech, 229–30, 240
Anderson, J. Richard, 214–15
animals, deception in, 80–89,
        90–93
aptitude in lie detection, 31–35
"arms race" conception of
        evolution, 93–96
Aronson, Elliot, 141
aspiration, 145–46
autism (autistic children),
        73–74

avatars, 236–38, 241, 243
averted gaze, 36–38, 235

Babiak, Paul, 219
Backstreet Boys, 163–64
Bad Apple Theory of white
        collar crime, 210–15, 219,
        222
Bad Barrel Theory of white
        collar crime, 215–19, 222
Barash, David P., 114
Barta, William, 105–6
Baumeister, Roy, 130
behaviors signaling deception,
        36–43, 169–70, 235, 251
Beijing Olympics (2008),
        181–83, 185–88
belief, concept of, 71–72
Big Brother (TV show), 188
Bigley, Elizabeth (a.k.a. Cassie
        Chadwick), 172–74
Big Tobacco, 9–10
Blair, Jayson, 198
Blanton, Brad, 247
blind dates, 148–52
Blow, Adrian, 101–2

bolas spiders, 86

Bond, Charles, 31, 36–37

born to lie. *See* childhood deception; evolution of deceit

Bridges of Madison County, The (movie), 105

Bright Shiny Morning (Frey), 192

broken trust (loving a liar), 97–120

  frequency of infidelity, 101–2

  Madison County model of infidelity, 104–9

  Primal Scream model of infidelity, 114–17

  problem of defining infidelity, 100–101

  restoring of, 119–20, 255–58

  self-blame and infidelity, 103–5, 109

  Sex and the City model of infidelity, 111–13

  social norms and infidelity, 109–12

Bryant, Kobe, 229

Bush, George W., 133–34, 212

business cards, 239

business (workplace) deception, 201–22

  Bad Apple Theory of, 210–15, 219, 222

  Bad Barrel Theory of, 215–19, 222

  degree falsification, 204–10

  work and the need to deceive, 219–22

butterflies, 84–85

Byrne, Richard, 91–92, 94–96

Calvin and Hobbes (comic strip), 88

Calvinball, 88–89

camouflage, 83, 84–85

career lies. *See* business deception

Carlsmith, James M., 126, 127

Carnegie, Andrew, 173–74

Casino Royale (movie), 32

Catch Me If You Can (movie), 176

CEO deceit, 210–19

Chadwick, Cassie (a.k.a. Elizabeth Bigley), 172–74

Chadwick, Leroy S., 172–73

charm and deception, 74–77

cheating

  with intent. *See* lies with intent

  in marriage. *See* infidelity

  on school tests, 57–60

Cheng Li, 182

childhood deception, 57–78

  age progression of, 64–66

  lovable liars, 74–77

  model liars, 66–74

  peeking experiments, 61–62, 63, 77

  school cheating scandals, 57–60

China

  Beijing Olympics (2008), 181–83, 185–86, 187–88

  business card etiquette, 239

Christmas extravagances, 93–94, 95

Clinton, Bill, 100–101

Clinton, Hillary, 160, 162

Coen, Joel and Ethan, 189–91

coercive interrogations, and false confessions, 122–23

cognitive dissonance, 125–28, 130, 134

cognitive misers, 47–48

Index

commonalties, as motivation for deception, 16–19

common conception of lies, 7–11

commonplace lies. *See* everyday lies

complicity with liars, 48–56

compliments, false, 48–55, 254

compulsive lying (mythomania), 7–10

confidence, and self-deception, 137–38

confidence games, 27–30, 79–82, 171–80

cooperation, 96, 139–40

cosmetic deceit, 143–62

blind dates, 148–52

job interviews, 153–55

political campaigns, 160–62

upward comparisons, 155–60

Cullen, Charles, 40

Cunningham, Michael, 150–52, 155–56, 159

Curtis, Tony, 176

Daedalus Capital Relative Value Fund, 167–68

daily lies, 11–26

Amanda and the Seven Dwarfs, 7–11

author's research on, 11–16, 18, 19, 21–22

motivations for, 16–23

myth of the little white lie, 23–26

Dallas Morning News, 58

Darwin, Charles, 83–84

death drive, 117

de Bruin, Gideon, 171–72

defensive driving in our social lives, 250–55

Defonseca, Misha (a.k.a. Monique De Wael), 194

degree falsification, 204–10

Deindividuation Hypothesis, 231–36, 237–38

Demara, Ferdinand Waldo, 174–76

DePaulo, Bella, 24–25, 31, 249

depression, 118, 136

depressive realism, 136

descriptive norms, 110–12

detecting deception, 31–35

physical clues, 36–43

Deterrent Hypothesis, 231–36

De Wael, Monique (a.k.a. Misha Defonseca), 194

DiCaprio, Leonardo, 176

Dietz-Uhler, Beth, 229–30, 240

Discovery Channel, 186–87

Doessekker, Bruno (a.k.a. Binjamin Wilkomirski), 194

Drigotas, Stephen, 105–7

Druen, Perri, 150–52, 155–56, 159

Dunlap, Albert J., 210–12

duping delight, 170–72, 195

Eastwood, Clint, 105

Edmondson, David J., 206

EEGs (electroencephalograms), 41

ego, 64, 136, 213–14

eHonesty, 236–41, 243

Ekman, Paul, 32–33, 34, 35, 170

election cycles, and cosmetic deceit, 160–62

Ellis, Joseph, 203

emotional betrayal. *See* infidelity

Employee Investment Savings Accounts (EISA), 164

Enron, 212, 215–18

escalation principle, 94

Essjay (Ryan Jordan), 226–28, 231

everyday lies, 11–26

  Amanda and the Seven Dwarfs, 7–11

  author's research on, 11–16, 18, 19, 21–22

  motivations for, 16–23

  myth of the little white lie, 23–26

evolution of deceit, 79–96

  in animals, 80–93

  "arms race" conception, 93–96

  mind reading, 89–93

  reproductive success and, 115–17

  self-deception and, 140

  tic-tac-toe or Calvinball, 88–89

excitement seekers, 171–72

eye contact, 36–38

fact-checking, 195–96, 197

false-belief tasks, 71–72

false compliments, 48–55, 254

false confessions, 122–24

falsehood bias, 253–54

Fargo (movie), 189–91

Fastow, Andrew, 216–17

FBI (Federal Bureau of Investigation), 33–34

Federer, Roger, 183–84

Festinger, Leon, 126, 127

fireflies, 85–86, 94

First Aid for the Betrayed (Alan), 117–18

Forbes.com, 197, 199

Ford, Charles V., 179–80

Forest Brook High School, 57–58

Forrest, James, 11

Founding Brothers (Ellis), 203

Fragments (Wilkomirski), 194

Franken, Al, 155

Frankenbiting, 187, 188, 190

Frank, Mark, 32–33

Freud, Sigmund, 117, 136

Frey, James, 191–93

frogs, 86

From Liar to Hire (Shulman), 220–21

functional MRIs, 41

Galanxhi, Holtjona, 236–38

gaze aversion, 36–38

Gentilia, Tiffany, 106–7

Genyue Fu, 65

Giddings, Elva, 79–80

Gillette Fusion, 183–85

Glass, Stephen, 196, 198

Gramzow, Richard, 137–38

Grant, Hugh, 16–17

Great Impostor, The (movie), 176

Grylls, Bear, 186–87

guilt, and infidelity, 118–19

halo effect, 211

Happ, Benjamin, 11

Harrison, William Henry, 160–61

Hartnett, Kelley, 101–2

Henry, Thierry, 183–84

He's Just Not That into You (Behrendt), 132–33

Hilton, Paris, 187

hognose snakes, 85

Hogue, James (a.k.a. Alexi Santana), 27–30, 48–49, 55

Index

Holmes, John, 138–39
homosexual infidelity, 116
Hornby, Nick, 16–17
House Subcommittee on Health
    and the Environment, 9
hummingbirds, 83

identity play online, 239–40
"I didn't do it" lies, 64
"I disagree with myself," 125–28
imposterism, 27–30, 143–46,
    172–76, 194–95
infants, deception in, 78
infidelity, 97–120
    frequency of, 101–2
    Madison County model of,
        104–9
    the mornings after, 117–20
    Primal Scream model of,
        114–17
    problem of defining, 100–101
    restoring trust, 119–20,
        255–58
    self-blame and, 103–5, 109
    Sex and the City model of,
        111–13
    social norms and, 109–12
injunctive norms, 110–12
Innocence Project, The, 122
insecurities, 21–22, 53, 133, 150
instinctual deception, 80–89
intent, lies with, 163–80
    confidence games, 176–80
    duping delight, 170–72
    imposterism, 172–76
    motives behind, 167–72
Internet deception, 223–44
    deterrence vs.
        deindividuation, 231–36
    eHonesty standard, 236–41
    the 1's and 0's of Internet

    lies, 226–31
    sock-puppeting, 241–43
investment model of
    commitment, 105–7
Iraq War, 199–200

Jakob, Bill A. (a.k.a. "Sergeant
    Bill"), 143–46
Jewell, Richard, 33–34
job deception. See workplace
    deception
job interviews, 153–55, 207–9
Joinson, Adam, 229–30, 240
Jones, Margaret B. (a.k.a.
    Margaret Seltzer), 193
Jones, Marilee, 152–53
Jordan, Ryan (a.k.a. Essjay),
    226–28, 231
joy of lying, 167–72
judgment heuristics, 44–45
Jukt Micronics, 197
"just being yourself," 19–22

Karadžić, Radovan, 174
Karr, John Mark, 121–22, 123
Kassin, Saul, 123
Kawagoe, Toshiji, 45–46
Keillor, Garrison, 135
Kelley, Jack, 198
Kincaid, Robert, 105

Lake Wobegon effect, 135–40
Lay, Kenneth, 215–17
leaders, and self-deception,
    133–34
Lee Chang-ha, 205
Lee, Kang, 65
LeRoy, J.T. (a.k.a. Laura Albert),
    194
Less Stress, More Success (Jones),
    153

Liar's Advantage, 27–56, 251
  physical clues to deception, 36–43
  truth bias, 43–48
  truth detection, 31–35
  Willing Accomplice Principle, 48–56
Liars Index, 205–6
lie detection, 31–35
  physical clues, 36–43
lie-detection skills, 31–35
Lies! Lies! Lies! The Psychology of Deceit (Ford), 179–80
"lies of social convenience," 23, 24, 165
lies with intent, 163–80
  confidence games, 176–80
  duping delight, 170–72
  imposterism, 172–76
  motives behind, 167–72
likability, as motivation for deception, 13–14, 18–19
Lin Miaoke, 181–83, 187–88
little white lies, 23–26
Living Colours, 223–24
living with lies, 245–60
  active honesty assessment, 250–55
  being honest about being honest, 258–60
  learning to trust again, 255–58
  motives for deception, 246–50
London *Sunday Times,* 186
lottery scams, 79–80
lovable liars, 74–77
Love and Consequences (Jones), 193
loving a liar. *See* infidelity

McCabe, Donald, 59, 60

McClellan, Scott, 133–34
MacGregor, Gregor, 28
Machiavellian intelligence hypothesis, 95–96
Mackey, John (a.k.a. Rahodeb), 241–43
Madison County model of infidelity, 104–9
Madoff, Bernard, 166, 176
Man vs. Wild (TV show), 186–87
marital infidelity, 97–120
  frequency of, 101–2
  Madison County model of, 104–9
  the mornings after, 117–20
  Primal Scream model of, 114–17
  problem of defining, 100–101
  restoring trust, 119–20, 255–58
  self-blame and, 103–5, 109
  Sex and the City model of, 111–13
  social norms and, 109–12
masquerading, 143–46, 172–76
Mean Business (Dunlap), 210
media-manufactured lies, 181–200
  memoir falsification, 191–96
  news that isn't worthy, 196–200
  reality bias, 183–86
  synthetic reality, 186–89
  truth brand, 189–92
Meet the Parents (movie), 38
memoir falsification, 191–96
Mendes, Wendy, 137–38
MetLife, 201
mind reading, 89–93

Index

mirroring behavior, 18–19, 68

mirror orchids, 85

Misha: A Mémoire of the Holocaust Years (Defonseca), 194

Mistakes Were Made (but Not by Me) (Tavris and Aronson), 141

modeling, 68

model liars, 66–74

monkeys, 90–93

monogamy, 100–101, 108, 110–14

morality, concepts of, 72–73

moral value of truthfulness, 66–67, 78, 258–59

motivations for deception, 16–23, 167–72, 246–50

Murray, Sandra, 138–39

Myth of the Little White Lie, 23–26

mythomania (compulsive lying), 7–10

Nah, Fiona Fui-Hoon, 236–38

National Archives (Washington, D.C.), 1–3

National Enquirer, 236, 238

nervousness, and lie detection, 40–41

New Republic, 196–97, 198–99

New Yorker, 227

New York Times, 15, 114, 182, 193, 197–98, 199

Nike, 229

Nitec Paper, 211

Nixon, Richard, 1–2

No Child Left Behind Act, 57–60

'N Sync, 163–64

Obama, Barack, 228–29

O'Leary, George, 206

online deception. *See* Internet deception

On the Origin of Species (Darwin), 83–84

opossums, 85

Oprah Winfrey (TV show), 191, 192–93

optimism, and self-deception, 137–38

ornamentation, 146–47

O'Sullivan, Maureen, 32–33

Paterson, David, 100

Paul (baboon), 91–92

peacocks, 83

Pearlman, Lou, 163–64, 166, 180

peeking experiments, 61–62, 63, 77

peppered moths, 83, 84

physical abuse, and false confessions, 122–23

physical appearances, and cosmetic deceit, 146–48

physical clues to deception, 36–43, 169–70, 235, 251

pigeon drops, 176–79

Pinocchio, 67

piping plovers, 87

plagiarism, 59, 203

"playing dead," 85

Plooij, Frans, 92

poker, 128–30, 131

political campaigns, and cosmetic deceit, 160–62

polygraph machines, 38–42, 169–70

Ponzi schemes, 164, 166, 167–69

portia spiders, 80–82, 84, 88–89

positive self-image, 20, 130–35.
    See also self-presentation
praying mantises, 84
Primal Scream model of
    infidelity, 114–17
primates, 90–93
protective lies, 50, 69–70, 102,
    130–31, 180, 248, 259
PRWeek, 201, 203
psychopaths, 219
puffing, 203
Purdue University, 203

Radical Honesty, 247–48, 259
Ramsey, JonBenét, 121–22,
    123
Rank and Yank, 216–18
rationalizations, 126–27
real estate market, 54–56
reality bias, 183–86
reality television, 186–91,
    198–99
Real World, The (TV show), 188
Reddy, Vasudevi, 78
regaining trust, 119–20, 255–58
reproductive success, 115–17
résumés, 152–53, 204–12
Richardson, Kevin, 163–64
Ridgway, Gary Leon (Green
    River Killer), 39–40
Romney, George, 160
Romney, Mitt, 160
Rousseau, Jean-Jacques, 62
Rowatt, Wade, 150–52, 155–56,
    159
Rudnick, Hilton, 171–72

Safstrom, C. Annette, 106–7
Santana, Alexi (a.k.a. James
    Hogue), 27–30, 48–49, 55
Sarkozy, Nicolas, 109

Saturday Night Live (TV show),
    155
Schlager, Seymour I., 202
Schlessinger, Laura, 103–4
scholarships, 202–3
school cheating scandals,
    57–60
Science, 203
Scott Paper, 210
Second Life, 243
Secret Service, U.S., 33
selective exposure, 131
self-deception, 121–41
    believing in yourself, 128–35
    cognitive dissonance and,
        125–28
    false confessions, 122–24
    Lake Wobegon effect,
        135–40
self-justification, 130, 141
self-presentation, 19–22,
    148–62, 248–49
    on blind dates, 148–52
    on job interviews, 152–55
    in political campaigns,
        160–62
    upward comparisons,
        155–60
    in the workplace, 220–21
Sex and the City (TV show),
    111–12
Sex and the City model of
    infidelity, 111–13
sex drive, 115–17
sexual betrayal. *See* infidelity
sexual selection, 83–84, 86
Shermer, Michael, 216–17
Shin Jeong-ah, 204
Short, Elizabeth, 122
Shulman, David, 220–21
Simple Life, The (TV show), 187

Index

Skilling, Jeffrey K., 215–17
skill in lie-detection, 31–35
Smith, John, 194
smudges, 24–25
social aptitude, and skill in lying, 74–77
social niceties, and lying, 6–7, 98, 146, 165, 258
social norms, 109–12, 217–18, 239–40
social parasites, 86
sock-puppeting, 241–43
South Korea, 204–5
Spears, Jamie Lynn, 70
Spielberg, Steven, 176
Spitzer, Eliot, 97–98, 99–100, 110
Spitzer, Silda Wall, 98
standardized tests, and cheating, 57–60
staphylinid beetles, 86
Stratford, Lauren, 28
Streep, Meryl, 105
Stuart Smalley philosophy of life, 155
subprime real estate market, 55–56
Sunbeam Corporation, 210–12
Survivor (TV show), 187, 190–91
swans, 113–14
sweating, 38–39, 235
Swenson, Debbie (a.k.a. Kaycee Nicole Swenson), 223–24
synthetic reality, 186–89. *See also* media-manufactured lies

Takizawa, Hirokazu, 45–46
Taleyarkhan, Rusi, 203
Talwar, Victoria, 63
Tavris, Carol, 141
Telling Lies (Ekman), 170

telltale signs of deception, 36–43, 169–70, 235, 251
Temptation Island (TV show), 188
temptation resistance paradigm (peeking experiments), 61–62, 63, 77
test performance, and cheating, 57–60
Texas Assessment of Knowledge and Skills (TAKS), 57–58
theory of mind, 71–72, 73, 89, 92–93
thermal imaging, 41
three-card monte, 178
tic-tac-toe, 88–89
Tirrell, Michael E., 214–15
Tracey, Michael, 121–22
Trans Continental Airlines, 164
trickery. *See* lies with intent
trust, regaining, 119–20, 255–58
truth bias, 43–48, 179, 184–85, 226, 252–53
truth brand, 189–92
truth detection, 31–35
  physical clues, 36–43
twinge of distress, 24, 249
Tyler, James, 156–59

upward comparisons, 158–60, 248
USA Today, 198

Voigt, Wilhelm, 28
Vonk, Roos, 50–54

Waller, James, 105
Wall Street Journal, 236, 238
Washington, George, and the cherry tree, 66–67, 78
Watterson, Bill, 88

Web of deceit (Internet
  deception), 223–44
  deterrence vs.
    deindividuation, 231–36
  eHonesty standard,
    236–41
  the 1's and 0's of Internet
    lies, 226–31
  sock-puppeting, 241–43
Weiss, Brent, 207–8
Werra, Jude M., 205–6, 211
*What Happened: Inside the Bush
  White House and Washington's
  Culture of Deception*
  (McClellan), 133–34
white collar crime
  Bad Apple Theory of,
    210–15, 219, 222
  Bad Barrel Theory of,
    215–19, 222
Whiten, Andrew, 91–92,
  94–96
Whole Foods, 241–43
Wikipedia, 226–28

Wilkomirski, Binjamin (a.k.a.
  Bruno Doessekker), 194
Willard, Greg, 137–38
Willing Accomplice Principle,
  48–56
Wilson, Laurel, 28
Winfrey, Oprah, 191, 192–93
Woods, Tiger, 183–84
workplace deception, 201–22
  Bad Apple Theory of,
    210–15, 219, 222
  Bad Barrel Theory of,
    215–19, 222
  degree falsification, 204–10
  work and the need to deceive,
    219–22

Yalincak, Ayferafet, 169
Yalincak, Hakan, 167–69, 180
Yang Peiyi, 181–83, 187–88

Zarrella, Ronald, 206, 209
zebras, 84
Zoey 101 (TV show), 70